TOTAL
WAR

CHARLES WINCHESTER

TOTAL WAR

Quercus

CONTENTS

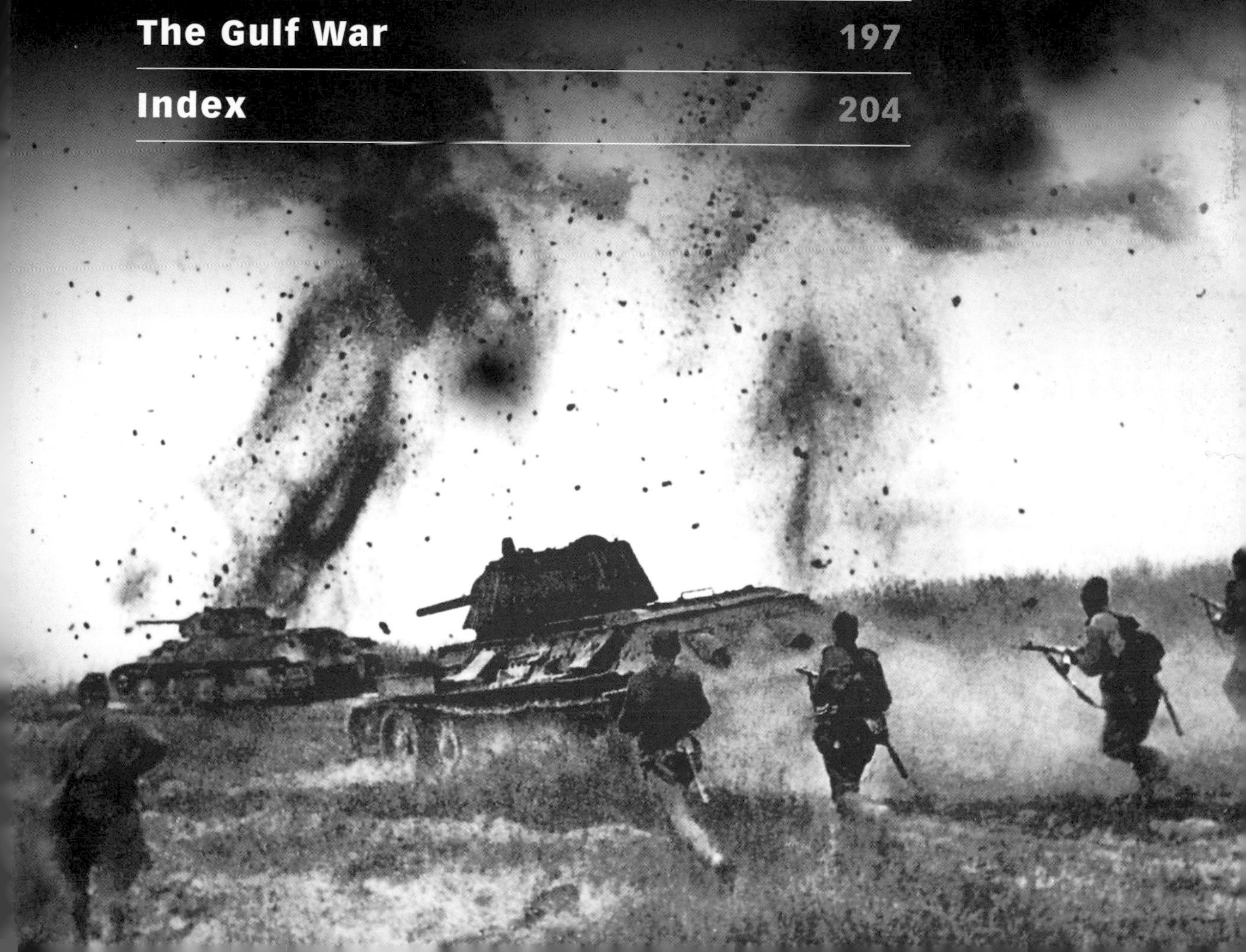

INTRODUCTION

The 20th century was the most violent in world history. The First World War (1914–18) caused the fall of the Russian, German, Austro-Hungarian and Ottoman Empires. This led to a drastic realignment of national boundaries across the world, and the creation of three artificial countries: Czechoslovakia, Yugoslavia and Iraq. The communist victory in the Russian Civil War and the great depression of the 1930s caused an equally radical shift in world politics. The result was a further series of conflicts across the globe as Germany and Japan attempted world conquest, and colonial territories regained their independence.

This book investigates the battles that changed the course of history and shaped the world we live in today. It is a strangely circular story in that recent crises have their origins in decisions taken after the First World War. Yugoslavia and Czechoslovakia have now reverted to their original constituent countries; only Iraq, assembled from three disparate provinces of the Ottoman Empire, still remains. The first major war of the 21st century has its roots in the great battles of the 20th.

Actions at sea best match the traditional concept of a battle: a climactic clash of arms that is decided in a day. Tsushima (1905) and Midway (1942) fit the bill: decisive victories both, one confirmed that Japan was now a world power; the other signalled she would not be for much longer. Where land battles end and campaigns – or wars – begin is a matter of debate. The 1967 Arab–Israeli War is referred to as such, although the armies and the area of operations were smaller than the Battle of Kursk (1943) or Operation 'Bagration' (1944). The Falklands War (1982) took place over distances that were daunting even by the standards of the Pacific War, but the forces involved were smaller than the various US Navy task forces at Leyte Gulf (1944).

The battles included here are some of the most decisive engagements of all time: the annihilation of the Russian fleet at Tsushima, the trouncing of the Allied armies in 1940 and the humiliation of the Arab forces in 1967 and those of Iraq in 1991. Yet even the most spectacular military victories in the Middle East often fail to deliver significant political gains. By contrast, some indecisive battles were pregnant with consequence. In terms of sailors drowned and warships sunk, the Royal Navy lost the Battle of Jutland, but its line-of-battle squadrons were hardly affected and the day after the battle it was the only operational fleet in the North Sea. The battle confirmed the pre-existing strategic balance and led the Germans to resort to submarine attacks on neutral shipping – bringing the USA into the war. Similarly, the Luftwaffe was defeated in the Battle of Britain, but its losses would not stop it wiping out the air forces of Yugoslavia, Greece and Russia the following year. What mattered in that vital summer of 1940 was that RAF Fighter Command did not lose.

The long-running war in Iraq (2003–) began in no small part thanks to errors of judgement by all the major players. A little more attention to history might have been helpful. The 20th-century's first great power conflict (1904–5) was driven as much by Russian racist assumptions of natural superiority as by greed and ambition in Tokyo. The story of 1914 is nothing if not a sorry saga of gross miscalculation. By contrast, the Battle of Britain is a perfect example of victory going to men who saw the fight coming, prepared for it with some forethought, and conducted it with ruthless professionalism. *Si Vis Pacem Para Bellum.*

TSUSHIMA
27–28 MAY 1905

'THE EXISTENCE OF OUR IMPERIAL COUNTRY
RESTS ON THIS ONE ACTION. EVERY MAN OF
YOU MUST DO HIS UTMOST.'
ADMIRAL TOGO

The Battle of Tsushima was the most decisive naval battle of the 20th century. Japan's annihilation of the Russian fleet struck a mortal blow, not just to Russian ambitions in the Far East, but ultimately to all European colonialism in Asia. Japan's transition from self-imposed isolation and obscurity to major regional power had taken less than 40 years: senior Japanese commanders in the Russo-Japanese War of 1904–5 began their military careers wearing armour and carrying swords.

Tsarist Russia underestimated its enemy and went to war with cheery insouciance. Racist stereotyping took the place of intelligence. Tsar Nicholas II had dismissed the Japanese as 'monkeys' and assumed his forces would cruise to victory. His advisers, above all the deeply reactionary minister of the interior, von Plehve, argued that a quick victorious war would stave off the revolutionary forces that threatened the tsarist regime. The theory did not work for him: the revolutionaries made their fourth and this time successful attempt to assassinate him in July.

Imperialism and its Discontents

The war began on the night of 8–9 February 1904 when the Japanese launched a surprise attack on the Russian Pacific Fleet in its anchorage at Port Arthur. Both sides had been preparing for conflict – one much more seriously than the other – and the Japanese had broken off diplomatic relations a few days previously. However, they did not bother with a formal declaration of war.

> 'In order to prevent revolution, we need a little victorious war'
>
> VYACHESLAV VON PLEHVE, RUSSIAN MINISTER OF THE INTERIOR

The two empires were both taking advantage of China's weakness to seize territory on the Asian mainland. Russia was steadily extending its control of Manchuria and had established a naval base at Port Arthur, on China's Liaodung peninsula, to supplement its existing port of Vladivostok. (The British and Germans had forced China to cede them naval bases on the opposite coast of the Yellow Sea at Wei-hei-Wei and Tsingtao respectively.) Within hours of their torpedo boats' attack on Port Arthur, the Japanese navy landed troops at Inchon, Korea. The Japanese army pressed north to engage the Russian forces in Manchuria, and to isolate and besiege Port Arthur.

Russia's large naval forces were divided into three widely separated forces: the Baltic, Black Sea and Pacific Fleets. The Black Sea Fleet was constrained by an international treaty that prevented it from passing into the Mediterranean, so could play no part in the fighting. The Baltic Fleet had already despatched the battleship *Oslyabya* and two cruisers to the east.

OPPOSITE: *Tsarevitch was the only Russian battleship to escape Port Arthur, seeking internment in China after the disastrous battle of 10 August. She survived 13 hits from 12-in guns with little damage, but one killed Admiral Vitgeft, throwing the squadron into fatal confusion.*

Tsushima

27 May 1905

06.15 The Japanese Combined Fleet leaves port.

13.39 The Japanese Combined Fleet sights the Russians and hoists battle ensigns.

14.05 The Japanese Combined Fleet turns in succession under fire from the Russian van.

14.10 Togo's battle line completes its turn.

14.12 The *Mikasa* is hit at a range of 5,500 yards.

14.16 The Japanese Combined Fleet opens fire, leading battleships concentrating on the Russian flagship *Prince Suvorov*.

14.43 The *Oslyabya* and *Prince Suvorov* fall out of line.

14.50 The *Alexander III* starts turning to the north and attempts to leave the battle line.

16.30 Contact between fleets lost in smoke and haze.

17.30 Russian line reformed and back on course but at very much reduced speed.

18.00 Battle resumed.

18.50 The *Alexander III* capsizes.

19.20 *Borodino* sinks.

19.30 *Prince Suvorov* founders.

28 May 1905

09.30 The Japanese Combined Fleet locates the Russians again.

10.34 Admiral Nebogatov signals 'XGE', which is 'I surrender' in the international signal code used at the time.

They got as far as the Horn of Africa before being recalled in January 1904, a fortnight before hostilities began. The tsar had decided to send his entire Baltic Fleet, together, retitled the 'Second Pacific Fleet', under the command of the famously louche chief of the naval staff, Admiral Zinovy Rozhestvensky. He had refused command of Port Arthur before the war, on the grounds that Russia's viceroy in the east, Admiral Alexeev, an illegitimate son of Tsar Alexander II, was a personal enemy. Nevertheless, as soon as Japan attacked, Rozhestvensky volunteered to lead the Baltic Fleet to the Far East.

Meanwhile, with seven modern battleships to Japan's six, the Russian Pacific Fleet was a match for the Japanese – on paper. But training standards in the tsarist navy were lamentable: signalling, gunnery and even steaming in formation proved a challenge. They were also unlucky. In March Admiral Oskar Stark was replaced at Port Arthur by Vice Admiral Makarov, a popular fork-bearded old salt who brought new purpose to the beleaguered fleet. He put to sea on 13 April, only for his flagship *Petropavlovsk* to strike one or more mines. He was decapitated and the battleship sank, taking him, his staff and her whole complement of 632 officers and men with her.

Preparations for the departure of the Baltic Fleet took so long that Rozhestvensky has been accused of dragging his feet. He was also having an affair with Makarov's widow, and it was an open secret in St Petersburg that this relationship predated the husband's demise. However, the

inefficiency of the Russian naval dockyard at Kronstadt was notorious. The tsar's decision was taken in April, but Rozhestvensky did not hoist his flag in the new battleship *Prince Suvarov* until 1 August, by which time the Japanese army had laid siege to Port Arthur. There, Alexeev had given operational control of the fleet to his chief of staff, Rear Admiral Vilgelm Vitgeft. He remained in harbour until 10 August, when, conscious that the Japanese front line was inching ever closer to the hills overlooking his anchorage, he sortied with the intention
of reaching Vladivostok.

The two fleets met in the Yellow Sea. After several hours of indecisive long-range gunfire, it was nearly dark and it looked as if the Russians would escape into the night. Then two heavy shells struck Vitgeft's flagship *Tsarevitch* in quick succession. The first struck the foremast and killed the admiral; the second killed the ship's captain and everyone on the bridge, and jammed the helm. The *Tsarevitch* turned 180 degrees and the rest of the fleet followed her, and then broke up in confusion as it became apparent no one was in charge. *Tsarevitch* limped into Tsingtao, where she was interned by the Germans. Most of the fleet returned to Port Arthur, where their eventual destruction was only a matter of time.

Rozhestvensky extracted his fleet from Kronstadt on 30 August, just as the Russian army in Manchuria fell back from its attempt to relieve Port Arthur by land. He steamed down the coast to Reval, where the Baltic Fleet remained for another month. There was some compensation for the admiral: two hospital ships with volunteer female nurses were attached to the fleet, and the head nurse became Rozhestvensky's new mistress.

A World Away from St Petersburg

The coal-fired warships of the early 20th century were ill-suited to long voyages without regular stops in port. Coaling ship was a hot, miserably arduous job even in harbour, but Rozhestvensky's fleet often had to coal at sea. The sailors were paying the price of their government's diplomatic ineptitude: Russia's only ally in this war was Montenegro. Britain was neutral, but had supplied the Japanese with most of their warships; many Japanese officers had trained in England, and had adopted all manner of British ways – painting their ships like the British and even making Nelsonic signals on the eve of battle. When jittery Russian gunners fired on British fishing boats off Dogger Bank, a British battle squadron formed an aggressively close escort to shepherd the Russians down the English Channel.

On 29 December, after three months at sea, Rozhestvensky and his fleet assembled off Madagascar. He and his modern battleships had rounded the Cape; his lighter warships traversed the Mediterranean and passed through the Suez Canal. They did not have radios, so it was not until they dropped anchor here that they learned of the fate of the Pacific Fleet. Four of the remaining battleships had been sunk by Japanese army heavy artillery in early December. The fifth, *Sevastopol*, was towed out of the harbour after suffering several hits from 11-inch howitzers, and was still there when the fortress surrendered on 2 January.

Disorder, Drunkenness and Mutiny

Rozhestvensky wanted to press on across the Indian Ocean and through Japanese waters to reach Vladivostok, preferably without engaging the Japanese. But with the sort of micro-management that invariably backfires, the tsar and his advisers overruled the admiral. The tsar ordered the despatch of the 'Third Pacific Fleet' – the elderly ironclad *Navarin* and three Ushakov class coastal defence ships that had remained in Kronstadt – to reinforce Rozhestvensky. These slow, obsolescent ships left the Baltic in February, commanded by Rear Admiral Nebogatov. Rozhestvensky's ships were left to swing at anchor in the tropics, accumulating cockroaches and grievances. The crews learned of the widespread disturbances in Russia, of which the killing of von Plehve had been but a part. There was disorder on some ships, morbid drunkenness on most of them and a mutiny on the battleship *Orel*.

In March, Rozhestvensky put to sea without telling his government, and steamed across the Indian Ocean, deliberately staying out of touch with St Petersburg. But when he put into French Indochina he was ordered by telegraph to wait for Nebogatov. Meanwhile, he landed 10 officers and 42 other ranks and sent them back to Russia, 28 with tuberculosis and 3 classified as insane. The 'Third Pacific Fleet' duly limped into Camn Rahn Bay; both fleets took on additional coal for the last leg of their journey and, on 9 May 1905, set course together for Vladivostok.

Little did the Russians know it, but the Japanese had not had it all their own way. They had maintained a close blockade of Port Arthur and they were not the only ones laying mines in the vicinity. On 15 May 1904, one of their six battleships, the *Hatsuse*, struck a mine in full view of the Russians ashore. The *Asahi* tried to tow her to safety, but *Hatsuse* hit another, which exploded her magazine. The *Yashima* also struck a mine and appeared to be towed away without difficulty, but she had been fatally holed. Once over the horizon, she capsized and sank. The Japanese kept her loss secret not only from the Russians but from the Japanese public.

The Japanese fleet that cruised off Japan to intercept Rozhestvensky was thus led by four British-built battleships and eight heavy cruisers. The cruisers' 8-inch guns lacked the crushing power of the battleships' 12-inch main armament, but they fired four times as fast and enjoyed an additional advantage in the fight that followed. Rozhestvensky had been obliged to overload his ships with coal, cramming every available space and leaving them lower in the water than their designers had intended. As a result, the armoured belt that protected the waterline was virtually submerged: hits on their less well-protected upper hull could open them to the sea.

Ironclad Obsolescence?

The warships at Tsushima had been built at the end of a century notable for a lack of naval battles. Technology advanced so quickly that warships were out of date within ten years of their completion. Gunnery remained an uncertain business: when Admiral Togo gave the four surviving Japanese battleships a practice shoot, they managed to hit with one in three rounds from their main armament: the target was a small island only 3,000 yards away. Nevertheless the Japanese entered the battle with almost every advantage. Their ships were excellent; their crews were well disciplined, and most had fought in several battles the previous year. The Russians were slowed by the addition of obsolete vessels, their crews verged on mutiny and their officers were sunk in fatalistic gloom. Rozhestvensky's second-in-command, Admiral Felkersam, went into battle already dead, his body in *Oslyabya's* chapel and his death concealed from the rest of the squadron. While this avoided further despondency among his superstitious men, it took no account of the effect on the chain of command if Rozhestvensky was hit – which is precisely what happened.

'The Japanese will annihilate us. Their ships are better and they are real sailors. I can promise you one single thing: we will all die, but never surrender.'

CAPTAIN BUKHVOSTOV OF THE *ALEXANDER III*, KILLED IN ACTION 27 MAY 1905

At a Range of 7,000 Yards

The Russian approach was detected by Togo's cruiser screen during the night, because the Russians complied with international law and kept their hospital ships illuminated. Togo's fleet sailed at 6.15a.m. and encountered the Russians some seven hours later. At 1.39 p.m. he hoisted his battle flag, a banner that would reappear in 1941 when the Japanese attacked Pearl Harbor. The Russians were on his bow quarter and in order to steam parallel to their line, he turned his ships in succession, allowing the Russians to engage each Japanese ship in turn. The range was nearly 7,000 yards, so the risk of a hit was not great; however, his flagship *Mikasa* was struck by several Russian 6-inch shells.

For about half an hour the two lines of warships steamed almost parallel, the range slowly closing to less than 6,000 yards. Rozhestvensky's flagship *Prince Suvorov* led the Russian line and attracted most of the fire as the faster Japanese fleet pulled ahead. *Suvorov* had much of her armament knocked out by 2.43 p.m. when the fourth in line, *Oslyabya*, veered to starboard and came to a stop, listing steeply to port. As her crew began to scramble out of every available hatch, the battleship rolled upside down and sank. Her steering jammed, *Suvorov* moved off to starboard. The next in line, *Alexander III*, followed the flagship for a moment, before Captain Bukhvostov realized what had happened and resumed course. Togo led his fleet across the path of the Russians just after 1500, concentrating all his guns on the head of their line. The Japanese pounded away for another hour, while the volume of Russian fire dwindled. The decks of *Alexander III*, *Borodino* and *Orel* were choked with bodies, fires raged out of control and repeated hits on the waterline left them wallowing lower and lower in the sea.

The sheer volume of smoke from so many coal-fired ships, allied to gunfire and explosions, reduced visibility to the point where the fleets lost contact. Rozhestvensky had been wounded several times, the last injury leaving him unconscious. His staff got him off the crippled battleship and on to a destroyer, coincidentally saving their own lives. For what exactly took place aboard the *Prince Suvorov* we only have their word to rely on: the battleship limped back into battle, a few guns bravely firing until she was torpedoed at dusk. She blew up with the loss of all hands.

The action was resumed at about 6.00 p.m., Togo pressing to close range to do as much damage as possible in the remaining hour of daylight. Poor damage control and bad communications aboard the Russian battleships – and possible design flaws – saw one after another suffer sudden, catastrophic loss of watertight integrity: sinking so quickly that hardly a soul escaped. *Alexander III* turned turtle at 6.50 p.m. taking 806 officers and men down with her; four survivors were plucked from the sea. *Borodino* capsized, one of her gun batteries still firing; only one of the 856 men aboard escaped.

Signal: 'I Surrender'

Japanese torpedo boats harried the Russians through the night and sank the old battleship *Navarin* by laying mines directly in her path. Dawn ushered forth a bright sunny day that gave the surviving Russian warships little chance of escape. Admiral Nebogatov surrendered the surviving units although a couple of light cruisers managed to slip away. Nearly 6,000 Russian sailors were taken prisoner; 4,830 were dead. The Japanese had lost 117 killed and 583 wounded.

American pressure helped bring both sides to the negotiating table a month later. Although Japan had the advantage, her economy could not sustain a long conflict; Russia still had 1 million troops in Manchuria, but could not sustain a long war either. Revolution was in the air. The Black Sea Fleet mutinied in June and the country was paralysed by strikes, rioting and rural uprisings. President Roosevelt hosted peace talks in New Hampshire which ended the war. When the Russian prisoners boarded ships to return from Japan, their officers had to ask for Japanese police to keep order.

A vengeful tsar had Nebogatov and some other officers court-martialled and imprisoned. Rozhestvensky, who had been greeted as a hero by revolutionaries and reactionaries alike on his return, was allowed to retire.

'THEY SHALL NOT PASS'
GENERAL PHILIPPE PÉTAIN

VERDUN
DECEMBER 1915– OCTOBER 1916

The Battle of Verdun lasted for most of 1916. The fighting there was so terrible, the casualties so horrendous, that it was more than just one battle among many: for France Verdun was The battle. The French stopped the great German offensive: but at hideous cost. Around 300,000 men – 140,000 German and 160,000 French – were killed there between February and October.

From 1917 towns and villages across France started to rename streets, squares and boulevards after Verdun – Paris has four, including the Avenue de Verdun. The battle cemented the reputation of Philippe Pétain as one of the greatest generals France has ever produced, and led to a sinister cabal of generals seizing power in Germany.

By Christmas 1914 the period of open warfare was over. The armies occupied a line of trenches that ran from the North Sea coast to Switzerland, leaving most of Belgium and a large part of northeastern France under German occupation. Ordered to liberate the lost towns and cities, the French army lost 350,000 dead and 800,000 wounded in 1915 during a succession of offensives that failed to crack the German defences. Every military development of the late 19th century – quick-fire artillery, magazine-loading rifles, machine guns and barbed wire – had increased the power of the defence. Nevertheless, the French planned to resume the offensive in 1916, by which time Britain's tiny pre-war army had been expanded into a continental-style massed army capable of landing a serious blow against the Germans. The target for the Anglo-French offensive was to be along the River Somme.

Falkenhayn's Plan of Slaughter

While holding off the French attacks in 1915, the German army had launched major offensives in the east, overrunning Serbia and Poland. But for General Erich von Falkenhayn, Chief of the German General Staff, this was just a necessary preliminary to another full-scale blow against France. He recognized the French army as the Allies' best weapon:'England's best sword', he called it. Britain's navy might rule the waves, but even the expanded British army was still only a fraction of the size of its German opponent.

From November 1915 the Germans began to assemble a massive striking force opposite Verdun, laying narrow gauge railways into the woods where an unprecedented number of heavy guns was assembled, together with vast stockpiles of ammunition. A historic fortress, surrounded by brick and concrete forts built in the late 19th century, Verdun was not a position the French would give up without a fight. And this was Falkenhayn's intention: as he put it, 'to bleed France white' in a battle of attrition in which

PREVIOUS PAGE: *French soldiers defended the ancient fortress town of Verdun against a succession of German attacks from February through June 1916, suffering hideous losses but stopping the German offensive in its tracks.*

regiment after regiment of the French army would be pounded to destruction by the most powerful heavy artillery in the world.

By January 1916 aerial photographs and statements from deserters led some of the French officers at Verdun to fear the worst. But their reports were disbelieved until the last moment. Had the German offensive began as planned, on 12 February, the German infantry would probably have broken through all the way to Verdun. However, a heavy snowstorm ushered in a week of severe winter weather. Gale force winds kept observation balloons and aircraft grounded, and constant snow showers left German artillery observers blinded. While tens of thousands of German infantry shivered in underground shelters, awaiting the order to attack, six French divisions arrived by rail and took up defensive positions around the town.

The Ground Quakes

Snow continued to fall at dusk on 20 February, but the forecast for the next day was clear and the German gunners were ordered to begin their bombardment at 4 a.m. the next day. Three 380mm long-range guns, originally built for the German navy opened fire in the darkness, their massive shells falling around the Meuse bridges and Verdun's railway station. Once German artillery observers could see their targets at first light, 1,200 guns opened fire, hitting the French frontline, the support trenches, artillery positions, command centres and supply dumps. For forty-five minutes up to 8 a.m. the German guns fired at maximum rate, with short-range mortars joining in a furious hurricane of fire that pulverized the French defences. The ground vibrations could be felt a hundred miles away.

The French were outnumbered 2:1 in infantry: 34 battalions versus 72, and they had only 270 guns and not much ammunition against 1,200 guns and 300 mortars. The Germans had seventeen 305mm heavy guns provided by their Austrian allies and thirteen of their own 'Big Bertha' 420mm super-heavy howitzers. These monsters had smashed concrete fortifications in Belgium and Russia and now proceeded to do the same to the forts surrounding Verdun. Ironically, the chain of 19th-century forts around the city had been disarmed in 1915 to provide artillery to support the French offensives. But now they were to be the focus of some of the most intense fighting of the war.

Fort Douaumont Falls

Two battalions of French light infantry, the 56th and 59th Chasseurs, led by Colonel Emile Driant, held their positions in the Bois des Caures with extraordinary bravery. Only one man in four survived the storm of steel that tore through their defences, but they counter-attacked during the night to regain some of their strongpoints. After a second hurricane bombardment, the survivors were driven out by 12 German battalions

Verdun

December 1915 Colonel Driant, an officer serving on the frontline at Verdun, complains that the defences of the sector have been seriously neglected. Meanwhile, General Falkenhayn orders the first major German attack in the West since April 1915, its objective: Verdun.

21 February 1916 German offensive begins, relying on very heavy artillery bombardments and short, sharp infantry attacks.

25 February The slow but remorseless German advance continues, and in a tragic-comedy of errors, Fort Douaumont is captured. The fortification has more symbolic than military value, but its loss deepens the gloom of local French commanders. General Pétain is appointed to command the Verdun sector.

6 March The Germans widen the scope of their offensive to include the left bank of the Meuse.

10 April Pétain issues his famous order of the day ending in 'Courage! We shall have them!' After a month of incessant attacks, the Germans have failed to take much more ground and casualties on both sides are soaring.

22 May The third French attempt to recapture Fort Douaumont fails.

8 June German troops take Fort Vaux after a week's heavy fighting around the ruined fortifications.

23 June The last major German push at Verdun captures the Thiamont redoubt but fails to break through to the last ridge overlooking the city.

July–October The Battle of the Somme draws off German reserves and forces Falkenhayn to scale back operations at Verdun.

24 October The French recapture Fort Douaumont.

and the gallant Colonel Driant was killed along with nine out of ten of his men. Their sacrifice helped delay the German advance long enough for the French to rush more troops to the threatened sector.

By 24 February the French commanders were planning to evacuate the right bank of the River Meuse as their positions were untenable, but Marshal Joffre decreed that anyone retreating could be court-martialled. He appointed General Pétain to take command of the Verdun sector on the 25th. The remaining civilians were evacuated from the city. Then came news that Fort Douaumont had been captured by the Germans. Although partly disarmed and prepared for demolition, the great brooding mass of the fort dominated the northern approach to Verdun. Pre-war French propaganda had grossly exaggerated the tactical importance of Douaumont and the other big forts. Now the government feared its loss would damage civilian morale, and pressured the generals to recapture it.

Pétain's Fever

Pétain spent 25 February touring the front in freezing weather and promptly went down with pneumonia the next day. He was sixty years old and in the pre-antibiotic era this was often a death sentence. His temperature soaring to dangerous heights, he managed the battle by telephone from under a pile of blankets, refusing his doctor's request that he relinquish command. Typically, he never mentioned this in his memoirs.

Brought back from retirement at the start of the war, Pétain was one of the few French generals to make successful attacks in 1915. He won the defensive battle for Verdun and would be called in to rescue the French army again in 1917 – and again in 1940. Had he died between the wars, he would be remembered as one of his country's greatest military commanders.

The systematic German bombardments and short, sharp infantry attacks had driven the frontline about six kilometres west. Since their guns had a range of nine kilometres at most, these now had to be brought forward over the devastated ground in order to continue the attack. From 28 February the weather improved, and melting snow reduced much of the battlefield to a quagmire. Their advance temporarily halted on the right bank, the Germans then opened a new assault on the left bank of the river. Through March and into April, the Germans shelled the French positions then attacked them with their infantry but the French now had plenty of artillery ammunition themselves. Woods were reduced to stumps and splinters, villages to a few smears of brick dust. All that remained was a churned mass of tortured earth with French and German infantry hunkered down amid the shell holes, fighting for places that only existed on the generals' maps.

In four months' fighting, the German army group on the left bank of the Meuse lost 69,000 men but advanced only three kilometres. Verdun had not fallen. However, the great Allied offensive planned for the Somme was delayed, and the French component much reduced, because of the incessant demands for more manpower at Verdun. However many troops Pétain received, he still seemed to ask for more. And he would only ever launch limited counter-attacks: Joffre wanted to retake Fort Douaumont. If this

The First Battle in the Air

VERDUN WAS THE FIRST BATTLE in which air operations were incorporated into both sides' plans from the start. The artillery fire with which General Falkenhayn intended to slaughter the French infantry was directed by aerial observation, and its targets were selected and monitored by aerial photography. The Germans formed the first dedicated fighter squadrons to protect their observation aircraft from French attack. The initial German offensive was supported by 270 aircraft. Nevertheless French ace Jean Navarre scored 12 kills over Verdun in his red Nieuport fighter, before being shot down and crippled in June. And it was above this battlefield that the famous squadron of American volunteers, *L'Escadrille Lafayette,* first saw action. German diplomatic protests to the still neutral USA prevented the French from calling it *L'Escadrille Americaine.*

irritated Joffre, the way that Pétain was hailed by the press as the 'saviour of Verdun' drove him to distraction. (Joffre set aside whole mornings to read his own fan mail which seemed to be diminishing.) On 30 April Joffre promoted Pétain to command Army Group Centre and General Robert Nivelle was placed in charge of the 2nd Army at Verdun.

Nivelle presided over a series of counter-attacks that failed to recapture Douaumont. Worse, the Germans took another of the pre-war forts, Vaux, in an epic week-long siege. Counter-attacks failed to relieve the surrounded garrison which surrendered when its water supply was exhausted. With Vaux in their hands, the Germans had one more ridgeline to conquer before they would be able to bring the Meuse bridges under direct artillery fire. But by mid-June Falkenhayn knew that a major Allied offensive was imminent on the Somme. Worse, the Russians had come to life again and inflicted a near-fatal mauling on the Austro-Hungarian army that would now have to be stiffened with German troops if it were to have any chance of holding the eastern front together.

Poison Gas and Counter-Attacks

The Germans tried to land the decisive blow before the Allied assault on the Somme. On 21 June they bombarded the French lines with a new type of poison gas, phosgene, against which existing Allied gas masks gave little defence. Around the village of Fleury and the ridge of Froideterre, French soldiers refused to give in and fought position after position to the last man. The Allies began a massive barrage of their own on 24 June: a fortnight of intense shelling along the Somme front, intended to destroy the German trenches and barbed-wire entanglements. The German emperor, who had come to Verdun in anticipation of the city falling into his hands, returned to his headquarters.

The sheer scale of the British effort on the Somme came as a disagreeable surprise to the emperor and his generals. Russia's resurgence tipped Romania into joining the Allies in August. As for 'bleeding France white', it was revealed that Falkenhayn had been concealing the extent of German losses at Verdun. And the French were still counter-attacking.

Falkenhayn's grand strategy had failed: he was sacked on 29 August. His successor, General von Hindenburg, ordered that there be no more German attacks on Verdun. But the battle was not over.

General Joffre's star was waning: his offensives in 1915 failed to liberate any significant French territory and now the Somme battle had not produced the hoped-for breakthrough. He visited the Verdun sector in September 1916 to hurry up plans for a major counterstroke there. Delayed by bad weather, the new Battle of Verdun opened on 22 October with massed French heavy guns neutralizing German artillery batteries and two gigantic 400mm rail guns cracking apart the concrete casemates of Fort Douaumont. When the infantry went over the top on 24 October they took all their objectives including Douaumont, regaining in a day what the Germans had taken four months to capture.

The Victory of Verdun

The last major action of the Verdun battle took place in mid-December when four French divisions launched a surprise attack on what the Germans now assumed was a quiet sector. Three hundred German guns and 11,000 soldiers were captured. After ten months of unprecedented casualties, the French army was attacking with as much panache as ever, but now supported by plentiful modern artillery.

Verdun cemented the military reputation of General Pétain, who would end the war a Marshal of France, the only man the politicians could turn to in 1940 once they had brought the country to ruin. By the end of 1916 half the German divisions on the western front had fought at Verdun, many went through the 'mill on the Meuse' more than once. Three-quarters of the French army fought at Verdun, divisions averaging two weeks in the line during which they could expect to lose a third of their men. Nevertheless, as Pétain had told his men, 'They shall not pass' – and they did not. From 1920 to 1980 it was celebrated in France as 'the victory of Verdun'. Since then, in a spirit of European unity, it is referred to as 'the Battle of Verdun': President Mitterrand and Chancellor Kohl met there in 1984 in a symbolic act of Franco-German reconciliation.

Forts Douaumont and Vaux are preserved as museums today, and large areas of shell craters are still visible beneath the conifer forests planted after the war. Nine of the villages were never rebuilt, and remain to this day, mute witnesses to man's blind indifference to his fellow man.

'FLEET ACTION IS IMMINENT'
SIGNAL FROM ADMIRAL JELLICOE TO THE
ADMIRALTY, 4.50 P.M., 31 MAY 1916

JUTLAND
31 MAY –
1 JUNE 1916

On the afternoon of 31 May 1916, Georg von Hase, gunnery officer of the German battlecruiser *Derfflinger*, was just sitting down in the wardroom for a cup of coffee. Some of his fellow officers had speculated they might encounter British warships off Norway, but so far this looked like another routine sortie. Hase had barely lit his cigarette when there was a thunder of drums and shouts to clear for action. Minutes later, Hase was at action stations, peering through his high-magnification Zeiss periscope.

At first, he saw nothing; then, a few cruisers in the distant haze. Some German torpedo boats raced past to shelter behind the 25,000-ton bulk of Hase's battlecruiser and her four consorts. The funnel smoke cleared. 'Suddenly my periscope revealed some big ships. Black monsters; six tall, broad-beamed giants steaming in two columns. They were a long way off, but they showed up clearly on the horizon, and even at this great distance they looked powerful, massive.' The biggest battleship action in history was about to begin.

Jutland was the only full-scale clash between the British and German battle fleets during the First World War. It was the last great naval battle decided by surface ships alone: there were no submarines present, and aircraft had little influence.

Maps of naval battles usually resemble a heap of spaghetti, but they can be untangled by patient observation and the manoeuvres of the rival fleets understood. However, the story of Jutland cannot be told so clearly: no participant had such an overview. As the British commander-in-chief, Admiral Sir John Jellicoe reported to the Admiralty, 'The whole situation was difficult to grasp, as I had no real idea of what was going on, and we could hardly see anything except the flashes of guns, shells falling, ships blowing up and an occasional glimpse of an enemy vessel.' The account of his opponent, Admiral Reinhard Scheer, sounds far more certain, but the German admiral was dissembling: every time he came into sight of the British line of battle he did so by accident – with the British steaming across his bows, bringing every gun to bear.

The strategic background to the battle was that pre-war German naval policy had failed. When he came to the throne in 1888, Kaiser Wilhelm II inherited the world's most powerful and professional army, backed by the fastest-growing industrial economy in the world. Obsessed with US naval captain Alfred T. Mahan's book *The Influence of Sea Power on History*, the young emperor ordered the construction of a modern battle fleet. His nautical fantasies were fed by his naval commander, Admiral Tirpitz, who persuaded

OPPOSITE: *A British dreadnought opens fire. Jutland was the last great battleship action in history, submarines and aircraft ultimately playing little part in proceedings. The big guns could hit targets ten miles away, with armour-piercing shells weighing up to half a ton.*

Losing the War in an Afternoon

WINSTON CHURCHILL DESCRIBED Admiral Jellicoe as 'the only man on either side who could lose the war in an afternoon'. Certainly, the British could not have continued the war had they lost control of their home waters to the High Seas Fleet. But it proved very difficult to inflict mortal damage on a battleship by gunfire alone – let alone on a squadron, or a fleet. The British battlecruisers were vulnerable because they were very lightly armoured: built in the belief that high speed and big guns were enough. German battlecruisers were almost as well protected as their battleships, accepting slightly lower speeds and lighter armament as the price of survival. Ironically, the man who did lose the war that afternoon was the German admiral, Reinhard Scheer. His confidential report to the German government accepted that the Germans could not defeat the British in a surface action. He recommended that Germany resume unrestricted submarine warfare: the U-boats duly attacked all shipping bound for the United Kingdom, including American vessels. The result: the United States declared war on Germany in 1917.

German political leaders that massive government spending on German heavy industry would end the capitalist cycle of 'boom and bust' – and banish the looming spectre of socialism. With the industrial working class now making up a third of the population, the pressure for democratic reform was becoming intolerable.

At the beginning of the 20th century, the British had the largest navy in the world, a position of global dominance enjoyed since they crushed the French and Spanish fleets at Trafalgar in 1805. The British were not about to concede maritime supremacy to Germany and so began an arms race that lasted until 1914, by which time the British had won. When Germany began to build its 'High Seas Fleet', the British maintained major naval forces in the Mediterranean and Pacific. These were brought back to home waters while British shipyards worked around the clock to out-build Germany. The shrill political rhetoric that accompanied Germany's naval programme poisoned Anglo-German relations. So when Germany went to war with France and Russia in 1914, the minority 'war party' inside the British cabinet was able to win the argument. Tirpitz's 'risk fleet' gamble was a busted flush: the Royal Navy was still far larger than Germany's and was now a declared enemy.

The British imposed a maritime blockade, preventing Germany from importing rubber, cotton, nitrates (for explosives) – all the strategic materials required for modern war. The narrow waters of the English Channel were defended by dense minefields, while the British battle fleet, based at Scapa Flow in the Orkney Islands, blocked German access to the Atlantic. To break the blockade, the Germans needed to sink a large number of British battleships. Since the British fleet was larger, they needed to lure an isolated squadron into an ambush by their main force: and this was the strategy behind a series of German raids on the British east coast from 1914–16. There had been some near misses, and one engagement between British and German battlecruisers in 1915. On 31 May 1916, both main fleets were at sea, on converging courses. Admiral Scheer had deployed a line of U-boats in the anticipated path of the British, and hoped to have Zeppelins to scout overhead as soon as the wind dropped. If he could smash a British squadron, he could change the course of the war.

The Fleets Sight Each Other – 15.20 hours

The British had captured copies of the German code books earlier in the war, and so had advance notice of Scheer's sortie. Nevertheless, it was the chance interception of a neutral steamer by light units from both fleets that brought about the action. After a brief clash between the cruisers and torpedo boats, the British and German battlecruiser squadrons sighted each other at about 3.20 p.m. hours: six British versus four German battlecruisers. The Germans steamed southeast, intending to draw the British on to the 22 battleships of the German battle fleet. The British should have had an overwhelming advantage at this point: Vice Admiral Beatty's six battlecruisers were supposed to be supported by Rear Admiral Evan-Thomas's 5th Battle Squadron: four massive fast battleships with the biggest guns of any warship then afloat. Unfortunately, Evan-Thomas missed Beatty's signal to turn and follow him. Displaying the lamentable lack of initiative that was prevalent in the Royal Navy at that time, Evan-Thomas steamed blithely on the opposite course for a good ten minutes. By the time he finally put his helm over, his mighty ships were trailing seven miles behind.

'There seems to be something wrong with our bloody ships today'

VICE-ADMIRAL BEATTY

'Q-turret has gone, sir'

Vice Admiral Hipper, commanding the German battlecruisers, gave the order to open fire at 3.48 p.m., his flagship *Lützow* engaging Beatty's flagship *Lion* at a range of eight nautical miles. The Germans fired four-gun salvoes every 20 seconds – and their shooting was extremely accurate despite the great range. HMS *Lion*, *Princess Royal* and *Tiger* were all hit. *Queen Mary* hit the *Seydlitz*, killing most of the 70-man crew in one of her great gun turrets. *Lützow* scored an equally devastating hit on *Lion*, blowing the roof off her amidships gun turret and causing a fire among the ammunition. An officer on *Lion*'s bridge remembered 'a bloodstained sergeant of Marines' with burnt clothes, arriving to make his report, 'Q turret has gone, sir. All the crew are dead and we have flooded the magazine.'

Shot and Shell

At the end of the battlecruiser lines, *Von der Tann* shot it out with HMS *Indefatigable*. After 15 minutes' shooting two successive salvoes from the German battlecruiser straddled the *Indefatigable* with gigantic shell splashes. One or more 11-inch armour-piercing shells struck home. She slowed, listing to port, then exploded with stunning force, sending one of her ship's boats hundreds of feet in the air. Just two of her 1,019 complement survived to be fished out of the water by a German torpedo boat a few hours later.

Queen Mary went up ten minutes later: blown in half by the explosion of her midships magazine. Eight men survived while 1,274 went down with their ship. At the same time, *Princess Royal*, next astern of Beatty's flagship, also vanished in a cloud of smoke and spray as a salvo struck the sea all around her. 'Chatfield,' Beatty remarked to his flag captain, 'there seems to be something wrong with our bloody ships today.'

Then came an electrifying signal from British light cruisers scouting ahead of Beatty's battlecruisers: HMS *Southampton* sent 'Have sighted enemy battle fleet'. Moments later, Beatty saw it himself and reversed his course and his role. It was now his job to lure the Germans on to the 24 battleships of Jellicoe's 'Grand Fleet'. The Germans certainly took the bait: Hipper turned to follow, and the German battleships went to full speed, their leading squadron opening fire on the British cruisers, then the battlecruisers – and then Evan-Thomas. Once again, Evan-Thomas missed the signal and, apparently unable to think for himself, steered his four battleships straight at the oncoming High Seas Fleet. HMS *Warspite*'s executive officer recalled 'an endless ripple of orange flashes all down the line'. Having belatedly turned, the four battleships steamed north, shooting it out with the German 3rd Battle Squadron, Scheer's most modern capital ships. These, the four König-class dreadnoughts, exceeded their designed speed trying to overhaul the British, such was the ferocious energy of their stokers.

Beatty lost visual contact with the Germans as he raced to position himself between Hipper's battlecruisers and the main body of the British fleet. This left Evan-Thomas as the most senior British commander in contact with the Germans, but he never informed Jellicoe what was happening until prompted by a radio signal from the admiral. The British were paying the price for their excessively centralized command system, which had grown up over the long years of peacetime – ironically, the officer responsible for the cumbersome signalling system was Evan-Thomas.

With tantalizingly little information coming in from his cruiser scouts and from his admirals currently engaging the enemy, Jellicoe had to decide when and where to deploy into line of battle. He had 24 battleships steaming in six parallel columns of four, an ideal

ABOVE: *Seen on his flagship* Iron Duke, *Admiral Jellicoe still carried a bullet in his shoulder, received while leading a bayonet charge ashore in China. At Jutland, he staged the greatest ambush in naval history, drawing the German fleet into a deadly trap from which it was very lucky to escape.*

Jutland

30 May 1916

22.30 British Grand Fleet puts to sea after radio intercepts confirm the German fleet is about to leave harbour.

31 May

02.00 German High Seas Fleet puts to sea, steering for the Dogger Bank area with its battlecruiser squadron probing ahead.

14.00 German torpedo boats close on a neutral steamer which has also drawn the attention of British light cruisers. The British sight their enemy and open fire at 14.28.

14.51 The German battlecruisers sight the British battlecruiser squadron and open fire a few minutes later at a range of 16,840 yards.

16.46 The British battlecruisers turn north, having sighted the main body of the German fleet.

18.25 The High Seas Fleet is ambushed by the British. Caught in line ahead, the Germans make an emergency 180 degree turn under heavy fire.

19.13 The High Seas Fleet blunders head first into the British battle line a second time and Admiral Scheer orders his battlecruisers on a 'death ride' to draw British fire while his fleet breaks contact.

20.30 Final shots traded between British battlecruisers and some of the German battle squadrons. During the night, the Germans slip astern of the British and creep back to harbour.

1 June

15.00 The German battle fleet anchors in Wilhelmshaven in no state to continue the battle. The Grand Fleet searches the North Sea for the enemy before turning for home.

---

formation for visual control, but not one in which to fight a battle. He could see gun flashes all along the horizon when, at 6.15 p.m., he deployed from the port column bearing southeast-by-east.

Scheer's first intimation that there were more British forces at sea came as his battle fleet's cruiser screen was engaged by British light forces, and some British destroyers attempted a torpedo attack on his battleships. Lieutenant Commander Tovey, in HMS *Onslow*, torpedoed the cruiser *Wiesbaden*, and engaged Scheer's battle line amid a storm of fire; he failed to get a battleship this time. (He had to wait until 1941 when he sank the *Bismarck*.)

Iron Duke Hits *König*

One moment Scheer was pursuing an outnumbered British force, probably to its destruction. Then the tables were turned. At 6.30 p.m., still steaming flat out in rough line ahead, he found the British main battle line across his line of advance. The smoke from the funnels and guns of over 200 ships ensured no one saw the battle lines in their entirety, Scheer recalling the horizon looked like 'a sea of fire' as gun flashes erupted all along the horizon. The Royal Navy's traditional obsession with rapid fire now came into its own: Jellicoe's flagship *Iron Duke* got off nine salvoes in the first four minutes, hitting *König*. An apparent explosion at the end of the British line marked the debut of the *Agincourt*: originally built for Brazil to a unique design with seven centre-line turrets, it had been widely rumoured that she would overturn if she fired all at once. Nevertheless, her captain ordered full salvoes: fourteen 12-inch guns fired together!

Sadly, there was an all too real explosion as Rear Admiral Hood's 3rd Battlecruiser Squadron entered the fray. Hood's squadron had accompanied Jellicoe but was sent to probe ahead of the main line, and quickly engaged the German battlecruisers. *Invincible's* shooting was excellent, scoring two quick hits on *Lützow* that led to severe flooding, but the German return salvo struck amidships and *Invincible* blew in half. The British achieved their rapid rates of fire by cramming the turrets with ammunition, and the giant bags of explosive propellant had black powder igniters. It literally took just a spark to trigger a catastrophic detonation.

Steaming Through Smoke

Scheer ordered 'battle about turn', a uniquely German manoeuvre in which the line of battle reversed course, starting with the rearmost ship. He sent torpedo boats forward to lay a smokescreen. For half an hour the British steamed south, all eyes peering into the murk until just after 7 p.m. they saw the Germans coming on again. Scheer had reversed course too soon and instead of running for his home port, he led his fleet straight into the British. His lead squadron was hit repeatedly. In a panic, he ordered another about turn and ordered his heavily damaged battlecruisers to continue forward and engage the British at close range, sacrificing themselves so the main line could escape.

Von Hase's ship, *Derfflinger*, was hit twice, two turrets and their whole crews were burned out by direct hits and the ship filled with poisonous fumes. He and his team donned gas masks. *Lützow* was left foundering; *Seydlitz* limped away shipping thousands of tons of water; *Von der Tann* had partial power failure and finished the engagement in darkness, with none of her big guns operational.

There were a series of desperate battles between small groups of ships during the night. British destroyers ran into the German heavy units and sank the old battleship *Pommern* with all hands. The British cruiser *Black Prince* gave the recognition signal to what her captain assumed was a British battleship squadron: but it was the High Seas Fleet and she was instantly illuminated with searchlights and shot to pieces. She caught fire and sank with her whole complement. In all these fierce little actions, British skippers simply assumed that their admirals knew what was happening so did not bother to signal them. As Jellicoe steered to intercept the enemy at first light, so Scheer's battered ships slipped past, astern of the Grand Fleet, and made for Germany. His course was known to the Admiralty in London, thanks to radio intercepts, but again, the message was not passed on to Jellicoe's flagship.

Dawn revealed the sea dotted with debris and the occasional survivors, but the Germans were long gone. It was with a sense of bitter disappointment that Jellicoe's fleet eventually set course for home. And although the Germans won the race to issue a triumphant and vainglorious communiqué, the strategic situation was unchanged by the Battle of Jutland. On 1 June there was only one operational battle fleet in the North Sea – and it was flying the White Ensign of the British Royal Navy.

THE SOMME

1 JULY – 20 NOVEMBER 1916

'IT MAKES ME SICK TO THINK
OF THE MIGHT-HAVE-BEENS'
GENERAL RAWLINSON, COMMANDER
BRITISH 4TH ARMY

The Battle of the Somme is notorious for the tremendous casualties suffered by the British army on the first day of the offensive. On 1 July 1916 the British lost 19,240 men killed, 35,493 wounded, 2,152 missing and 585 captured; German casualties were 10,000–12,000 including about 2,000 prisoners.

However, the battle lasted until 20 November, and by then the slaughter was no longer one-sided: about 300,000 men lay dead; in round numbers 100,000 British, 50,000 French and 150,000 German. (The statistics of the Somme have been disputed ever since, thanks to chaotic record-keeping and some sleight of hand in official histories.)

'. . . up the line to death.'

The impact of so many deaths is difficult to overstate, especially for the British who had no experience of military casualties on this scale. The way their army had been recruited meant that the losses were not evenly distributed, but concentrated among particular communities; the virtual annihilation of some units gave the impression that a whole generation had been wiped out. In reality, the British were paying the penalty for their haphazard, if gallant, recruiting system that had created the largest volunteer army ever seen in Europe.

In December 1915 the Allied leadership resolved to make near simultaneous attacks on the Germans in the summer of 1916. The British and French would combine forces to make a major push in the Somme sector, where their respective front lines met. None of the major offensives made by the French alone in 1915 had had any success in ejecting the Germans from French soil. This time, they would be fighting alongside a massively enlarged British army. Meanwhile, the Russians, who had been driven out of Poland in 1915, would return to the fight with an attack aimed at Germany's weak ally, the Austro-Hungarian Empire. Italy, seduced into joining the Allies by promises of Hapsburg territory, would strike another blow against the Austro-Hungarians.

Unfortunately for the Allies, the Germans did not sit and wait to be attacked. They did not even wait for the end of winter. In February 1916, the snow still on the ground, they attacked the old French fortress at Verdun, and came very close to capturing the city. The French rushed in reinforcements by railway and managed to arrest the German advance. But they became involved in a terrible attritional struggle there that compelled them to scale back their commitment to the planned offensive on the Somme. Understandably, they pressured the British to attack as soon as possible. General Haig wanted time to train his vast but inexperienced army, yet however much he would have

OPPOSITE: *The iconic image of the battle of the Somme: British soldiers struggle through barbed wire under enemy fire. In fact, the Germans counter-attacked with typical vigour throughout the five-month campaign.*

preferred to attack in late summer, the needs of the alliance had to come first. It was agreed that the attack would take place at the end of June.

'Hour after hour they ponder the warm field . . .'

The rolling hills of the Somme countryside that reminded many British soldiers of southern England also made for excellent defensive positions. The chalk ridge that ran from Thiepval to Morval gave the Germans a splendid view to the west, and they fortified a number of villages on the forward slope, facing the direction from which the British would attack. They constructed very deep dugouts in the chalk hillsides, impervious to all but a direct hit from a very heavy gun. The basements of the village houses were connected by trenches and tunnels, and concrete strongpoints, bristling with machine guns, were sited so that their fields of fire overlapped. Allied soldiers attacking any one position would come under fire from one or both flanks. Successive lines of trenches, several hundred yards apart, were protected by dense thickets of barbed wire, some of them hidden in the long grass.

'The enemy must not be allowed to advance, except over corpses'

GENERAL ERICH VON FALKENHAYN, CHIEF OF THE GERMAN GENERAL STAFF

The Germans were completely confident of holding their ground against the British. In 1914 the German political leadership had accepted war with Britain as the price of their invasion of Belgium with the utmost insouciance. Germany had 100 divisions of highly trained soldiers; Britain had 6. Rapid expansion of its pre-war army by mass voluntary enlistment during 1915 had enabled the British to mount some small scale-attacks on the Germans. None succeeded, and after another fiasco, at Loos in September, the British commander was sacked, and replaced by General Haig. The German assessment of the British army in early 1916 remained the same: it had grown enormously, but its officers and men were merely enthusiastic amateurs. In March–April, when Verdun was almost within their grasp, the German high command toyed with a follow-on attack against the British. They made some local attacks and captured several positions the British had only just been entrusted with by the French. It made for a frosty start to planning the battle.

The sad truth was that the British were amateurs. Like the Army of the Potomac in the Civil War, the British Expeditionary Force had expanded from a tiny pre-war army into a mighty host. Few of the volunteer soldiers had any previous military experience, and officers were catapulted into senior rank for which they had no preparation. Many senior positions were filled by 'dugouts', retired officers who had done some soldiering, but only in small-scale colonial operations. Haig was one of the few true professionals who understood what his men faced: he had translated German manuals before the war and knew just how well trained and equipped the kaiser's armies were.

The 'Pals Battalions'

UNLIKE THE MAJOR EUROPEAN POWERS, which conscripted a varying proportion of their young men every year, the British army of 1914 was a volunteer force of long-service professionals. Most of the soldiers in this (by continental standards) tiny army were dead, wounded or promoted by the end of the year. Lord Kitchener, secretary of state for war, called for volunteers to fill up the ranks. The response from the British public was incredible: by summer 1916 General Haig had 600,000 men in 56 divisions and several hundred thousand in training. It was a true citizen army in which factory and office workers often joined-up together, retaining hierarchies and comradeship from the civilian workplace into the army. It was an army like no other, and whatever its professional shortcomings, there was no doubting its determination. The downside to such local recruitment was that when battalions suffered heavy losses, they could have catastrophic effects on small, close-knit communities, leaving whole streets in mourning.

Every man in the British army from Haig down to the newest recruit took great pride in the sheer number of artillery pieces assembled for the offensive. One conspicuous problem with the limited British attacks in 1915 had been the shortage of guns – and ammunition. Now, thanks to sterling efforts on the home front, there were just over 1,000 field guns assembled behind the front line. Another 182 heavy guns and 245 howitzers would contribute to a bombardment that was scheduled to last for a week. Day after day, night after night, the British guns pounded the German trenches, barbed-wire barricades, artillery positions and headquarters. The first rudimentary attempts to direct fire from aircraft and captive balloons were supplemented by photo-reconnaissance flights. The technology was primitive in the extreme, but recognizably modern techniques were developing quickly in the white heat of combat.

Storm of Shrapnel

The bombardment sounded like the wrath of God. For more than 12 miles, the German front line was engulfed in a storm of earth and dust, peppered with angry flashes as 1.5-million shells detonated on the heads of the defenders. Except that they didn't. The ammunition had been supplied by factories tooled-up in great haste and quality control was very poor. Dud shells are still being dug out of the Somme chalk nearly 90 years later. When the high-speed railway line was built across the Somme region in 1990, 23 tons of unexploded ordnance was found along the route.

Less than 10 per cent of the 12,000 tons of high explosive fired came from guns heavy enough for the shells to penetrate deep enough to cave in the German dugouts. The thousand British field guns mostly fired shrapnel: shells with a small bursting charge that exploded in the air, showering the target with small steel projectiles like a giant shotgun. Lethal against men in the open, it made no impression on the German trenches and did not, as was hoped, have much effect on the barbed wire either.

'. . . earth set sudden cups in thousands for their blood . . .'

The British also tunnelled under the German trenches and set off a series of gigantic mines just before they attacked. These were extremely spectacular and blew the trenches, wire and unfortunate defenders to kingdom come. Unfortunately it proved very hard to win the race to occupy the craters: the Germans recovered their wits and counter-attacked like the experienced professionals they were.

At 7.30 a.m. on 1 July, the bombardment finally stopped. Moments later it resumed, now concentrating on the second and third German lines so the British infantry could assault without being struck by their own artillery. Then everything went wrong. The British infantry advanced towards the German front line, walking steadily across several hundred yards – sometimes half a mile – of 'no-man's-land'. They expected to be counter-attacked once they had occupied the German front line, so they carried a heavy load of ammunition. Follow-up parties came on with sandbags, picks and shovels to re-fortify captured positions. But in many places the wire thickets remained, impenetrable.

> ' The Somme was the muddy grave of the German field army '
>
> CAPTAIN VON HENTIG, GERMAN GUARD RESERVE DIVISION

German machine-gun teams raced up from their dugouts, deployed their weapons and fired on the serried lines of khaki. The British had lost the race to the German parapets, and now paid a dreadful price. Battalion after battalion was shot down in no-man's-land. Flares soared above the German lines, signalling that they were under attack. In response, the German gunners manned their pieces and opened fire. Despite the best efforts of the British fliers, many German artillery batteries had remained hidden. Hundreds of heavy guns opened fire, shelling the British troops now pinned down in no-man's-land. In some sectors, the German counter-bombardment was so heavy that it flattened the British front-line trenches too – and the support battalion waiting its turn to attack.

Portable radios had yet to be invented, runners and their messages simply vanished, and even the telephone lines buried beneath the earth were soon cut by shell fire. With no easy way of communicating, the British infantry were left to die while the artillery continued to fire on the German second and third lines. There were a few isolated break-ins, but the day was a disaster for the British. The French did far better on their sector, largely because the French sensibly backed their smaller operation with proportionally much more artillery: they had something like a 10:1 advantage in guns, compared to the British 2:1.

Communications were so slow that it took several days for the extent of the disaster to become known. Nevertheless, the British continued to attack, every day saw another bombardment, another rush of men into a storm of shot and shell. From 2–13 July the British suffered another 25,000 casualties in some 40 attacks characterized by lack of preparation, hasty execution and tactical failure. In the south, the French continued to advance, capturing position after position (and 8,000 prisoners) until they had driven the Germans back nearly six miles. Only a rush of reinforcements to the sector prevented the liberation of Péronne.

'Only the stuttering rifles' rapid rattle . . .'

On 14 July the British attacked just before dawn. In a very professional operation, the assault troops were assembled close to the German front line overnight, without the Germans detecting them. At 3.20 a.m. the British artillery began another bombardment, and the Germans took cover. But this time the guns ceased fire on the front line after only five minutes, and the British infantry raced forwards. The Germans lost the contest and, instead of shooting down the British in no-man's-land, there was a desperate fight with bayonets and grenades. Almost every objective was taken, and there was even a cavalry charge that evening. The 7th Dragoon Guards and 2nd Deccan Horse lowered their lances and speared a number of Germans lurking in standing crops outside High Wood, before dismounting to hold off a counter-attack.

The Somme campaign settled into a rhythm of attack and counter-attack that lasted from mid-July until mid-September. Every day saw one or two small-scale operations somewhere along the front. Most cost the British dearly and few gained any significant amount of ground; the front line hardly moved during all this time. Nevertheless, 40 German divisions were sent to the Somme, as the daily attrition rate consumed unit after unit. Few British attacks failed so completely that the Germans were not forced to counter-attack to recapture lost positions. The iconic image of the Somme is a line of 'Tommies' climbing out of their trench, picking their way through their own defensive wire, and advancing into no-man's-land under a hail of bullets. Yet it was an equally common sight to see groups of men in field grey, rushing from crater to crater, more and more remaining on the ground as British machine guns found the range. German counter-attacks on Delville Wood frequently lost half their men just getting on to the start line: co-ordination between the British infantry and their supporting artillery had improved markedly.

By the end of August the fighting on the Somme had cost the Germans more men in two months than in six months' fighting at Verdun. Ultimately 138 German divisions served on the Somme in 1916, compared to 75 at Verdun. One German soldier remembered the unceasing fury of the British artillery, 'The English bombardment kept increasing in intensity at the turn of each hour. Even when night settled over the mutilated fields of France, there had been no let up . . . The few remaining defenders of this section of the Western Front had become nothing more than crawling animals, seeking refuge in ever fresh-made holes. They slid from one crater to another in vain search for food as well as protection. But neither could be found.'

The last major Allied attack took place on 15 September. The artillery laid on another massive shoot, firing some 800,000 shells. Most memorably, the attack included 48 tanks of which 21 got into action, the first tank action in history. Their descendants would one day dominate the battlefield, but the tanks of September 1916 were mechanically unreliable death-traps; highly inflammable and barely bulletproof. The attack broke through to the German third line, but German reinforcements arrived to seal the breach.

Ill-advised British attempts to continue the offensive into the autumn piled up a lot of dead in the muddy wreckage of the German lines. Heavy rain turned major sectors of the battlefield into foetid swamps. Survivors of both battles argued over which mud was worse, that of the Somme or Passchendaele in 1917. The final attacks lasted from 13–18 November and witnessed the capture of Beaumont-Hamel, one of the objectives of 1 July.

War of Attrition

At a cost of 419,654 killed, wounded and missing, the British had liberated a two-mile strip of blasted countryside and shattered French villages. French losses had reached 204,253 and they had advanced up to five miles. It is not easy to justify an operation of war in which you lose five men for every inch of ground recaptured, but it had cost the Germans about 500,000 casualties too. By the end of 1916 the Germans had lost so many of their peacetime-trained officers and NCOs that senior commanders detected a marked loss of competence. By contrast, the British had learned a great deal. It was no longer a case of amateurs versus professionals.

The Somme brought home to the Germans the folly of accepting war with Britain. The Russian and Italian offensives of 1916 had all but knocked out Austria-Hungary. Now the Germans faced another major army on a European scale, and one that was increasingly well equipped and competently led. And its fighting spirit was undaunted. One of the Germans' more dispiriting discoveries was that captured British soldiers regarded their imprisonment as merely temporary, were confident the Union Jack would be flying over Berlin by 1917 and, in many cases, were only angry that they were not able to have another 'crack at the Hun'.

AMIENS
8–12 AUGUST 1918

'THE BLACK DAY OF THE GERMAN ARMY'
GENERAL ERIC LUDENDORFF

Once the USA had joined the alliance against Imperial Germany, the kaiser's generals could no longer play for time. Within a year – 18 months at most – the British and French armies would be joined in Europe by several hundred thousand US troops, tipping the military balance irrevocably against Germany. In March 1918 General Ludendorff gambled on all or nothing.

He began a series of offensives against the British and French, endeavouring to win the war before America could tip the scales. Although they gained some spectacular successes, by July the German attacks had run out of steam. Their failure meant there was now no prospect of Germany winning the war. The British and French counter-offensives that followed, above all the attack of the British 4th Army on 8 August, ensured Germany would lose.

The Allies Come Off the Ropes

Although severely shaken by mutinies in 1917, the French army had recovered sufficiently to administer a sharp defeat to the Germans in July 1918, at the Second Battle of the Marne. Ludendorff postponed the next major offensive he had planned and it was never revived. Germany's strategic situation was now bleak in the extreme. Ludendorff had reorganized the German army during the winter of 1917–18, concentrating the fittest and best soldiers into special 'attack divisions', which obviously diminished the quality of the other units. The defeat of Russia produced a one-time bounty: many of the forty German divisions there were moved by rail to the western front, and their best troops transferred to the attack divisions. The so-called 'Kaiser's Battle' beginning on 21 March 1918 ultimately cost Germany nearly 1 million casualties, most of them from the elite attack divisions.

Morale in the German army began to sag. The best motivated soldiers were dead or in hospital. The army could censor men's letters home, but could not prevent wives and mothers writing with news of what was happening in German towns and cities. The naval blockade of Germany had already caused the awful 'turnip winter' of 1916, and by 1918 shortages of food and fuel affected every family, from dukes in their palaces to the working-class tenements of Berlin. Germany could not look to its allies either: the situation was even worse in the Austro-Hungarian Empire, which was teetering on the brink of complete disintegration.

Another 'Big Push'

If the mood in the British army was far from the bold confidence it exuded on the eve of the Somme, there was a grim determination to see the thing through. The British had

---

PREVIOUS PAGE: *German prisoners of war carry wounded men to the rear, passing a British tank on its way up the line. In August 1918, the British army managed to co-ordinate tanks, infantry and aircraft together: the true birth of modern warfare.*

survived the heaviest blow the Germans could land. What remained to be seen was whether the Germans could stand the counterpunch.

The ground selected for the first major British counter-offensive was the open plateau east of Amiens, not much cut up by shell craters and good going for the massed tanks that would play a key, if sometimes overstated, role in the operation. The German advance in this sector had been halted in April, but until mid-July the Germans had remained confident they would resume the attack soon. They had therefore not troubled to fortify their positions with their customary zeal.

The British did not have 'attack divisions' in the German sense, but they did have the Australians and Canadians. Whereas British divisions had been reduced from 12 infantry battalions to 9, as the manpower crisis bit, Australian and Canadian divisions remained at full strength. Both were supremely confident, well-trained and battle-hardened formations. The British 4th Army comprised the Canadian Corps of four large divisions; the Australian Corps, with five large divisions; the British III Corps with four British divisions; and an attached US division. Three cavalry divisions stood by to exploit any breakthrough. Three tank brigades, including eight battalions of Mk V heavy tanks, two of Mk IVs, two of Whippet light tanks and one of armoured cars gave an armoured strike force of 342 heavy and 72 light tanks. The British commander-in-chief, Sir Douglas Haig, had been an early advocate of tanks, pressing for 1,000 of them after their tentative debut on the Somme in 1916, but production could not be accelerated that quickly. By contrast, the German high command dismissed the whole concept; General Ludendorff did not see his first tank until February 1918.

> 'Some of the great set-piece battles of World War II are merely sophisticated variations on the theme of Rawlinson's Battle of Amiens'
>
> GENERAL H ESSAME

Metal Monsters Churning Mud

The British attack at Cambrai in November 1917 was the first effective use of armour. However, most of the 378 tanks were out of action within a day or so, and the Germans recaptured almost all their lost positions within a week. Unable to move much faster than a man on foot, the early tanks were blind monsters, lurching across the battlefield, drawing enemy fire until they bogged down or were knocked out. But in the six months since Cambrai, the British had developed techniques in which the infantry and tanks worked together. At Amiens each leading battalion was supported by four tanks that would crush barbed wire and destroy machine-gun posts, with their guns or, if necessary, by ramming.

Cambrai was important for another reason, not as immediately obvious as the grand spectacle of the tank assault. The British artillery had improved its techniques, and proved able to register its guns on target 'blind', by means of good mapping and aerial survey, instead of firing ranging shots which were adjusted by an observer. A German battery bracketed by ranging shots knew what was about to happen and would usually move to another position. 'Silent' pre-registration meant the British were able to strike their targets by surprise. So additional artillery pieces deployed in the 4th Army sector in July 1918 did not signal their arrival by firing ranging shots. They calculated their precise position, the exact location of their targets, and adjusted their aim and ammunition accordingly. The Germans would have no indication they were about to be attacked until a storm of steel burst about their heads.

The Germans came close to discovering what the British were planning just 48 hours before the attack. The highly aggressive Australians had been persistently raiding the German lines, so the Germans brought forward the high-quality 27th Württemberg division to do likewise. Just after everyone had relaxed after the dawn 'stand-to', the Württembergers attacked a section of trenches that the Australians had seized a few days earlier. It was held by British troops from III Corps and the attack caught them in the middle of an inter-brigade relief: in the resulting chaos the Germans penetrated half a mile into the British lines and captured 200 men. The British 18th Division counter-attacked and regained the ground, but there was no telling how much the prisoners knew, and if any of them had blurted something out under interrogation.

Fog in a Summer Dawn

The night of 7/8 August was quiet and still; in the early hours of the morning mist rose from the River Somme, thickening before dawn to form a dense fog, so that the promised RAF support was reduced to a single pilot in a Handley-Page bomber. He stooged about as low as he dared, in the hope that the noise of his engines would make it impossible for the Germans to hear the clatter and roar of several hundred tanks arriving on the front line. The Australian Corps commander, Sir John Monash, described the tension on the eve of this, his greatest battle. Standing in their trenches, 100,000 infantry were waiting for the word to go: 'All feel to make sure that their bayonets are tightly locked, or to set their steel helmets firmly on their heads; company and platoon commanders, their whistles ready to hand, are nervously glancing at their luminous watches, waiting for minute after minute and – giving a last look over their commands – ensuring that their runners are at their sides . . . overhead drone the aeroplanes, and from the rear, in swelling chorus, the clamour of the tanks grows every minute louder.'

The British, Australian and Canadian commanders looked at their watches with the same compulsion as the infantry in the trenches and the gunners crouched around their pieces. Then, at 4.20 a.m. they saw a great blaze of light all along the eastern horizon as 2,000 guns opened fire at maximum rate. For veterans on the 18-pounder field guns this could mean a round fired every few seconds, the gunners working in a superbly choreographed routine either side of the breech as it slammed back at full recoil.

A line of earth and steel fountains erupted 200 yards in front of the British infantry. With remorseless precision it began to move eastwards, a 'creeping barrage' behind which the attackers advanced. In the awful arithmetic of war, the attackers knew that they would lose fewer men if they kept as close behind the barrage as possible. Inevitably, some shells fell short, scything down the advancing infantry with a hail of sharp steel fragments.

'War was return of earth to ugly earth.'

Most German artillery positions were battered with shellfire, some blinded by smoke shells and few in communication with their frontline as all the wires were cut. In just three hours the Australians had taken all their initial objectives. They reorganized, and then struck on to take their second and third lines, destroying any German strongpoints that held out with a combination of tanks, machine guns and pin-point artillery fire. By the afternoon, armoured cars managed to pass across no-man's-land and venture down a road, overrunning the headquarters of the German 51st Corps and some very surprised staff officers. The Canadians faced stout resistance in some sectors, but their long experience served them well and most German positions were suppressed, surrounded and stormed. With mortars, light machine guns and grenade launchers, the infantry were no longer the hapless lines of riflemen the Germans had faced on the Somme two years earlier.

The British 1st and 3rd Cavalry Divisions advanced to exploit the breakthrough and this time they advanced through the infantry by noon and pressed forward to exploit the victory. Serious opposition was dealt with by

Amiens

21 March The first major German offensive in the West since Verdun (February–July 1916) achieves great success against the British 5th Army.

28 March While the British 5th Army continues to retreat in disorder, a second German offensive at Arras is stopped in its tracks within 24 hours.

18 July The series of German offensives ends with the second Battle of the Marne, a French counter-attack that reveals the French army has recovered from the mutinies of autumn 1917.

6 August A German raid captures 200 prisoners on the Amiens front, some of which knew that the British were poised to make an attack of their own.

8 August Nevertheless the attack at Amiens takes the Germans completely by surprise and their entire position collapses. British cavalry, armoured cars and light tanks penetrate behind the front line to overrun headquarters and even capture a train full of reinforcements.

10 August The German retreat brings them on to the old Somme battlefield where the wilderness of old trenches and craters enables them to form a new defensive line.

11 August General Rawlinson terminates the operation having captured some 30,000 Germans and 500 artillery pieces. General Ludendorff has a mental breakdown.

dismounting and attacking with rifles and machine guns, but to their astonished delight, they found many Germans did not even try to defend themselves. Some 3,000 Germans dropped their weapons and surrendered. The 5th Dragoon Guards famously captured a trainload of German reinforcements, taking 600 men prisoner. Whippet light tanks were involved in some exciting incidents too, although it proved impossible to co-ordinate them with the much faster-moving cavalry.

As the summer sunshine broke through the fog, the RAF intervened in style, making incessant attacks on the Somme bridges over which any German reinforcements would have to come. The Battle of Amiens pointed the way to the future in so many ways, and the aerial battle was no exception. Low-level attacks pressed home with great gallantry in the teeth of heavy anti-aircraft fire are incredibly dangerous. The 700 sorties made that day resulted in 96 aircraft destroyed or written off: a completely unsustainable casualty rate.

The Ghosts of 1916

With its customary professionalism, the German staff managed to feed in six new divisions overnight and three more during 9 August. They slowed, but could not stem the British onslaught. By 10 August the Germans had been pushed back to the old Somme battlefields and it was here, in the wilderness of old trenches, overlapping shell craters and rusting barbed wire, that the Battle of Amiens ground to a halt. There were only 38 tanks left operational and the battle had moved far beyond the range of the British artillery. Unlike the grisly offensives of 1917, the Amiens operation was closed down as soon as it bogged down. In any case, the damage had been done. For the first time in the war, German soldiers were giving up, sometimes whole units together. The number of prisoners exceeded the number of dead or wounded. At least 18,000 Germans surrendered to the British and another 11,000 during the supporting French attack on the southern flank. Five hundred German artillery pieces were taken, in many cases because German infantry refused to fight a rearguard action to give them time to limber-up and escape.

From 21–23 August the British 3rd Army attacked south of Arras. The troops were mostly fresh conscripts; there were no big Dominion divisions present, and the German commander, von Bülow, was so confident that he was planning an attack of his own. But once again, cutting-edge artillery tactics, massive firepower and new tactical methods by the British infantry smashed through the defences. Ten thousand Germans surrendered.

As report after report of such moral collapse reached him, Germany's supreme warlord, General Erich Ludendorff, finally cracked. Bad-tempered meetings ended in shouting matches. The German generals began to put out feelers to the politicians they had shouldered aside. Someone would have to negotiate.

THE BATTLE OF
THE ATLANTIC
1939–45

'THERE CAN BE NO QUESTION OF LETTING
UP IN THE U-BOAT WAR. THE ATLANTIC IS MY
WESTERN BUFFER ZONE.'

Adolf Hitler, May 1943

The Battle of the Atlantic was Winston Churchill's name for the German attempt to impose a maritime blockade on the United Kingdom. Before the war, Britain imported 60 million tons of goods per annum, and strategic planners calculated that, even with the imposition of rationing, the country could not continue to fight with less than 47 million tons a year.

If the Germans could reduce the influx of food and raw materials entering the UK below a certain threshold, Britain would be forced to make peace. The campaign was at its most intense between mid-1941 and mid-1943, when Germany seemed dangerously close to strangling its island enemy. Practically every necessity of life was rationed, and the rations subsequently reduced. As an example of how deep-reaching it became, in January 1942 it was decreed that powdered milk damaged in transit could be used to feed cats employed in vermin destruction at warehouses containing more than 25 tons of food.

A Never-Ending Battle

The German navy had lost out to the army and air force in the Nazi rearmament programme, which had been predicated on there being no war before 1948. During the 1930s the navy spent most of its budget on surface warships, above all, a new programme of very expensive battleships. The outbreak of hostilities in 1939 found the Germans with only 20 or so ocean-going U-boats in service. Not until July 1940, when it became clear Britain would not give in, did U-boat construction receive priority. The U-boat commander, Admiral Karl Dönitz, had 28 U-boats in service by then but estimated that he would need 300 to strike a mortal blow: it would take him two years to assemble a fleet that size.

The British merchant marine began the conflict with some 3,000 ocean-going vessels and about 1,000 coasters. Hitler invaded a number of countries distinguished by their large merchant fleets: Norway, the Netherlands and Greece, inadvertently making his own navy's task considerably harder. Although German U-boats had wreaked havoc against British shipping in the First World War, anti-submarine warfare was an unfashionable activity in the inter-war Royal Navy and a dire combination of overconfidence and ineffective weapons and tactics handed the Germans the initiative from the start. There was an inexplicable slowness in organizing ships into convoys: in 1939 the handful of U-boats at sea sank more than 100 ships, almost all sailing individually and quite unable to defend themselves.

Marshalling 20 or 30 merchant ships – each with different cruising speeds and all with famously independent skippers – into a convoy was no easy business. It demanded

PREVIOUS PAGE: *More than 30,000 seamen lost their lives as they strove to keep Britain in the war. Here, another merchant ship lies blazing, one of the 3,500 vessels sunk by German submarines during the battle.*

an enormous administrative effort in the ports and naval escort vessels that were few and far between. But it had to be done. In the vastness of the Atlantic, it was no easier for a U-boat to find a whole convoy than it was to find a single ship, and from the instant convoys were insisted upon, the U-boats were condemned to spend day after day on the surface, their lookouts sweeping the horizon with binoculars.

'I've just seen down your funnel . . .'

The U-boats are better thought of as submersibles rather than true submarine vessels. Underwater, they relied on electric power and while they could put on a quick burst of speed in an emergency, to do anything more than creep along at 3 knots exhausted their batteries in a few hours. They spent much of their time on the surface, where their diesels gave them enough speed to out-run many of the British escort vessels. The diesel engines also recharged the batteries.

> 'Cease firing. Gosh what a lovely battle.'
>
> LEGENDARY U-BOAT HUNTER CAPTAIN FREDERICK WALKER AFTER A 15-HOUR FIGHT RESULTING IN THE SINKING OF U-473, MAY 1944

The U-boats' design made few concessions to human comfort. They stank of crowded humanity, oil, mould and damp clothes. Most of the men 'hot bunked', and there was little water to be spared for washing or shaving. The second toilet was usually employed as additional storage space. Fresh food spoiled quickly and poor diet often had additional gastrointestinal consequences.

The Royal Navy's escort vessels were not noted for their creature comforts either. The 'Flower' class corvettes, typical escort vessels, were equally cramped, very wet, and although based on the design of a whaler, very exciting places to be during an Atlantic gale. As one signalled to another, 'I've just seen down your funnel: fires burning brightly'.

The 'Wolf Packs'

The fall of France in 1940 transformed the war at sea: instead of having to pass up the North Sea and around Scotland to enter the Atlantic, the U-boats could be based on the French Atlantic coast. The Germans constructed massive concrete submarine pens there: impervious to bombing attack and post-war demolition crews. The giant pens at Lorient remain there to this day. Dönitz established his headquarters in France from which he exerted a very personal control over the battle. He deployed his submarines in long patrol lines: once a submarine located a convoy, it would send a radio signal and Dönitz would order all nearby boats to the scene. Mass 'Wolf Pack' attacks made under cover of darkness could be devastating. In the early days, the bolder U-boat commanders came in on the surface, trusting to the low silhouette of their conning tower to keep them invisible from the ships' lookouts. Approaching with the wind behind them blowing spray into the eyes – and optics – of the lookouts, they would launch a fan of torpedoes into the heart of the convoy, calculating that if they missed the ship they were aiming for, there was a good chance of striking another.

The crews of the escort vessels found it a frustrating business, searching empty sea for hours, days and weeks, as a convoy made its stately progress across the ocean. For the seamen aboard the merchant ships, death could come at any moment. Bulk ore carriers sank in seconds; oil tankers immolated whole crews in fireballs that acted as beacons for any U-boat unsure of the convoy's position. A man could live for only a few minutes in the North Atlantic in winter. And if the oil-choked survivors did make it into the ship's boats, they often found nobody would stop for them. Some were picked up by escorting warships, and some by other merchant ships; but U-boats regularly torpedoed ships that had stopped to rescue survivors.

Hundreds of merchant ships, totalling 3.6 million tons (grt) were sunk by the 'Wolf Packs' during 1941. The U-boatmen called it the 'Happy Time'. The British had too few escort vessels to cover the convoys and their pre-war confidence in 'ASDIC' (sonar) was not borne out by experience. It was useless against a submarine on the surface in any case. Nevertheless, British and Canadian shipyards delivered 1.2 million tons of new shipping that year and saved another 3 million tons by reorganizing port procedures and rethinking import requirements. The British also placed orders for another 7 million tons with US shipbuilders.

In December 1941 Hitler declared war on the United States, four days after Japan attacked Pearl Harbor. One reason for this fatal error on his part was the very active part played by the theoretically neutral US Navy in guarding merchant ships in the western Atlantic. News of this other war was passed among the convoys at sea that month, leading to the celebrated exchange of signals between a westbound and an eastbound convoy:

'Commence hostilities with Japan.'
'Permission to finish breakfast first.'

Enigma

With the declaration of war, Hitler ordered Dönitz to send some of his long-range submarines to attack shipping off the US coast and in the Caribbean. This was the U-boats' second 'Happy Time' as the US Navy was very slow to organize convoys and relations between it and the US Army Air Force were lamentable. There was no blackout along the coast, so ships were silhouetted against the lights by night, easy targets for the waiting U-boats.

Dönitz's command method involved a great deal of radio signal traffic between his headquarters and the U-boats. It was encoded with the famous 'Enigma' machines and the British success in breaking the German codes played a key role in defeating the U-boats.

ABOVE: 'We who are about to die, salute you': new U-boat crews salute Admiral Dönitz (second left) after completing their work-up in the Baltic, January 1944. By this date, the hunters had become the hunted: submarine losses were catastrophic and many convoys got through unscathed. One in three U-boat personnel would die in their 'iron coffins' as Hitler insisted the campaign continue, hoping it would postpone the cross-channel invasion.

By monitoring the German signals it was possible to reroute convoys away from known concentrations of submarines. When the Germans changed their procedures in February 1942 and it was no longer possible to decode the signals, Allied shipping losses mounted rapidly. By mid-1942 Dönitz had 250 U-boats in service and by his calculations should have been poised for victory. In November the U-boats sank a record 700,000 tons of shipping and the total Allied losses for the year reached 6 million grt.

The British broke the code again in early 1943 and were able to decipher most U-boat signals for the rest of the war. Dönitz reduced his headquarters staff to a handful of personally vetted officers, convinced that there was a security leak, but to the end the German navy believed its Enigma system was too complex to be decoded.

The second killer blow to the U-boats came from the air. Near the continental United States or Great Britain, the submarines' actions were restricted by the presence of patrol aircraft. They could only come up for air to recharge their batteries by night, and with the advent of airborne surface search radar, even that became dangerous. But until early 1943 there had been a wide gap mid-Atlantic, beyond the range of Allied aircraft. Eventually, sufficient long-range machines were prised away from the 'bomber barons' and devoted to anti-submarine patrols. In late 1942 the Royal Navy introduced its first 'escort carrier', a converted merchant ship carrying a handful of anti-submarine aircraft and a few fighters to strike back at German long-range anti-shipping bombers. The *Audacity* was torpedoed and sunk, but not before she had proved her worth: her air group forced the U-boats to stay submerged and lose contact with the convoy as well as bringing down several very surprised Focke-Wulf FW 200 Condors.

Listening Devices and Depth Charges

The Royal Navy's early efforts against the U-boats may have been tragically amateurish, but by 1943 it was extremely professional. New tactics evolved all the time, rapidly disseminated across the fleet. Every convoy action was subjected to statistical and tactical analysis: the birth of modern 'operational research'. Standard tactics were perfected and rehearsed.

The balance of technological advantage swung like a pendulum, first favouring one side, then the other. The British fitted radar on their escort vessels; the Germans added radar-detectors to their submarines; the British developed devices that detected the German detector; and so on. The increasing air threat led to heavy anti-aircraft armament being installed on some U-boats, but their attempts to shoot it out with attacking aircraft were generally unsuccessful.

The battle came to a dramatic climax in the spring of 1943 when a succession of convoys was subjected to incessant U-boat attacks. Dönitz had more than 100 operational U-boats but was aware that his codes had been broken at the last moment.

Several convoys suffered high casualty rates, one ship in five was sunk, but the escorts and air patrols found and sank U-boats day after day. In April 15 U-boats were sunk. In what the U-boat men called 'Black May' the Allies sank 41: a third of the operational fleet. Dönitz recalled his surviving submarines to rethink strategy and tactics.

The Battle of the Atlantic had been won: in 1943 the U-boats sank 3 million tons of shipping, which was more than compensated for by 11 million grt of new vessels, especially the utilitarian 'Liberty' ships built in record time in American yards. Dönitz sent his men back into the fray later that year, but no longer with the hope of winning the war. From the summer of 1943 until June 1944 Hitler regarded them as his front-line defence against Allied invasion. Unfortunately for the U-boat men, the hunters were now the hunted. There were now sufficient escorts to form 'support groups'; independent of the convoys, these squadrons of dedicated warships could support a convoy in trouble or be vectored towards a U-boat patrol line. Improved sonar and new anti-submarine weapons proved deadly effective, especially when co-ordinated by experienced commanders like Captain Frederick Walker.

The Merchant Marine – Unsung Heroes

The Germans developed a *Schnorchel* (snorkel) device that enabled the U-boats to use their diesel engines underwater. It was effective when it worked, but made conditions inside the boats even more disagreeable, filling the hull with fumes, reducing oxygen levels and causing fluctuations in air pressure. (U-577 famously completed an underwater passage of the Atlantic in order to escape to Argentina.) To attack the escorts, they developed homing torpedoes that locked on to their enemies' sonar signals. Rubber-based coatings on the U-boat hulls helped to hide them from sonar scans. By 1945 sleek new submarines with massive battery capacity and the ability to maintain high speeds underwater were being assembled in Norway, ready to renew the fight. The war ended before these advanced craft could be deployed in meaningful numbers.

Of the 41,000 U-boat crew who served in the Second World War, 30,000 died in their submarines. A similar number of Allied seamen went down with the 3,500 merchant and escort vessels sunk by U-boats and the 1,500 lost to air attack, mines and surface raiders. For the UK's civilian population, the psychological effects of rationing would endure for decades after it ended. As SOE agent and author George Millar put it, 'there was hardly an infant in the land, let alone a parent, who did not realize that much of the food, and all of the petrol, had to be brought to Britain in ships whose seamen, in the night as well as the day, faced and often found a horrible death.'

SEDAN

10–15 MAY 1940

'IT IS MIDNIGHT IN EUROPE'
MACKENZIE KING, CANADIAN PRIME MINISTER

The Second World War began in September 1939 with the German invasion of Poland; yet after a brief flurry of activity in the west, it became known as 'the phoney war'. British and French forces entered Belgium, but there was no thought of an Allied attack across the Rhine.

Having declared war on Germany, the Allies sat and waited nine months for Hitler to invade. The Germans would be coming from the same direction as in 1914 – as in 1870 or 1814 for that matter – nevertheless, when they did, they pulled off one of the greatest surprise attacks in military history. In six dramatic weeks, France was defeated and compelled to sign an armistice on 22 June. Only Britain, with her empire and Commonwealth, was left in the war against Nazism.

Blitzkrieg

On paper, the rival armies looked very similar in May 1940. France fielded 79 divisions plus 13 fortress divisions; Belgium had 22; and Britain just 10: a total of 124. Germany had 135 but added 12 to the Allied order of battle by invading the Netherlands. France's fortress divisions occupied Europe's latest and most famous fortification, the Maginot Line. Stretching for 140 kilometres along the Franco-German frontier, this chain of steel and concrete forts owed much to the lessons of Verdun, where permanent fixed defences like Fort Vaux had proved difficult and costly to capture. Built between 1930 and 1937 it was intended to delay any German attack in the centre and south, while the bulk of the French army deployed to Belgium to meet the main German thrust. This depended on the Germans repeating their invasion strategy of 1914 – which they fully intended to do right up to the last moment – and on Belgium playing a full role in the defence of the west. Unfortunately for France, in 1937 the Belgians cancelled their 1920 defence treaty with France, and declared themselves neutral. So when the French finally advanced into Belgium, there was little co-operation with the Belgian army, and no defensive positions prepared.

Neither side enjoyed a significant advantage in weapons and equipment. The German and French armies consisted of infantry divisions with horse-drawn guns and transport, little changed from 1914. The Allies had 11,000 artillery pieces to about 8,000 German. The Germans had ten tank divisions, with a total of 2,445 vehicles, of which some 1,400 were light tanks armed only with machine guns. The French had about 3,000 tanks, all with better guns, although handicapped by the use of a one-man turret which reduced their rate of fire; the 313 Char B1s heavy tanks were all but immune from German anti-tank guns, and potentially a very important asset. The British shipped 310 tanks to

OPPOSITE: *Parisians gather to watch German soldiers marching through the French capital in 1940, having destroyed the French, British and Belgian armies in a matter of weeks.*

Explanations and Excuses

THE FRENCH DEFEAT IN 1940 was so sudden and shocking that it continues to resonate into the 21st century. At an army inquiry held in 1950 the commanders of 1940 were blamed by the generals of the 1950s for failing to modernize in time, and for Gamelin's bungled deployment that neglected to provide any reserve. The generals blamed the soldiers, citing the spread of panic that often preceded rather than followed a German attack. Everyone blamed the politicians of the Third Republic who had turned the army into a virtual militia by reducing the term of service to less than a year. There were certainly scenes of panicked flight, but also tough resistance: the Germans buried nearly 30,000 of their soldiers, so clearly someone stood and fought. Given the great disparity in populations and industrial output between Germany and France, perhaps 1940 was less of an aberration and more a repeat of 1870. The French Second Empire had been crushed in a short summer campaign, which also ended at Sedan.

France, mostly big, fast 'cruiser' tanks with excellent anti-tank guns but lightly protected. They also brought some Matilda infantry tanks, armed only with machine guns but so thickly armoured as to be impervious to almost any German weapon.

Von Manstein's Strategy

France had three heavy and three light armoured divisions in 1940, but these only accounted for 960 tanks. The rest were scattered among the infantry corps in the belief that such wide integration would bolster the infantry all along the line. The Germans chose to concentrate all theirs in their panzer divisions, and to concentrate most of them for one giant armoured punch. There had never been tank operations on such a scale before, so no one knew which approach would prove correct.

Hitler liked to pose as a decisive leader, but he postponed the invasion many times between the fall of Poland and 9 May when he gave the order. The original German war plan was a cautious advance into Belgium, a far cry from the bold sweep towards Paris the Germans tried in 1914. But on 10 January a German aircraft crash-landed in Belgium; on board was a staff officer with details of the invasion plans in his briefcase. In the rethink that followed this comic lack of security, future Field Marshal Erich von Manstein persuaded Hitler to attempt a far more imaginative strategy. While the Allies poured reinforcements into Belgium, Manstein proposed to rush most of the German panzer divisions through the Ardennes forest, outflanking the Maginot defences. If they could cross the River Meuse, they could cut towards the coast, chopping the Allies in two.

The French general staff had considered the possibility of a German strike through the Ardennes – and concluded that it would take so long that a counter-attack could be organized at leisure once their spearheads appeared at the Meuse crossings.

Panzergruppe Kleist

From 10–12 May the 1,600 vehicles and 134,000 men of *Panzergruppe Kleist* drove along the narrow roads that snake through the forested hillsides of the Ardennes. Nobody noticed. To the north, the French moved not only their best troops but even the only army they had kept in reserve, in an attempt to support the Dutch. They reinforced the Maginot Line with another 30 divisions. At Hannut in Belgium on 14 May the first great tank versus tank battle in history took place. Two French light armoured divisions held off two German panzer divisions, knocking out 165 German tanks for the loss of 105 of their own. But it did not matter, because 24 hours earlier, the leading elements of *Panzergruppe Kleist* had reached the Meuse at Sedan – and crossed it.

The French had chosen to defend the Ardennes sector with their least effective forces. The two infantry divisions holding the line at Sedan were both second-line formations; the average age of the ordinary soldiers was 31 and 19 out of 20 officers were reservists, mostly in their forties and fifties.

While the correlation of military forces was well balanced on the ground, the Germans enjoyed a considerable advantage in the air. The Germans had about 4,000 aircraft operational on 10 May compared to 3,000 Allied, of which 1,368 were French and mostly unserviceable. Equally

Sedan

9 May 1940 Hitler orders the invasion of France, Belgium and the Netherlands.

10 May The invasion begins. British prime minister Neville Chamberlain resigns and is replaced by maverick MP Winston Churchill at the head of a coalition government.

13 May German troops emerge from the Ardennes, taking the Allies by surprise. They establish bridgeheads across the Meuse under cover of repeated air attacks.

14 May German aircraft carpet bomb Rotterdam to compel the Dutch to surrender. Allied air attacks on the Meuse crossings fail to stop the expansion of the bridgeheads.

15 May Poorly co-ordinated and local counter-attacks by French tanks fail to halt the German drive westwards. RAF bombers attack the Ruhr industrial region that night, beginning a strategic bombing campaign against Germany that will last five years.

20 May German troops reach the Channel, cutting the Allied armies in two.

22 May RAF loses its last airfield in France and operates from southern England to cover the withdrawal of British troops from Dunkirk.

26 May The British begin to evacuate their forces, abandoning their tanks, artillery and vehicles.

31 May President Roosevelt introduces a massive programme of rearmament in the United States.

4 June The evacuation from Dunkirk is completed. Churchill makes his 'we shall fight them on the beaches' speech.

10 June Paris falls.

22 June France signs armistice.

3 July British naval forces attack and destroy the French fleet at Oran in Algeria.

importantly, the Germans had invested heavily in anti-aircraft weapons and had 9,300 guns in place; the Allies had only 3,800 – and just a single battery covering Sedan.

Panzergruppe Kleist comprised five panzer divisions, three under General Guderian and two under General Reinhardt. According to French doctrine, Guderian should have spent days, perhaps a week, preparing his assault across the Meuse. However, his attack was hasty, even by German standards; he did not even wait for his full force to emerge from the Ardennes. French engineers had blown the bridges and zeroed-in their heavy artillery on the approaches to the main crossing points. The big guns opened fire on the morning of 13 May, but their shooting was soon interrupted. Every few minutes, half-a-dozen Junkers Ju-87 Stukas would plummet from the sky, coming down almost vertically with sirens screaming for added psychological pressure. They pulled out at 1,500 feet as their bombs impacted with deadly accuracy. As the Stukas banked away, so a flight of twin-engined bombers would conduct a level bombing attack, coming in at ever lower altitudes as pilots realized no one was firing back.

Domination from the Air

For hour after hour, the bombing continued: a total of 310 sorties by Dornier and Heinkel level bombers and more than 200 dive-bomber missions. The unremitting ferocity of the bombardment would have unsettled veteran troops, but the French soldiers were completely inexperienced reservists. Then, at 4 p.m. came a massed raid by Stuka dive bombers at the same time as Dornier 17 medium bombers laid stick after stick of bombs on the French infantry holding the riverbank.

Under cover of the massed air attack, German troops paddled across the river in rubber dinghies. They were sitting ducks, but few soldiers of the 147th Fortress Infantry Regiment even raised their weapons. Some of the French positions had been empty for some time before Colonel von Balck's 1st Infantry Regiment lobbed stick grenades into them. The German bombing raids had severed the French telephone lines; without radios, the French units had no means of communication and could not direct the fire of their supporting artillery. Even if they had, by that evening there was no one on the end of the line: the gunners had fled.

It was the same story to the north at Dinant where General Hoth's two panzer divisions had reached the Meuse, and summoned hundreds of German bombers to blast the defenders' positions. By midnight on 13 May the Germans had established a bridgehead five kilometres deep at Sedan. They were across at Houx also, and dug-in three kilometres on the west bank. At Monthérme, 32 kilometres north of Sedan, French North African troops fought hard and although Reinhardt's men got across, they found it impossible to advance for the next two days until other French units on the flanks had run away.

Defending a river line sounds easier than it is: throughout history attacking forces have usually found a way to cross. The defence stands or falls by its ability to counter-attack, and the Germans were acutely aware how vulnerable they were. The Sedan bridgehead depended on a 16-ton capacity bridge laid by their engineers: trucks and light tanks could pass but their Panzer III and Panzer IV medium tanks were still on the east bank. All their crossing points were terrible bottlenecks, exposed to air attack and artillery bombardment. It was not an unusual situation in historical terms, but one which the French army of the 1930s simply was not ready for: its doctrine of methodical battle was just too slow. The French army's telephone network was too vulnerable and not fast enough for modern battle. Neither, it must be said, were many of its generals. Three French tank divisions were sent to support the 2nd Army but they took 48 hours to mount a succession of hesitant, small-scale counter-attacks. While Guderian raced westwards, co-ordinating his corps from a bank of radios in his command vehicles, his French opponents sat by the telephone waiting for orders, for fuel, reinforcements – or air support.

‘I remember every detail. The Germans wore grey. You wore blue.’

RICK, IN *CASABLANCA*

As the German bridgeheads expanded, capturing or repairing permanent bridges and laying more pontoons, the Allied air forces finally appeared over the Meuse. Some 150 bombers and 250 fighters were engaged, but German fighters and the intense light flak over the river inflicted terrible losses: the British lost 30 out of 71 light bombers in one sortie. Two pontoons were put out of action.

'The front is broken . . .'

The Germans expanded their bridgeheads faster than the French could deploy troops to stop them. They continued to push west with a cavalier disregard for their flanks that alarmed some of Hitler's most senior generals. French Prime Minister Paul Reynaud telephoned his new British opposite number on 15 May, saying 'The front is broken near Sedan; they are pouring through in great numbers with tanks and armoured cars'. Churchill flew to France to inject some backbone, but it was all too little too late. The French sacked their commander-in-chief, General Gamelin, on 19 May, replacing him with General Weygand who had boasted in 1939 that 'The French army is a more effective force than at any other time in its history'.

On 20 May German tanks reached the Channel coast at the mouth of the Somme, cutting the Allied armies in two. The commander of the British Expeditionary Force ordered a limited counter-attack near Arras that briefly arrested the progress of the German 7th Panzer Division, but its commander, Erwin Rommel, was soon on the move again. The roads were choked with refugees, the French army was melting away in chaos and disorder, and the British fell back to Calais and Dunkirk where they were rescued by the Royal Navy. The 'miracle of Dunkirk' was largely made possible by the stout resistance of French troops around Lille and in the Pas de Calais, but this was quickly forgotten in light of subsequent events. The British were also fortunate that Hitler became as jittery as some of his high command; fearing a counter-attack on his strung-out tank units, he ordered them not to press home an attack on Dunkirk.

The End of the Beginning . . .

Belgium surrendered on 28 May and the Germans turned south to attack the French army along the Somme and Aisne where it had finally assembled a new frontline. On 5 June the Germans opened their new offensive, and were surprised to encounter much fiercer resistance. They had averaged 1,500 casualties per day from 10 May to 4 June, but this rose to 5,000 per day 4–18 June as the French stood and fought. German casualties reached 163,000, including 29,000 dead by the time hostilities ceased; some 90,000 Frenchmen died and 200,000 were wounded. With their northern armies dispersed, and deserted by their British, Belgian and Dutch allies, the French were too heavily outnumbered to last much longer. Paris was evacuated on 10 June and on 22 June France was forced to sign an armistice. The battle for France was over. The Battle of Britain was about to begin.

'I AM NOT IN THE MOOD FOR A VICTORY PARADE. WE AREN'T AT THE END YET.'

ADOLF HITLER, PARIS, 28 JUNE 1940

THE BATTLE OF BRITAIN

10 JULY–31 OCTOBER 1940

Between 26 May and 4 June about 240,000 British soldiers were evacuated from Dunkirk, leaving behind almost every tank, artillery piece and vehicle the British Expeditionary Force had taken to France. Some 120,000 French troops were brought to safety too, but most of them elected to return to France for the final few weeks of futile resistance. Germany had conquered Poland, Norway, Denmark, the Netherlands, Belgium, Luxembourg and France.

Only Britain was left, and a strong body of opinion in Parliament said that it was time to recognize the inevitable and make peace with Germany – with Adolf Hitler. Had Germany not been ruled by the Nazi dictator, or had Winston Churchill not been appointed prime minister of Great Britain, then a compromise peace may well have been negotiated in the summer of 1940. Churchill had recognized the evil of Nazism for what it was, far earlier than most British politicians. By his refusal to treat with Hitler, Churchill brought about the Battle of Britain. His famous speeches defined the struggle in apocalyptic terms: as a fight to the death between Western civilization and a new dark age of racist barbarism. His leadership – and the spectacle of German aircraft bombing England – united the country as never before, or since.

'If the English surrender too, this is going to be a long war'

(Apocryphal comment by one Scottish soldier to another as they embarked from Dunkirk, June 1940)

After the war, one of Hitler's most senior commanders, Field Marshal von Rundstedt, said that the most decisive battle of the conflict was the Battle of Britain. He may have said so just to irritate the interrogators, who were Russian, and presumably expecting him to name Stalingrad; but Hitler launched his invasion of Russia with the explicit aim of removing Britain's only remaining potential ally in Europe. In doing so, he committed Germany to a two-front war, the very error for which he had criticized the German military leadership in the First World War. Hitler's failure to make peace with or conquer the British Isles led directly to his fatal gamble in the east.

The speed of the German victory in May 1940 stunned the whole world, including Hitler and his generals. Hitler assumed he could make peace with Britain, and assumed, correctly, that a large proportion of the British political establishment could see the rational case for ending the war. To the amazement of his generals, Hitler ordered a partial demobilization of the German army. Not until 16 July did Hitler realize that Churchill would not negotiate, and order the German high command to prepare to invade Britain.

PREVIOUS PAGE: *The battle made the British Supermarine Spitfire fighter the most famous aircraft in the world. Improved versions would fly for the rest of the war and still be in frontline service into the 1950s.*

German High Command Think it Over

On a clear day the white cliffs of Dover are easily visible from Cap Blanc Nez in France. From here, German generals peered at their last remaining enemy through binoculars, and pondered how to invade. German admirals were wholly negative; having lost half their destroyers to the Royal Navy during the invasion of Norway in April, they were acutely aware that the British outnumbered and outclassed them completely. Only if Germany had complete air superiority would they dare risk their warships in the English Channel. The specialist landing craft later developed by the Allies for the D-Day landings did not exist: the Germans planned to land their soldiers from Rhine barges and other shallow-draught vessels assembled in the Pas de Calais. The invasion plan, Operation 'Sealion', made so many optimistic assumptions that it is hard to see many generals taking it seriously; the preparations should perhaps be seen more as a bluff. Churchill's confidence in the outcome can be gauged by his despatch of most of the battle-worthy tanks in the UK to the Middle East on 10 August. On the other hand, the German invasion plan of May 1940 had been a fearsome gamble that worked. The British were right to treat the risk of invasion as extremely serious. Yet there could be no thought of invasion while British aircraft patrolled the coast.

Hitler gave the Luftwaffe from 8 August to 15 September to gain air superiority over southern England. The Germans had about 4,000 aircraft available, of which 1,000 were Messerschmitt Bf-109s – short range interceptors; and 1,300 were twin-engined bombers. The British had some 750 single-engined fighters: Hawker Hurricanes and Supermarine Spitfires.

Dowding, Park and Radar

Although the British were outnumbered, they enjoyed many advantages, none of which were known to the Germans as they progressed from attacks on coastal convoys to raids on airfields in Southern England. In contrast to the shambolic state of the British army in 1939–40, RAF Fighter Command, established in 1936, was the best fighter interceptor force in the world. German bombers had attacked London during 1917–18 and the British had studied that campaign in great detail. By 1940 the British had established a command system that would co-ordinate defending fighter aircraft. The sound-ranging devices of 1918 had been replaced by the world's first radar network, supplemented by thousands of observers. Churchill's romanticism of 'the Few' notwithstanding, the RAF had more than 400,000 men and women devoted to stopping the German onslaught. In this battle, national characteristics were reversed: it was the British who were the well-prepared professionals; the Germans were the amateurs who lost. Without the comic inefficiency of Nazi industrial policy the Luftwaffe could have been substantially larger, and have had heavy bombers of the sort entering service with RAF Bomber Command.

The Battle of Britain

3 June 1940 The evacuation from Dunkirk ends in the early hours of the morning with the departure of the last British ships.

4 June Churchill delivers his 'we shall fight them on the beaches' speech, coining the name 'Battle of Britain' and defining its purpose.

10 June Italy declares war on Britain and France now it appears that they will lose the war.

22 June France signs an armistice with Germany.

16 July Hitler issues the directive for Operation 'Sealion', an amphibious invasion of Britain, to be preceded by an aerial campaign intended to achieve air superiority over the potential invasion beaches and ports.

1 August Hitler sets 19–26 September as the date for the invasion of Britain.

12 August German aircraft attack British radar stations.

15 August The Germans make a maximum effort involving 2,000 sorties against targets in England. Intensive air raids continue through the rest of the month.

20 August Churchill delivers his 'Never in the field of human conflict' speech.

24 August German bombers strike London at night.

25 August RAF bombers strike Berlin at night.

7 September Germans begin a series of major raids on London.

continued on opposite page

Nevertheless, military forces have often entered battle with the odds stacked in their favour, only to lose because of incompetent leadership. Again, the British were fortunate in Air Chief Marshal Sir Hugh Dowding's foresight and the inspiring commander of 11 Group, Air Vice Marshal Sir Keith Park, whose fighter squadrons in southern England bore the brunt of the struggle.

From June until 12 August, German aircraft attacked shipping in the Channel with the explicit aim of bringing on battles between British and German fighters. Field Marshal Kesselring, commander of the German 2nd Air Fleet in 1940 and one of the best of Hitler's generals, thought the British were ducking the challenge. 'Our difficulty was not to bring down enemy fighters – in Galland, Molders, Oesau, Balthasar, etc., we had real aces, while the huge figures of aircraft shot down are further proof – but to get the enemy to fight.' Actually, the German pilots were claiming about three 'kills' for each British aircraft they shot down (the RAF were doing the same) which made them think they were winning. What they had not realized yet was that the British had expert pilots of their own: they just did not put their faces on the covers of glossy magazines.

Kesselring's comment also reveals the poverty of Luftwaffe strategy from the battles over the Channel to 'Eagle Day' – 13 August – on which the German bombers began a six-week campaign of raids inland. The Germans attacked many airfields, but dissipated their effort against some facilities used by British bombers and seldom managed to inflict enough destruction to put the airfields out of use for more than a few hours. The raids looked spectacular from the air, with buildings collapsing and fires raging, but RAF fighters were widely dispersed around their fields, in individual shelters that protected them from all but a direct hit. In any case, most were airborne, directed by radar operators to intercept the bombers. The German 'plan' amounted to attacking an almost random variety of targets – so poor was their intelligence effort – with their bombers, while the likes of Galland and Molders shot down any British fighters they chanced to meet.

Dogfights in the Summer Skies

The air battles were visible from the ground, contrails criss-crossed the sky and occasionally a parachute blossomed as another aircraft plummeted to earth. British pilots who baled out of a stricken fighter had an excellent chance of living to fight another day; Germans who survived became prisoners-of-war. On 15 August the Germans made their greatest effort to date: air strikes from France and Belgium supported by a long range sortie from their 5th Air Fleet based in Denmark and Norway. The latter flew across the North Sea without Bf-109s which lacked the range to accompany them: they were so badly mauled by British fighters that they never returned in daylight. German aircraft flew 2,000 sorties that day for the loss of 75 machines. Over-claiming by German fighter pilots left them thinking honours were even, but the pilots dubbed it 'Black Thursday' nonetheless. They would have been even more despondent if they knew British losses were only 34.

The Luftwaffe underestimated the initial strength of the RAF and the rate at which the British could manufacture new aircraft. By mid-August German intelligence reports predicted that the RAF was down to 300 fighters: the true figure was 855 in frontline squadrons plus 289 in store and another 84 with training units – a total of 1,438. Luftwaffe aircrew became sceptical of their own briefings. Told on a daily basis that the British were down to their last few squadrons, they found every raid met the same highly aggressive response.

The British defensive system was like nothing the Luftwaffe had encountered before. The Germans did not know whether to concentrate their raids on airfields, radar sites, aircraft factories or on prestige targets like London that the RAF would be forced to come up and defend. The 2nd and 3rd Air Fleets developed their own bombing policies which were only occasionally co-ordinated. German bombers and German fighter aircraft could not communicate in the air because the fighters' radio sets could not operate on more than one frequency. The Messerschmitt Bf-110 twin-engined long range fighters proved too vulnerable to Hurricanes and Spitfires and many were sent back to Germany

continued from previous page

15 September Another maximum effort by the Germans compels the RAF to put up every airworthy fighter: later known as 'Battle of Britain Day'.

17 September Hitler postpones 'Sealion'.

30 September The last major German daylight raid on London.

October 1940–May 1941 'The Blitz' – German bombing raids on London and other cities continue through the winter and spring.

for conversion to night-fighters. Junkers Ju-87 Stukas, dive bombers so effective over Poland and France, were massacred whenever the British intercepted them, and they were withdrawn. While the Battle of Britain drew on, British bombers began to raid deep into Germany during the night.

The first major German attack on London took place on 7 September. Successive raids stoked huge fires in the East End that guided in another wave of bombers during the night. How seriously the bomb aimers strove to hit military targets like docks, gas works and factories remains moot: the result was a lot of houses wrecked and hundreds of civilians killed or injured. After a week of daily raids, on 15 September the Luftwaffe made a maximum effort which led to fierce aerial battles above London that afternoon. The leading bomber squadron lost 6 out of 25 aircraft, and many of those that returned had wounded men on board. They had been attacked by so many British fighters the Spitfires were queuing up to engage them. By nightfall the Germans had lost 56 aircraft: not as many as on 15 August, but this was after a month of aerial battles that they thought they had won. Yet there were just as many British fighters as ever, and flown with the same implacable determination.

German bombers appeared on British radar screens as they formed up over their airfields in France, a process that took a good 20 minutes. The bombers headed for England, joined en route by their escorting fighters which could cross the Channel in only six minutes. The fighters preferred to fly independently, seeking out and hopefully catching a British squadron by surprise. In fighter combat, most 'kills' occurred when one formation 'bounced' another, usually from out of the sun; most victims never saw their attacker. However, German commanders often insisted on keeping their fighters close to the bombers to protect them.

'Scramble!'

The RAF pilots began their day before dawn, some ready to scramble at a few minutes' notice. It was a fine judgement for the controllers: radar plots were uncertain and the Germans often made feint attacks to cover the real raids. It took a Hurricane 15 minutes to reach 20,000 feet; scrambling too early might leave the fighters out of position to intercept, but a late order could be worse. Pilots could be scrambled five or six times a day, and the British found that a handful of fighters could attack much larger enemy formations with confidence. Small groups of aircraft were hard to see, and with the advantage of surprise they could swoop on a German formation, shoot a couple down, and vanish before the Bf-109s could react. Sometimes it was the other way around.

The fighter aircraft of 1940 demanded physical strength to fly, and they were unforgiving machines. Veterans estimated you had eight seconds to escape a burning Spitfire. Archibald McIndoe's burns unit at East Grinstead pioneered modern plastic

The Aces

SINCE THE FIRST WORLD WAR a fighter pilot who shot down five or more enemy aircraft had been called an 'ace'. The Germans feted their most successful pilots in both world wars, while the British establishment disliked what it saw as the glamorizing of a select few at the expense of the vast majority. However, on both sides a tiny minority of pilots – no more than 5 per cent – accounted for about half the kills. And the casualties were concentrated among the inexperienced: the typical fighter kill involved one formation 'bouncing' another, usually from behind and out of the sun. In a few seconds, a couple of aircraft would be sent spinning down, trailing smoke. Whether their aircraft bore the German cross or the British roundel, the doomed pilots would usually be the new replacements on their first or second mission.

surgery techniques to treat the dreadful injuries sustained by RAF pilots. The Spitfire and Bf-109 were so close in performance that the skill of the pilot usually made the difference between victory and death. The Hawker Hurricane was outmatched by the Messerschmitt – on paper – but accounted for more German bombers than the glamorous Spitfire.

The War in the Air Changes Direction

Hitler postponed 'Sealion' indefinitely on 17 September, and from the end of September the Luftwaffe switched to night raids on London and other British cities. The end of German attempts to win air superiority over the invasion beaches marked the end of the Battle of Britain.

Kesselring had wanted to try an airborne landing in June, and could not understand why the Luftwaffe's parachute troops factored little in 'Sealion', especially after their successes in Belgium and Holland in May. He ended the battle convinced his fighter pilots were winning; although they did overclaim, post-war research shows they averaged about 1.2 British fighters for every one they lost. Unfortunately for them, they needed to shoot down something like a 5:1 ratio to have the White Cliffs of Dover all to themselves. The Germans lost so many bombers that the campaign could not have continued much longer even had the autumn weather not reduced the opportunities for daylight raids. Some 1,300 German aircraft were lost and since German replacement rates were far lower than British, the Luftwaffe declined in strength by about 25 per cent during the battle. Fighter Command had not only driven off the Luftwaffe, it had severely dented its strength and reputation. And although it lost 1,000 fighters during the battle, it actually increased its frontline strength by 40 per cent between July and November 1940. The home defence system created and commanded by Sir Hugh Dowding had fulfilled its mission to the letter. British strategic planning and management had triumphed over German improvisation.

BARBAROSSA

22 JUNE–5 DECEMBER 1941

'BEFORE THREE MONTHS HAVE PASSED,
WE SHALL WITNESS A COLLAPSE IN
RUSSIA, THE LIKE OF WHICH HAS NEVER
BEEN SEEN IN HISTORY'

ADOLF HITLER, 22 JUNE 1941

Operation Barbarossa, Hitler's invasion of Russia,

transformed the course of the Second World War. By the time it began, on 22 June 1941, Germany had defeated all but one of the countries it had attacked: only Great Britain remained in the fight. Communist Russia had allied itself with the Nazis.

The Russo-German Pact of 1939 remains one of the most cynical alliances in world history. It enabled Stalin to occupy Lithuania, Latvia and Estonia and murder thousands of their citizens, as well as seize eastern Poland with similar consequences for her people, especially the 15,000 military officers put to death in Katyn Forest.

Hitler Goes East

Hitler had always intended to attack Russia, to destroy the communist regime and exploit the peoples and natural resources of Eastern Europe as a giant slave colony. German plans for the occupation of western Russia called for the extermination of Jews, communists and much of the wider civilian population too: a biblical war of conquest with modern weapons. The dire performance of the Russian army in its invasion of Finland (December 1940) suggested the Wehrmacht would make short work of Stalin's forces. British and American intelligence independently concluded that the Russians would probably lose in a matter of months. Russia's intelligence operatives predicted the timing and scale of the invasion, but Stalin could and did shoot messengers bringing bad news. In consequence the Russian army was not deployed for defence, and its formations were not prepared for battle.

The German invasion forces were divided into three Army Groups. Army Group North was to advance from East Prussia, through the Baltic States and on to Leningrad. Army Group Centre was to pass north of the Pripyat marshes, heading for Moscow. Army Group South occupied a start line that arced from southern Poland to Romania. The Soviet equivalent of an Army Group was a 'Front'. The North Front faced the Finns and the German army in Norway; the North-West Front held the Baltic States; the Western Front faced Army Group Centre; and the South-West Front held a line from southern Poland to the Hungarian border. Armies assembled opposite Romania were organized into a fifth Front, the Southern, a few days after the invasion.

Each German invasion since 1939 had opened with a devastating air attack, and the Luftwaffe showed it had lost nothing of its edge despite the losses over Britain and Greece. It destroyed 800 Russian aircraft on the ground, while another 400 were shot down in some very one-sided air battles.

OPPOSITE: *Two million Russian soldiers were captured during 'Barbarossa': their survival rate in German captivity was even lower than that of Americans captured by the Japanese. Almost all were dead by the spring of 1942.*

The German Army Groups advanced in two echelons: the panzer divisions and motorized divisions grouped together into four Panzer Groups, one each in the north and south and two for Army Group Centre. The Panzer Groups cut through the front line and pressed on, trapping the Russian armies between them and the mass of infantry divisions hurrying along behind.

'Lightning War' Again

Army Group Centre's Panzer Groups drove 200 miles in five days, reaching Minsk in a pincer movement that cut off most of the Russian 3rd, 10th and 13th Armies – 350,000 men were taken prisoner. Army Group North made rapid progress too, helped by the fact that the road network in the Baltic States and Belorussia was more extensive than in the regions south of the Pripyat. The Panzers reached the River Dvina on 26 June. Army Group South encountered the largest concentrations of Russian tanks and General von Kleist's 1st Panzer Group faced several major counter-attacks. Army Group Centre made faster progress than Army Group South, and captured Smolensk on 26 July. The exhaustion of fuel and ammunition as well as stiffening Soviet resistance on the high road to Moscow forced a halt at this point.

As the Germans swept across the southern Ukraine, the huge Russian forces around Kiev became dangerously exposed. Hitler ordered the 2nd Panzer Group, hitherto part of Army Group Centre, to head south from the Smolensk sector. Meanwhile Army Group South's 1st Panzer Group headed north from Kremenchug on the River Dnepr. On 16 September, the armoured pincers met, trapping 4 Soviet armies totalling nearly 50 divisions. According to Soviet figures, the South-West Front had 677,000 men in late August, of which 150,000 escaped and 527,000 were captured.

2 Million Prisoners

On 8 September 1941 the German High Command decreed that Soviet prisoners of war had forfeited their rights. Nearly 2 million Soviet servicemen had been captured, winter was approaching and no provision had been made to deal with so many captives. Some army units machine-gunned their POWs on receipt of the decree. The majority of the prisoners were herded into vast barbed-wire enclosures, and left to starve and freeze to death in conditions of indescribable squalor. The mass surrenders of 1941 suggested that large elements of the Red Army were no more ready to die for their country than those of France in 1940. The populations of the Baltic States and the Ukraine welcomed the Germans as liberators; the photographs of armoured cars driving through cheering crowds look just like Western Europe in 1944. If the Nazi regime had not treated these people and its prisoners with such beastliness, Germany would probably have won the war.

Stalin had the unfortunate commander of the Western Front, 44-year-old General Dimitri Pavlov, and his staff arrested as traitors. They were tortured into confessing they had betrayed their men at the Battle of Minsk. The atmosphere of paranoia persisted for years: between the German invasion and the end of 1942, more than 2 million people were despatched to the dreaded gulag labour camps. By bullet, starvation or gas chambers – pioneered in Russia before the war – Stalin's regime had already murdered between 16 and 19 million people before the war. He killed more communists than Hitler.

Destination Moscow

On 6 September Hitler demanded a maximum effort to capture Moscow before winter. The city was a key industrial centre at the hub of the Soviet rail network. Its fall might bring down the communist regime altogether, but even if Stalin remained in control, the loss of the capital would hamper Soviet strategic movement, logistic arrangements and military production. As usual, the Germans planned to isolate the city rather than embroil themselves in an urban battle: 3rd and 4th Panzer Groups were to bypass Moscow to the north, the 2nd Panzer Group to the south. The assault began on 2 October, and brought about two more battles of encirclement. Another 650,000 Red Army soldiers passed into captivity.

Hitler was staking everything on his mechanized units, but his elite armoured forces were sadly depleted by the fall of 1941. For example, 2nd Panzer Group had advanced 1,200 miles in three months; the wear and tear on vehicles (not to mention crews) depleted the tank regiments as fast as actual battle. Nevertheless, the Panzer Groups made a brisk start and cut off the 19th, 20th, 24th and 32nd Soviet armies at Vyazma. 2nd Panzer Group broke through to Orel, encircling the Russian 13th and 50th armies too.

In Moscow Communist officials packed their bags and burned a mountain of paperwork as the regime implemented its emergency plan to transfer most government departments to Kuibyshev, 600 miles away. Alexander Werth, the British correspondent in Moscow observed the stampede to the east on 16 October, and how it suddenly stopped when it was announced that Stalin would be staying in the Kremlin.

A World of Rain and Mud

Three developments helped stiffen the tyrant's resolve. A light fall of snow dusted German positions on the night of 6 October, heralding not winter but the rains that turned the dirt roads into a sticky morass every autumn. Russians call this time of year the *rasputitsa* – the 'time without roads'. There were 750,000 Soviet troops in the Far East, and Stalin's intelligence sources now confirmed that the Japanese planned to attack the United States, not Russia. The Red Army in Manchuria was able to supply a steady stream of replacements to the formations defending Moscow as well as 10 fully equipped divisions.

The third reason for Stalin's confidence was the success with which the Red Army mobilization system was creating new units. Between July and 1 December 1941 the Red Army mobilized 143 new rifle divisions and replaced 84 rifle divisions that had been destroyed. The population of the pre-war USSR was more than twice that of Germany, which the Germans obviously knew, but the efficiency with which that manpower was put into uniform was a disagreeable surprise to German intelligence.

On 7 November the first really hard frost occurred, and the mud solidified. It was also the day that the Soviet regime traditionally held its great military parade through Red Square. With German reconnaissance patrols approaching the outlying stations of the Moscow metro, the central committee was astonished when Stalin announced his intention to hold the parade as usual.

The German advance resumed as soon as the ground hardened. The 1st Panzer Group approached Rostov and German forces swept into the Crimea, driving the Russians back on the great naval base at Sevastopol. The key industrial city of Kharkov and the whole Donbass region, economic powerhouse of the USSR, was overrun. Despite the daytime temperatures averaging minus 5 degrees Celsius, the heavily depleted battalions of Army Group Centre battered their way towards Moscow. On 28 November, elements of the 7th Panzer Division forced a crossing over the Moscow–Volga canal. Some troops were within 12 miles of the city, and in the cold clear air, the distant spires were visible through binoculars. Their reports generated great excitement at Hitler's headquarters, but few front-line officers believed they would enter the city. German losses had been horrendous, units were at only a fraction of their theoretical strength, the Red Army was contesting every yard of ground with stubborn bravery – and supplies were running dangerously low.

Operation Barbarossa set world records for the speed of military advances, and for the numbers of prisoners captured – and murdered. Although only a quarter of the German divisions in Russia were mechanized, their demands for POL (petrol, oil, lubricants) and ammunition were insatiable. As the Germans moved deeper into Russia they depended on the Russian rail network, which – as known from the First World War – was built on a wide gauge incompatible with German rolling stock. Also, the tracks could not carry as heavy a load as German railways. Even when the rails were converted to German gauge, all facilities like water towers were built for Russian engines and were too far apart for German ones.

Neither could supplies be brought forward by truck. Even the mechanized formations had no spare vehicles to shuttle back and forth between railheads: they needed every truck they had. The German army had seized vehicles from all over Europe because its own industry was delivering only a fraction of the quantities required. In 1941 the Germans had more than 2,000 different vehicles in service.

ABOVE: *Russia's dirt roads dissolved into liquid mud during the autumn rains and again in the spring when snow-melt also led to the rivers flooding. This imposed a seasonal rhythm on operations which these German soldiers struggle to defy, manhandling a truck through the quagmire.*

The Russian roads proved even worse than had been assumed and fuel consumption reached 330,000 tons per month, rather than the 250,000 budgeted for. Germany only had two or three months' supply of oil in reserve and it was discovered that captured Soviet petrol was unsuited to German engines. The army's head quartermaster, Generalmajor Friedrich Paulus, conducted a wargame in December 1940, which demonstrated that German logistic arrangements would collapse before they reached the upper Dnepr. However, as the date for the offensive drew nearer, the German planners persuaded themselves that if the army could not sustain a campaign on this scale for six months, then it would have to be won in three.

Hitler's Two Armies

THE PANZER DIVISIONS made the headlines, but there were only 21 in the whole army and 2 of them were in North Africa by 1941. The tank divisions fought in association with a dozen *panzergrenadier* divisions – infantry in half-tracks and lorries. The rest of the 120 or so German and allied divisions that took part in Barbarossa were infantry formations that marched on foot. Their artillery batteries were horse-drawn, as were their machine-gun and mortar companies. Most of Hitler's army advanced at the same pace as Napoleon's invaders in 1812.

Frozen Tanks, Frostbitten Men

December 1941 found the German army tantalizingly close to Moscow, but with no prospect of advancing further. The thermometer sank to an average minus 12 degrees Celsuis every day, although plunging to minus 20 on occasion. Without winter clothing the soldiers froze: more than 100,000 frostbite casualties were reported that month. Without winter equipment, heaters, special oils and lubricants, tanks and aircraft ceased to function too. Such was the chaos at the railheads far to the west, that even had the army possessed adequate quantities of cold-weather gear, it is unlikely it could have been brought forward.

On 5 December the Russians counter-attacked. The temperature that day peaked at minus 15 and the snow was about a metre deep. The German army had little air support: the Luftwaffe found it took five hours to get a bomber airborne. The Red Army placed greater reliance on artillery than aircraft, and its heavy guns and Katyusha rocket launchers functioned without apparent difficulty. Once driven out of their positions, the Germans found it impossible to dig new trenches in the frozen ground. Nocturnal temperatures were so cold that even the smallest villages assumed tactical importance. The dilemma was whether to try to survive in the open or seek shelter in a village that was likely to be on the Russian gunners' maps too.

Barbarossa had failed. Moscow had not fallen and Stalin's regime was more firmly entrenched than ever. German industry and its armed forces were only prepared for a short, sharp conflict, not a protracted war of attrition. By contrast, Russian industry – indeed, the whole of Soviet society – had been reorganized during the 1930s for precisely this sort of struggle. Heavy industry, like the heavy tank factory in Leningrad, had been evacuated to the Urals despite the pace of the German advance. Nevertheless Hitler demanded that his soldiers stand fast, ready to try again in the spring. The Führer's confidence never wavered. In the wake of Japan's attack on Pearl Harbor, he declared war on the USA.

'NONE OF OUR CARRIERS ARE OPERATIONAL'
ADMIRAL NAGUMO TO ADMIRAL YAMAMOTO, 9.30 P.M., 4 JUNE 1942

MIDWAY
4–7 JUNE 1942

The Battle of Midway, fought six months to the day after Pearl Harbor, ended the unbroken run of Japanese victories that had followed their attack on the US Pacific Fleet. In a few hectic hours, four of the six Japanese aircraft carriers that had attacked battleship row lay on the ocean floor, 17,000 feet from sunlight; 200 of their veteran aircrew were dead; and Japan's war of conquest was over. The planned invasions of Fiji, Samoa and Hawaii were postponed, never to be revived.

Having shattered the US Pacific Fleet at Pearl Harbor, Japan had then destroyed the British position in Malaya, inflicting the worst defeat the British Empire ever suffered, the surrender of Singapore. They conquered the Philippines, where US and Filipino forces were progressively destroyed until the survivors surrendered in May 1942. The Japanese seized islands all over the Pacific in order to create a chain of airbases which would support their formidable battle fleet. Their intention was make the cost of reconquest prohibitive for the Allies, and then to negotiate from a position of strength. There were two fundamental problems with Japan's strategy: Japanese leadership was lethally divided between factions for whom assassination was just a standard tool of politics; and the Allies were not about to negotiate, at any price.

> ‘Send out the rest and we'll get those too!’
>
> JUBILANT US NAVY PILOT OVERHEARD FROM USS *ENTERPRISE*, 6 JUNE 1942

Even as the tide of Japanese conquest surged across the Pacific and south Asia, the US Navy struck back with raids by carrier-borne aircraft on Japanese-held islands, Wake, Kwajalein and Makin, and then, in April, with the audacious raid on Tokyo by B-25 bombers launched from USS *Hornet*.

In May, the Japanese invasion of Port Moresby, New Guinea was frustrated by the US Navy at the Battle of the Coral Sea. But the US aircraft carrier *Lexington*, pride of the pre-war fleet, was sunk and the *Yorktown* badly damaged. Since the *Saratoga* had been torpedoed by a Japanese submarine in January, and was still under repair, the Japanese carrier force now outnumbered that of the Americans by a good margin.

What Was Yamamoto's Plan?

The Japanese naval commander, Admiral Yamamoto, therefore determined on a new offensive in the central Pacific. Unusually among his peers, he had spent time in America, and understood that Japan's industrial output was dwarfed by that of the USA and so knew that his numerical superiority would not endure long. However, speculation about

PREVIOUS PAGE: *Douglas SBD Dauntless dive-bombers landed the vital blow at Midway, putting armour-piercing bombs through the decks of the Japanese aircraft carriers and sending the pride of the Imperial fleet to the bottom of the Pacific.*

his strategic plan which led to the Battle of Midway continues to this day. The admiral himself was killed in 1943, and his fleet commander would later commit suicide after the fall of Saipan in 1944. The few surviving senior commanders were adept players of the blame game.

Yamamoto's battle plan involved a maximum effort by the Imperial Navy's Combined Fleet, eating deeply into its strategic oil reserves, to send more than 150 warships far across the Pacific to seize the western end of the Aleutian and Hawaiian island chains. Lying at the northwestern end of the Hawaiian island chain, Midway atoll comprises two sub-tropical islands, encircled by a coral reef, and uninhabited until 1903 when the Pacific telegraph cable was laid through them. Just before the war, the US established an airbase on the eastern one, imaginatively named 'Eastern Island'. From there, US reconnaissance aircraft could range far across the central Pacific.

Yamamoto presumably assumed the Americans would react, as they had at Wake, by despatching a carrier task force to support their garrison. He seems to have dismissed the possibility that the Americans might detect his approach and react before the invasion fleet appeared off the atoll. Worse, Yamamoto scattered his fleet into numerous task forces widely spread across the globe, as if the objective was to give a job to every Japanese admiral. So when battle was joined at Midway, the Japanese contrived to be outnumbered in aircraft – only slightly – but it was another step towards an entirely avoidable defeat. Even more strangely, the ground force ratios make no sense. One or two air strikes were to precede the landing of an assault force that was no larger than the defending garrison, and would require six trips by its five little landing craft to get ashore. Had the invasion force actually attacked Midway, it is hard to see it faring any better than that at Wake Island when, on 11 December, US Marines beat off a Japanese assault: the only time an amphibious landing failed during the Second World War.

A Dot in a Vast Ocean

Yamamoto had played a key role in honing Japan's naval aviation to its pre-war pitch of perfection. He had opposed further battleship construction, recognizing that the future belonged to air power, not battlewagons, however big their guns. Yet for the Midway operation, he flew his flag in the super-battleship *Yamato*, built despite his protests from 1936–41. Even more curiously, he stationed himself – with two other massive battleships – 300 miles, or almost 24 hours' steaming, behind Nagumo's carriers.

Yamamoto retained one small escort carrier to provide reconnaissance and anti-submarine patrols for the battleships, which was prudent. Admiral Kondo was ordered to follow the invasion force more closely; his squadrons also required air support, thus taking the light carrier *Zuiho* and her 31 aircraft out of the picture too. Most crucially, the diversion of two carriers capable of carrying 80 aircraft to cover the raid on the Aleutians proved worse than pointless. The defending US Task Force 8 stood well off to the east, and the landings on Attu and Kiska were not opposed. The Japanese air raid on Dutch Harbor on 3 June failed to divert any US forces to the area; worse, one of the escorting Japanese fighters crash-landed almost intact and was restored to flying condition in America, where its performance could be minutely analysed.

The Japanese assumed that America could deploy only two aircraft carriers (*Hornet* and *Enterprise*), shipping about 155 aircraft between them. The Japanese had last seen USS *Yorktown* in apparently sinking condition at the end of the Battle of the Coral Sea. However, she had been saved, taken into dockyard hands, and repaired at breakneck speed. *Saratoga* was still on the US east coast, completing repairs after being badly damaged by a torpedo in January. (In another testimony to American engineering skill, she was already working up a new air group and arrived in Pearl Harbor at the end of the battle.)

Codebreaking

Once the Japanese squadrons departed to their widely separated positions, they were ordered to maintain radio silence, but the mission had already been compromised by US and British codebreakers. The American fleet commander Admiral Chester Nimitz remained ashore at Pearl Harbor to co-ordinate the US response, working from a reasonably good picture of where and when the Japanese were likely to appear. Task Force 16 (*Hornet* and *Enterprise*) commanded by Rear Admiral Spruance (in the absence of his sick commander, Vice Admiral Halsey) would rendezvous with Task Force 17 (*Yorktown* and a cruiser/destroyer escort) on 2 June some 300 miles northeast of Midway. Nimitz knew that with three US carriers and the aircraft stationed on Midway he would have about the same number of aircraft as the enemy.

However, the odds were still not even. What the Americans struggled to accept was that their aircraft were substantially inferior to those made in Japan. Japanese aircraft had far longer range, so could land the first blow. Their fighter, the Mitsubishi A6 Zero, completely outmatched the Grumman F4F Wildcat; their torpedo-bomber, the Nakajima B5N2, was the best of its type in the world; the Japanese dive-bomber, the Aichi D3, carried a slightly smaller payload than the Douglas SBD-3 Dauntless, but its strike radius was 600 – as opposed to 300 – miles. And that was against the newest US machines. The Marines air group on Midway included 20 obsolete Brewster F2A-3 Buffalo fighters of which just one survived the 4 June air battle. They also had to attack the Japanese fleet with the 16 equally dated Vought SB2U Vindicator dive-bombers. Twelve were shot down.

The Battle of the Coral Sea, a month previously, had been the first time naval forces clashed without surface ships sighting each other. They fought solely by air strikes, conducted over ranges of several hundred miles. Thus *Yorktown* was the only carrier on either side at Midway to have experience of this novel form of warfare – and much of her

Order of Battle

Japanese forces (*numbers of aircraft in parentheses*)

- Mobile Force (Vice Admiral Nagumo): four aircraft carriers – *Akagi*, *Hiryu*, *Kaga*, *Soryu* (296), two battlecruisers, two heavy cruisers, one light cruiser, twelve destroyers, five fleet oilers.
- Midway invasion force (Vice Admiral Kurita): four heavy cruisers, two destroyers, one light cruiser, ten destroyers, twelve transports carrying 5,000 troops (2nd Special Naval Landing Force, some army detachments and two construction battalions).
- 1st Fleet (Admiral Yamamoto): three battleships, one escort carrier, *Hosho* (18), three light cruisers, eight destroyers, two fleet oilers.
- 2nd Fleet (Vice Admiral Kondo): one aircraft carrier, *Zuiho* (31), two battlecruisers, four heavy cruisers, one light cruiser, seven destroyers, four oilers.
- 2nd Battleship Division, 1st Fleet (Vice Admiral Takasu): four battleships, two light cruisers, twelve destroyers, two oilers.
- 5th Fleet (Vice Admiral Hosogaya): two carriers – *Ryujo* and *Junyo* (80), three heavy cruisers, five destroyers, three oilers.
- Aleutians invasion force (Rear-Admiral Omori): two light cruisers, seven destroyers, three transports (1,750 troops and 700 construction troops).

US Navy

- Task Force 17 (Rear Admiral Fletcher): one carrier, *Yorktown* (71), two heavy cruisers, six destroyers.
- Task Force 16 (Rear Admiral Spruance): two carriers – *Hornet* and *Enterprise* (155), five heavy cruisers, one light cruiser, nine destroyers, two oilers.
- Midway atoll (78).
- Task Force 8 (Rear Admiral Theobald): five heavy cruisers, thirteen destroyers, two oilers.

air group had been changed. For almost all aircrew involved, this was the first time they had attacked an enemy carrier group – or defended one of their own.

On the afternoon of 3 June, the Japanese invasion force was bombed from about 12,000 feet by nine Boeing B-17 four-engined heavy bombers from Midway. They missed, and identified their targets as battleships. At 4.30 a.m. on 4 June, still some 200 miles away from the atoll, Nagumo launched 35 Nakajima B5Ns, carrying bombs instead of torpedoes, and 36 Aichi D3s dive-bombers to soften-up Midway, ahead of the amphibious landings. The bombers were escorted by 36 Zero fighters. An hour later, a US flying boat from the island located Nagumo's carriers, and another one saw the formation of Japanese aircraft en route, now 150 miles from their target. Every airworthy aircraft on Midway was scrambled.

The US Marine Buffalo fighters managed to bounce the incoming raid, shooting down three B5Ns before they were set upon by the escorting Zeros and massacred. Three more Japanese aircraft were brought down by American anti-aircraft guns. Some fuel tanks were set alight, but the AA fire was undiminished as the bombing finished. Lieutenant Tomonaga, the Japanese raid commander, radioed back to say that a second strike would be required to suppress the US defences.

ABOVE: *Japanese admiral Yamamoto was one of a handful of senior Japanese officers to have visited America and thus had some idea of what they were up against. But his intricate plan for the Midway battle took little account of American reaction, and this gigantic operation collapsed in confusion.*

Tomonaga's Signal

Admiral Nagumo had kept half his aircraft back, armed for an anti-shipping strike, just in case the Americans had wind of the operation and their warships put in an early appearance. But according to all the reports from his and other reconnaissance aircraft, there was no sign of any US surface ships in the vicinity. On receipt of Tomonaga's signal, Nagumo briefly considered his options. At 7.15 a.m. he ordered his second strike aircraft to be rearmed for a ground attack mission. To swap bombs for torpedoes on the B5Ns and blast bombs for armour-piercing ones on the dive-bombers would involve moving many aircraft back down into their hangars and back again. It would take about an hour. What he did not know was that the US carriers had not only located his position, but at 7.00 a.m. Spruance launched a strike from *Enterprise* and *Hornet* at the extreme range for his aircraft. Fletcher held his aircraft back for an hour, remembering how at Coral Sea the Japanese had operated two widely separated carrier groups. At 8.00 a.m. *Yorktown's* first strike thundered down the deck.

Half an hour into the rearming process, Nagumo countermanded his orders. At 7.28 a.m. a Japanese aircraft reported unidentified American warships 240 miles from Midway. Just as the Japanese started to swap bombs for torpedoes, some B-17s arrived overhead, forcing the Japanese carriers to take evasive action, although no hits were scored. Sixteen Dauntless dive-bombers from Midway arrived moments later, but were driven off by the Zeros. The old Vindicator dive-bombers found their target at 8.20 a.m. and attacked the battlecruiser *Haruna* without effect. About 40 minutes of air attacks from Midway cost the Americans 19 aircraft shot down. They inflicted little damage, but forced the Japanese carriers to manoeuvre defensively, just as their own aircraft were returning from attacking Midway.

At 8.20 a.m. the Japanese reconnaissance aircraft updated its report to identify an aircraft carrier with the US force it was shadowing. Nagumo's heart must have sunk at the news: his first strike needed to land and his second strike was not ready yet. But the attacks from Midway ceased, his aircraft landed, and the rearming and refuelling was nearly complete by 9.18 a.m. when his carriers reformed, set course for the American squadron and worked up to 28 knots. Their decks were crowded with bombed-up aircraft and strewn with fuel lines, but they would be ready for take-off in an hour or so. Moments later, the US carrier aircraft arrived overhead. Not that much overhead in the case of the first torpedo squadron to attack, all the obsolete Devastators from Torpedo Squadron 8 (VT-8) were shot into the sea during a low-level attack. The Japanese carriers did not even take evasive action as Zeros chopped plane after plane into the sea. But the attacks by VT-8, VT-3 and VT-6 in their more modern Grumman Avengers dissipated the Japanese fighter screen.

Aircraft Carriers Burn

Kaga was a few minutes away from launching her aircraft at 10.27 a.m. when dive-bombers from *Enterprise* swooped from high altitude. A 500-lb bomb landed in the middle of 25 torpedo bombers, waiting to take off. Another struck a refuelling cart which blew up, killing most personnel on the bridge. An armour-piercing 1,000-pounder penetrated into the engine room before detonating; the conflagration there accounted for most of the 800 men who died aboard her. Three 1,000-pounders tore through *Akagi's* deck, causing sympathetic detonations throughout the ship. *Yorktown's* dive-bombers targeted the *Soryu* with similar effect. In a few desperate minutes, three of Japan's fleet aircraft carriers were ablaze from stem to stern.

'Straight through her flight deck . . .'

Hiryu was not hit and launched two waves of aircraft that found *Yorktown* and crippled her. However, a second American strike found *Hiryu* at 5 p.m. and put three bombs straight through her flight deck. She caught fire and blazed until the early hours of the morning when she foundered.

Nagumo's bomber pilots reported sinking two US carriers, but his reconnaissance flights claimed to have identified another four carriers, six cruisers and fifteen destroyers north of Midway. He withdrew, only to be sacked by Yamamoto who ordered his various battleship units to close for surface action. Not until midnight on 5 June did he accept that the Americans were not going to oblige him. The Japanese turned for home.

Yorktown stayed afloat, even after she was abandoned, and there was some hope of salvaging her on 7 June. Unfortunately she was found by the Japanese submarine I-168 and torpedoed, this time fatally. Nevertheless, Midway had overturned Japan's advantage in aircraft carriers and enabled the American counter-attack to begin within two months, at Guadalcanal.

EL ALAMEIN
23 OCTOBER–
5 NOVEMBER 1942

'THE BATTLE WHICH IS NOW ABOUT TO
BEGIN WILL BE ONE OF THE MOST
DECISIVE BATTLES IN HISTORY. IT WILL
BE THE TURNING POINT OF THE WAR.'
Lieutenant General Bernard Montgomery,
message to the British 8th Army, October 1942

El Alamein was the most famous battlefield victory

won by the British Empire in the Second World War. Every previous British success in North Africa had been followed by a swift German recovery, counter-attack, and the sacking of the British commander. This time, Field Marshal Rommel's Panzerarmee Afrika retreated for good.

The British general was promoted and went on to command the Normandy landings in 1944, where he defeated Rommel a second time. In 1946 he became Chief of the Imperial General Staff and was ennobled as Viscount Montgomery of Alamein. Unfortunately, he was an unpleasant egotistical braggart who had alienated even his closest friends by the end of his life. Disentangling the real story of El Alamein from the foundation myths of the Montgomery legend was to take sixty years.

'Militarily, this is the most difficult period . . .'

Montgomery's battle was actually the second battle of El Alamein. It was to this position that the British 8th Army had withdrawn in June 1942, after its defeat at the Battle of Gazala and the fall of Tobruk. General Auchinleck, commander-in-chief of the British Middle East Command, sacked the army commander and took personal charge. He redeployed his men where there is only a 40-mile gap between the Mediterranean coast and the Qattara Depression – an impassable sand sea beneath cliffs several hundred feet high. Rommel was accustomed to beating the British by wide outflanking of their open, southern flank. Here, at the tiny Egyptian railway halt of El Alamein, he would have much less room for manoeuvre.

From 1–4 July, Rommel's army attacked, but was beaten back. Mussolini, who had flown from Italy with a white horse on which to parade through Cairo, sulked back to Rome. From then until 31 July, when Auchinleck called a halt, the British went over to the offensive, picking – whenever they could – on the Italian divisions which comprised half of Rommel's army. Rommel confessed to his wife, 'Militarily, this is the most difficult period I've been through'. He was beaten – but not fast enough to satisfy Winston Churchill.

The prime minister had promised 'blood, sweat and tears', but the first half of 1942 witnessed a terrible run of defeats: the surrenders of Singapore in February and of Tobruk in June; the retreat of the 8th Army into Eygpt, compounded by the aerial onslaught against Malta; the humiliating escape of the German battleships *Scharnhorst* and *Gneisenau* through the English Channel in broad daylight. Churchill's party lost a by-election in June when an independent candidate, a former communist, roundly beat the Conservative candidate. Churchill faced a vote of no confidence in the House of Commons on 1 July.

PREVIOUS PAGE: *A German tank crew surrender to a bayonet-wielding 'Tommy' in a scene from* Desert Victory, *an Oscar-winning British film made in 1943 to celebrate victory in the battle for North Africa.*

He had seen off a similar challenge in January by 464 votes to 1; this time 25 MPs voted against him and another 40 abstained.

Learning that Auchinleck wanted more time to prepare a new offensive against Rommel, Churchill sacked him, as he had done his predecessor in similar circumstances. However, his intended replacement, the bluff, hearty veteran general 'Straffer' Gott, was killed when a transport aircraft was shot down. The second choice, recommended by General Sir Alan Brooke, was a whippet-thin ascetic, Lieutenant General Bernard Law Montgomery, OC South-Eastern Command in the UK. He flew to Egypt, fired anyone too closely associated with the old chief, and set about reshaping the army. Ironically, his first demand of Churchill was that he wanted the same breathing space requested by Auchinleck before assaulting Rommel.

'Tanks . . . under-gunned and . . . unreliable'

Montgomery inherited a plan of campaign from Auchinleck, although he would deny this to his dying day. He also inherited an army unique to the mid-20th-century British Empire and Commonwealth: British, Australian, New Zealand, Indian and South African divisions – although no Canadians – plus Free French and Polish contingents. The commanders of the Australian, New Zealand and South African forces had right of appeal to their national political leadership in extremis, an option that was exercised more often as the campaign unravelled.

> 'If he is disagreeable to those about him, he is also disagreeable to the enemy'
>
> WINSTON CHURCHILL IN A LETTER TO HIS WIFE, DESCRIBING GENERAL MONTGOMERY

For try as he might, Auchinleck was unable to resolve deep-seated organizational, sociological and technical problems that handicapped the British army in the Desert War. The shortcomings of the hardware attract the most attention: many British tanks were under-gunned and mechanically unreliable, inferior to German panzers. The Germans were quicker to upgrade their anti-tank gun batteries, and employed them with greater skill. The British could not even get the little things right: their sharp-cornered petrol tins sprung leaks so everyone used German ones – jerry cans – when they could. American tanks and bigger anti-tank guns improved things in time, but the software problems were more intransigent – some not resolved by the end of the war. Co-ordination between infantry and armour was lamentable compared to the German integration of panzers and panzer-grenadiers. While deriding the Germans as unable to think for themselves, the truth was the polar opposite. British operations were characterized by a crippling want of initiative and drive.

Montgomery had no shortage of drive. His great achievement was to impart his personal confidence and energy to the 8th Army; above all, to connect with the ordinary soldiers in a very modern way. He was a patrician, socially inept in private, but he knew how to work a crowd. He embarked on a furious round of training and reorganization, while making frequent addresses to the troops. Unlike his predecessors, he was fully aware that his soldiers were civilians in uniform; that they had strengths and weaknesses quite different from those of long service professional soldiers. He wore a variety of headgear obtained from his units, sporting every one of their badges. Montgomery was like no other officer the men had ever seen: a British celebrity general.

The 8th Army Gets its 'Tommy Cookers'

In addition to rebuilding his army's morale, Montgomery restored its equipment. American tanks were key: M4 Shermans with engines that did not break down every few miles and a 75mm gun. British tank crews blackly referred to their tanks as 'Ronsons', after the cigarette lighter advertised to 'light every time'. In fact, Shermans burned just as well (the Germans named them 'Tommy Cookers'), thanks to the way their ammunition was stored, but they evened the odds against Rommel's panzers. In tanks, artillery and aircraft, Montgomery would outnumber the Axis by a substantial margin. Rommel's supplies had to run the gauntlet, across a Mediterranean infested with British submarines. One of Rommel's worst decisions had been to reject a planned attack on Malta in 1942 in favour of pushing on to Egypt. The island – submarine base and unsinkable aircraft carrier – endured a horrific aerial blitz, but did not surrender. By late summer 1942, Axis supplies were running low: although ammunition would remain

Lili Marleen

ROMMEL CALLED THE NORTH AFRICAN CAMPAIGN 'war without hate'. It was not marred by atrocities, the region was thinly populated so civilian casualties were minimal, and the exigencies of life in such a hostile climate sometimes led soldiers of both sides to make common cause in the name of survival. Water was shared. Casualties were rescued without hindrance. The campaign even had its own song, 'Lili Marleen'. Recorded in 1939 by Lale Andersen, it was broadcast frequently on Radio Belgrade in 1941 when the Germans took control of the station – not as a matter of policy: they just did not have many records. 'Lili Marleen' was an immediate hit with the German troops in Africa, who wrote in to request it. The Nazi regime ordered it to stop, thinking the lyrics sad and defeatist, but gave way in the light of popular demand – and a BBC report that Lale Andersen had been sent to a concentration camp for communicating with a Jewish director she used to work with. Eventually, the song was used to sign off the programme every night on Radio Belgrade. British authorities frowned on their troops singing a German song, but sing it they did, often in German – as some veterans are still wont to do. US authorities were equally disapproving, thinking the heroine of the song was a prostitute, but their ban did not work either. It was later recorded by Marlene Dietrich, Perry Como and Carly Simon, among others. 'Lili Marleen' remains the most famous German song of all time.

plentiful, Rommel's command was critically low on petrol, restricting the movement of his tanks.

Montgomery corrected a long-standing problem within the 8th Army by locating his headquarters close by that of the Desert Air Force, and integrating air power with his ground operations as never before. German soldiers were used to having the sky above them dominated by the famous fighter aces of the Luftwaffe. They still got on the front page of *Signal* magazine, but seldom by attacking British bombers, which ranged unchecked over the Libyan coastal highway along which all Rommel's supplies had to pass.

Miles and Miles of Sand

The blistering pace of Montgomery's reorganization of his command was not driven just by the traditional goading of the prime minister. Churchill and his new general both knew that in November the Desert War would be transformed by Anglo-American landings at the other end of North Africa – Operation 'Torch'. The attack at El Alamein would be the last time the British army fought the Germans on its own. With Eisenhower's armada en route to Morocco and Algeria, the British needed a victory they could call their own, despite the obvious truth that Rommel would be unable to remain inside Egypt while another massive Allied army threatened Libya from the west.

Montgomery planned to fight the sort of set-piece battle that the 20th-century British army had excelled at since 1917. Based on good intelligence and incorporating an elaborate deception plan, it would be a step-by-step, grinding battle of attrition which did not demand the flair or tactical initiative that was the hallmark of the German army in general, and Erwin Rommel in particular. It would be in overwhelming force, with twice as many tanks, three times as many aircraft and vastly more heavy artillery than the defenders possessed. It would also enjoy a hidden advantage in intelligence. The British famously had ULTRA, the ability to read many German coded signals, so Rommel's reports and the responses from Hitler were read and understood by his opponent. Auchinleck had destroyed Rommel's equivalent, a specialist unit of English-speaking Germans who were expert at monitoring the 8th Army's radio signals. ULTRA intelligence discovered the location of Rommel's radio-interception unit, just behind the lines, and an Australian infantry brigade launched a surprise attack that – coincidentally as it appeared – overran Rommel's SIGINT unit and killed its CO.

Attack and Counter-Attack

Montgomery's battle began with a time-on-target barrage from up to 744 guns: the artillery batteries timed it so the first shells struck their targets at the same time, right across the front line. The Axis front line was protected by the biggest minefields ever laid, a 'devil's garden' of 500,000 anti-tank and anti-personnel mines through which the British

ABOVE: *The controversial victor: General Montgomery was a dedicated and highly competent officer, with a flair for public relations. He was unable to accept that his victory at Alamein owed anything to the efforts of his predecessors, and went to unseemly lengths to write them out of the battle's history.*

infantry and engineers would have to clear a path before their armour could push through. The shelling began on the evening of 23 October and lasted for more than five hours, before the infantry assaulted in the eerie light of a full moon. By chance, the battle opened with Rommel in Germany, where he was receiving medical treatment for stomach and skin conditions brought on by too much time in the desert. Worse, Georg Stumme, the tank general brought in from the Russian front to command in his absence, was killed under fire; German communications were paralysed by the bombardment, and local counter-attacks launched by the Afrika Korps led to heavy losses.

Montgomery had told his men and his prime minister that the battle would unfold by successive phases, in a week of heavy fighting that would end in victory. Everything would go according to plan. However, after seven days there was still no breakthrough. Churchill railed at Alan Brooke, demanding to know why 'his' Monty had allowed the battle to peter out, why 'he had done nothing for three days and was now withdrawing troops from the front'.

Afterwards, Montgomery claimed it had all gone according to his master plan. In fact, he spent the last few days in October reshaping his battle in the light of experience. He was not the first general to lie in such a way: it created an aura of omniscience that would give his army a psychological advantage in future battles. Montgomery's worst problem was the exasperating inability of the British tank formations to co-ordinate with the infantry – or even each other. Fortunately, when Rommel returned he ordered his last armoured reserves to the south, where he always tried to break through. Montgomery struck in the north.

Montgomery said he was 'a very nice chap'

From 1–3 November, the 8th Army battered away against weakening opposition and on 4 November the British armour finally broke through into open country. Rommel ordered a withdrawal, countermanded it after a hostile signal from Hitler, and then decided to reinstate the order. In the disorderly retreat that followed, the Italian infantry divisions – with little motor transport – were abandoned to their fate. The German paratroop contingent, originally trained to attack Malta but deployed to the desert as infantry, hijacked some British lorries with which to effect their escape. General von Thoma, the Bavarian aristocrat in command of the Afrika Korps, donned his dress uniform and took charge of a handful of tanks that formed the rearguard. Iron Cross on his breast, Knight's Cross at his throat, he disdained retreat and was the only survivor when his tank caught fire. Taken prisoner, he dined with Montgomery that night, who thought him 'a very nice chap'.

Alamein restored the British army's confidence in itself. It gave rise to the Monty legend that would help carry it across the Channel to victory in 1944; and for the first time, the home audience could enjoy it too. The documentary *Desert Victory*, released in March 1943, won director David Macdonald an Oscar. While some of the footage was faked – Australian infantry attacking a position that was actually their own field kitchen – much else was genuine: one cameraman was killed, seven were wounded and six captured during filming. Combat footage is so commonplace today, it is important to note that this was the first time since 1917 that a 'battle film' of this type was released in Britain.

Axis losses at El Alamein were about 17,000, or roughly the number of casualties German forces sustained every week on the Russian front, month after month, year after year. Rommel accepted that he would never again be able to menace Egypt and the Suez Canal, but he did not accept that defeat at El Alamein – or 'Torch', which took place on 8 November, meant the Axis war in North Africa was over. Indeed, the Germans proceeded to expand their bridgehead in Tunisia faster than the Allies could reach it. By the turn of the year, the British and American forces were strung out along a wide front to the west of Tunis, the 8th Army had yet to arrive in strength, and Rommel's thoughts turned to counter-attack – this time against the Americans.

STALINGRAD

27 JULY 1942–
2 FEBRUARY 1943

'I DON'T WANT A SECOND VERDUN'
ADOLF HITLER, SPEAKING IN MUNICH, 8 NOVEMBER 1942

The Battle of Stalingrad was the bloodiest battle of the Second World War. The Russian army sustained over 1 million casualties; Germany lost 800,000 men, and its last chance to make a success of the invasion of Russia. It was a turning point in world history.

The German invasion of Russia, launched in July 1941, had ground to a halt in the snow outside Moscow in December, a few days before Pearl Harbor. In these circumstances, Hitler's declaration of war on the USA seems as bizarre today as it did to his more globally minded generals. In 1942, Hitler gambled that the German army could seize Russia's oilfields in the Caucasus, easing the oil shortage that bedevilled the German war machine, and depriving Russia of its main source of fuel. The German army would strike past the junction of the rivers Don and Donets, seizing Rostov on one flank and Stalingrad on the other.

July saw such rapid German advances that the Soviet official history tried to explain this as a deliberate strategy to draw the Germans on to defeat. The German 6th Army reached the suburbs of Stalingrad on 23 August. But, unlike in 1941, the Germans no longer had enough tanks to bypass the city on either side and cut it off. They were going to have to make a frontal attack.

The city hugged the west bank of the Volga for 15 miles. At the heart of the city lay three large manufacturing complexes: the Red October steelworks, the Barrikady ordnance factory and the Stalingrad tractor factory, which actually built tanks. All three became centres of resistance. The city centre was defended by the Russian 62nd Army with some 54,000 men, 900 guns and mortars and 110 tanks. The German 6th Army had 25 divisions, with more than 100,000 men committed to the battle for the city, supported by some 2,000 guns and 500 tanks.

The battle for the city began in earnest on 13 September. The German 295th, 71st and 94th Infantry Divisions and 29th Motorized Division, supported by 14th and 24th Panzer Divisions, launched an all-out attack which overran the low hill where the Soviet 62nd Army's HQ had been located. The railway station was taken and the 71st Division advanced far enough to bring the Volga landing stage under fire.

In the City of Rubble and Ruins

In ferocious house-to-house fighting, most of the city's wooden buildings were destroyed, leaving the soldiers to fight over rubble, through cellars and among the giant industrial complexes that resisted the heaviest bombardment. Because each assault left the attackers

OPPOSITE: *Russian soldiers in insulated winter gear aim their superbly reliable PPSh sub-machine guns in a wartime film of their most famous victory. Stalingrad removed any prospect of German victory in Russia and exposed just what a colossal gamble Hitler's invasion had been.*

so disorganized, short of men and ammunition, counter-attacks often succeeded, and the same objective could change hands repeatedly. The 62nd Army bled to death, fighting on in an ever-shrinking bridgehead. Drafts of replacements were fed in, just enough to keep the units operational, although divisions were often reduced to little more than battalions.

General Friedrich von Paulus, commander of the German 6th Army, flew to Vinnitsa for a meeting with Hitler on the eve of the September offensive. The very same day, Russian generals Zhukov and Rokossovsky presented their plan for a counter-offensive to Stalin. They foresaw how the battle for the city would soak up most of the 6th Army, leaving its long flanks guarded by second-rate units.

The Red October Steelworks

The ruins of the tractor factory were finally captured; by November only 10 per cent of the city remained in Russian hands. The 6th Army gathered itself for a final effort before winter. On 11–12 November it attacked the Red October steelworks with nine divisions. The same night, German intelligence repeated its warnings about Russian armies massing along the 180-mile front held by Romanian, Italian and Hungarian forces.

Three Soviet fronts (roughly equivalent in size to a German army), with a combined strength of 1.1 million men, 894 tanks and 12,000 guns, began the great winter offensive on 19 November. At Stalingrad itself, the dawn was barely perceptible, the gaunt silhouettes of the ruined tower blocks hidden in the fog. More than 1,200 Soviet aircraft had been deployed to support the fronts. The sudden concentration of Russian fighters and the onset of severe weather ended the Luftwaffe's domination of the Stalingrad area.

The Russians swept through the Romanian and Italian armies, Luftwaffe field divisions, and other second-rate formations dotted along the south bank of the Don. When the two Russian spearheads met at Kalatsch on 23 November, the encirclement was completed. The Russians had trapped more than 300,000 German and allied troops in the Stalingrad pocket: the entire 6th Army and most of the 4th Panzer Army.

Desperate Measures for Desperate Times

NI SHAGU NAZAD!– not a step backward! – was the theme of Stalin's Order 227 read out to Red Army units on 28 July 1942. It seemed nothing could stop the German 6th Army racing across Russia all the way to the Volga: whole units of the Red Army were fleeing eastwards, abandoning their weapons. Stalin had his security forces enforce discipline with the utmost savagery: some 13,500 Russian soldiers were shot for cowardice or desertion and many more consigned to newly created *strafbats* (penal battalions). These suicide units were employed as human mine-detectors or to spearhead assaults: spectacular acts of bravery were required to win transfer back to a regular regiment. Casualties averaged six times that of a normal infantry unit.

The encirclement caught the Germans without their winter clothing which was still at supply depots outside the perimeter. Once again German soldiers would have to endure sub-zero temperatures, wearing standard uniforms padded with newspaper and straw. And the army had food and fuel only for a week. Although a defensive front was quickly established facing west, there were no real defensive positions on the open steppe. The troops entrenched themselves as well as they could in the frozen earth.

Reichsmarschall Göring told Hitler he could supply Paulus's men by air: a blatant untruth made in an attempt to regain the Führer's favour. About 500 transports and bombers were lost, trying to shuttle supplies to the 6th Army. The Russians deployed anti-aircraft guns along a corridor, and deployed squadron after squadron of new fighter planes. More than 1,000 German aircrew perished in an operation that delivered an average of 100 tons of supplies a day: about 5 per cent of what the 6th Army required to move, fight – and eat.

Field Marshal von Manstein was ordered to take command of Army Group Don on 26 November. Hitler insisted that the 6th Army remain in Stalingrad, rather than try to escape. He told Manstein it would be the springboard for a new offensive in 1943 which would see German forces advance through the Caucasus and link up with Rommel's army in Africa. Hitler was lying: unlike Manstein, he knew Rommel had just been defeated at El Alamein and was in full retreat.

> 'A few trips to the front could easily have shown him . . . the fundamental errors that were costing so much blood. Hitler and his military advisers thought they could lead the army from maps.'
> ALBERT SPEER

Before examining the German attempts to rescue the 6th Army, it is important to understand what was happening further north. Many books have been written on the Stalingrad campaign that fail to mention an even larger battle that took place at the same time and which had profound consequences for Paulus and his men.

Germany's biggest and most powerful army, the 9th, commanded by Walther Model, was fighting for its life in November 1942. Arguably, the fate of the 6th Army was largely determined by the battles around Rzhev that embroiled 6 German tank and 17 infantry divisions, preventing the transfer of significant German reserves to help rescue the 6th Army. When the German high command reviewed the Stalingrad situation map, it was at all times conscious that another army was also engaged in a life-or-death struggle. Model was the definitive glassy-eyed fanatic, and if he said he could spare no reserves, the situation had to be grim indeed.

Operation 'Mars' opened on 25 November. Seven Russian armies, including 83 divisions, took part in the operation: more than 800,000 men and 2,350 tanks. Fierce fighting lasted until 15 December (as Hoth's Panzer corps got within 50 miles of the 6th Army's positions). It was a disaster for the Russians: their losses here approached 500,000 dead, wounded and missing. German intelligence correctly estimated Russian tank losses at 1,700 – more than the number of tanks allocated to the Stalingrad offensive. Zhukov's meat-grinder cost the Red Army more than ten men for every German casualty: a ratio that even Soviet manpower reserves could not sustain. Few commanders in history have kept their heads, let alone their jobs after such a fiasco; but Stalin retained both Zhukov and Konev, recognizing perhaps that neither had any political ambition.

Operations 'Winter Storm' and 'Thunderclap'

There could be no help for the 6th Army from the substantial German forces in western Europe either. They had been on high alert since 8 November when an Anglo-American army landed in North Africa. German forces in the occupied zone of France were ordered to take control of the Vichy state and seize the French battle fleet at Toulon. Only after the danger of an amphibious invasion of southern France had passed were the armoured formations released to the eastern front.

General Hoth began the Stalingrad rescue mission on 12 December. It was planned to unfold in two stages: Operation 'Winter Storm' would punch through the Soviet encirclement to link the defenders of Stalingrad to the rest of the German army; then in Operation 'Thunderclap' the 6th Army would escape westwards along the corridor carved by Hoth's Panzers.

The 6th Panzer Division began the relief attempt with 160 tanks, but 23rd Panzer had only 40 operational tanks on 18 November. The 17th Panzer Division had 60. Despite facing substantially larger Soviet forces, Hoth's 57th Panzer Corps fought its way forward about 30 miles in 12 days. On the morning of 17 December, the Germans captured two crossings over the River Aksay, bringing them within 45 miles of the 6th Army's perimeter. Then came the crushing news; a new Soviet offensive had opened northwest of Stalingrad. The Italian 8th Army and Romanian 3rd Army along the River Tschir had been badly beaten.

Manstein was obliged to detach 6th Panzer to deal with the new threat, leaving Hoth to battle on alone. Grinding through the Soviet lines had reduced the Panzergruppe to just 35 tanks. The sound of the fighting could be heard from within the pocket. The 6th Army prepared its three strongest divisions to attack at Karpovka as soon as Hoth's troops were within 20 miles – there was not enough fuel for a longer advance. Starting with the Volga front, the encircled army planned to retreat southwest, units leapfrogging back with the army's remaining 100 or so armoured vehicles providing flank protection.

On clear nights, Hoth's soldiers could see flares on the distant horizon, rockets arcing high above the Stalingrad perimeter. But the relief effort was faltering. If the 6th Army was to escape, it would have to try to break out.

ABOVE: *Russian soldiers in action against the last pockets of German resistance in the industrial buildings of Stalingrad. German counter-attacks continued well into January, long after all hope of rescue had vanished.*

The order was not given. Conscious that the army had so little fuel left, that it would soon be compelled to abandon its vehicles and guns, neither Manstein nor Paulus would take responsibility for the break-out, an operation that would have seen the remains of the 6th Army try to fight its way across 30 miles of open steppe with nothing but rifles and shovels, abandoning their sick and wounded comrades to the enemy. Yet there can be no doubt that this superhuman task would have been made with exceptional determination, and, as several of Paulus's officers said at the time, better to escape with 6 divisions than lose all 20.

By 31 December, Hoth's relief force had been driven back beyond its start line and the German defensive front along the Don had collapsed. The Russian offensive had blown a gap more than 200 miles wide, and the entire German Army Group in the Caucasus was in danger of being cut off.

The 6th Army was doomed. Several officers shot themselves. An understandable – but unedifying – scramble took place among the Nazi leadership to extract friends and relatives from Stalingrad before it was too late. Albert Speer tried and failed to get his brother out. Air crew landing at Pitomnik in mid-January had to resort to their personal weapons to fight off attempts to storm the aircraft. Discipline was maintained with the same savage methods the Soviets had already resorted to. Paulus had 364 of his men shot for cowardice in just one week; 18 more than Field Marshal Haig had executed in the British army during the whole of the First World War.

Frostbite, Malnutrition and Disease

All able-bodied men in the pocket were combined into 'fortress battalions'. The Luftwaffe ground personnel, Flak crews, clerical staff and all rear echelon services took up rifles instead. The rapid exhaustion of medical supplies left the sick and wounded to suffer in the most revolting conditions, their numbers overwhelming the medical staff. Dysentery and typhoid fever swept through the starving units and dressing stations alike. There were more than 50,000 wounded men in the pocket. Thousands had reached the field hospital at Gumrak only to be stacked into unheated freight cars at the railway station. The novel *Forsaken Army*, written by a survivor, describes how medical teams let the badly wounded freeze to death overnight rather than prolong their agonies in the hellish dressing stations. Standing orders forbade leaving the wounded to the enemy, so as the perimeter contracted under steady Russian pressure, aid posts were cleared and the casualties moved into the city.

Paulus rejected an offer to surrender on 9 January and directed that flags of truce were to be fired on in future. The next day the Russians attacked the western perimeter, where the defences, such as they were, stretched across the bare steppe. The perimeter was penetrated by tanks after a concentrated artillery barrage, and in temperatures of minus 30 degrees Celsius, the German survivors fell back towards the city itself. There was no intermediate defensive line, nothing on which to build a new position. Pitomnik airbase was overrun on 16 January, leaving the small strip at Gumrak the 6th Army's only contact with the outside world.

Paulus: 'I have no intention of shooting myself for that Austrian corporal.'

The renewed Soviet offensive overran the Hungarian 2nd Army in the Don Bend, destroying it in a series of battles around the small town of Voronyets. This was the blackest day in the history of the Hungarian army: of the 270,000 men in the Hungarian forces there, 130,000 were killed, captured or posted missing. The Russian breakthrough in the Hungarian sector led to the capture of many of the airfields from which the Stalingrad airlift was being mounted. By mid-January 1943 the nearest German-held airfields were more than 200 miles from the city.

The German forces in Stalingrad suffered about 60,000 casualties in December and another 100,000 in January. On 22 January, Gumrak – the last airfield – was overrun. The Luftwaffe had evacuated 34,000 wounded during the siege, but that left tens of thousands of men to wait for death in conditions of indescribable horror.

Paulus capitulated on 30 January. The 6th Army had been split in two by the final Russian attacks, and Strecker's 11th Corps, holding the tractor factory and Barrikady ordnance works, held out until 1 February. Its commander made one last radio call before surrendering. A party from Strecker's headquarters broke out of the city as it fell, as did elements of the 71st Infantry Division and an unknown number of little groups. A few were seen by German aircraft, but were all swallowed up on the vast frozen steppe, never to be seen again. German aircraft flying over the city on 2 February could see no sign of movement among the ruins.

Henderson Field. The island would function as an unsinkable aircraft carrier for the rest of the campaign – its air group dubbed 'The Cactus Airforce', after the code name for the island.

Fail to Plan . . .

The next night witnessed one of the most catastrophic Japanese intelligence failures of the war. In the macho culture of both the Japanese army and navy, learning the enemy language was regarded as suspect, and intelligence officers were treated with contempt, sometimes excluded altogether from planning operations. The Japanese assumed the US Marines operated in the same way as the Japanese naval infantry, so they landed several hundred naval troops and 1,000 soldiers to destroy what they thought was an equivalent lodgement of Americans. On the night of 21 August some 2,500 Japanese tried to overrun 11,000 dug-in US Marines. Most died in a hail of fire and the Marines counter-attacked at dawn, driving a few survivors into the jungle and killing their commander.

Admiral Yamamoto did not wait to learn the result of the battle before ordering a counter-strike by the Japanese navy. His objective was not the island, but a decisive naval victory that would reverse the judgement of Midway. He ordered the fleet carriers *Shokaku* and *Zuikaku* to form a task force under Admiral Nagumo; Rear Admiral Hara commanded a smaller force, based around the light carrier *Ryujo*; both were preceded by a surface action group under Rear Admiral Abe – two battlecruisers and four cruisers. The heavy cruiser squadron at Rabaul would also sortie, covering Admiral Tanaka's destroyers and transports that carried 1,500 troops to Guadalcanal.

With the *Wasp* detached to refuel when battle was joined, the combined American air groups totalled 177 aircraft to 176 Japanese. On 24–25 August the fleets clashed in a furious exchange of air strikes known as the Battle of the Eastern Solomons. Reconnaissance aircraft mis-identified enemy ships they found, or reported them in the wrong position, or missed them altogether. Air strikes were launched and found their targets, but neglected to report what they had encountered – or where. Aircrew and anti-aircraft gunners reported wildly inflated numbers of enemy planes shot down.

The 'Tokyo Express'

A few things were certain, *Ryujo* was sunk by US dive-bombers, putting up such a feeble anti-aircraft barrage that all the bombers returned home. One Douglas SBD lowered its undercarriage to slow its dive and so make sure of a hit. *Enterprise* escaped damage from a Japanese air strike by steaming in a circle at 27 knots with full rudder. She was accompanied by the battleship *North Carolina* which erupted in fire from bows to stern, prompting an anxious call from Admiral Kinkaid on *Enterprise*. The battleship was not hit: this was her formidable anti-aircraft battery in action – 100 guns. Several US fighters were lost to their own anti-aircraft barrage as they chased Japanese bombers into it. Of one flight of 36 Aichi D3 dive-bombers, 20 were shot down as well as 6–8 accompanying Zeros. Admiral Fletcher was told 70 Japanese aircraft had been downed; on the other hand the surviving Japanese aircrew told their admirals they had hit two US carriers and a battleship.

The Japanese troop convoy was found and subjected to repeated air attacks by US aircraft from Guadalcanal. The survivors returned to Rabaul, from whence they were shipped to the island by Tanaka's destroyers under cover of darkness. 'The Tokyo Express' managed to land some 5,000 troops by the end of the month, making sure to be well clear of land by dawn.

The Submarine Factor

Neither fleet managed to land a decisive blow on 24–25 August, but *Enterprise* was damaged and left for repairs. A week later a Japanese submarine evened the odds with a torpedo attack on the USS *Saratoga*. Her air group was flown to join the Cactus Air Force but the carrier would be out of action for three months.

On 15 September another Japanese submarine skipper, Commander Takaichi Kinashi, fired a fan of six extremely well-aimed torpedoes, putting one in the *North Carolina*, blowing off the bows of the destroyer *O'Brien* and slamming three

Guadalcanal

1942, May US intelligence learns the Japanese are building an airbase on the island of Tulagi.

19 June US establishes a new command, the South Pacific theatre, under the command of Vice Admiral Robert Ghormley.

7 August US forces land on Guadalcanal and its outlying islands. Japanese aircraft attack the beachhead.

8 August Japanese air raids continue. That night, Japanese cruisers defeat an Allied naval squadron off Savo Island. US surface fleet withdraws from the area.

18 August Henderson Field declared operational.

29 August Japanese begin to land reinforcements on the island, at night, using destroyers soon dubbed 'The Tokyo Express'.

11 October Battle of Cape Esperance: US surface action group defeats Japanese cruiser force at night, off Guadalcanal.

14 October Japanese battle cruisers bombard Henderson Field under cover of darkness.

24 October Japanese begin landing another wave of reinforcements.

26 October Battle of Santa Cruz sees the loss of USS *Hornet*.

12 November Japanese battlecruisers try to shell Henderson Field again, but are intercepted and the *Hiei* is sunk.

30 November Japanese surface units win the Battle of Tassafaronga against a US cruiser force.

12 December Japanese high command accepts defeat on Guadalcanal and orders the evacuation of remaining ground troops.

1943, 14 January Japanese evacuation begins.

9 February Japanese evacuation completed.

into the *Wasp*. Sympathetic detonations followed 20 minutes later and the ensuing fires proved impossible to control. She sank that evening, leaving *Hornet* the only American carrier left afloat in the South Pacific.

Japanese actions in the Solomons were handicapped by bitter inter-service rivalry. The army regarded Guadalcanal as a tiresome distraction from its invasion of New Guinea, but further defeats on Guadalcanal led General Hyatutake, commander of the 17th Army, to send additional reinforcements. On 9 October he established the army headquarters on Guadalcanal, signalling that the army was finally giving priority to this sector.

On the night of 11–13 October a Japanese cruiser squadron closed Guadalcanal to shell the airfield. It was intercepted by US cruisers off Cape Esperance; one Japanese cruiser was sunk and the Japanese admiral killed. The next night, the Japanese returned with two battlecruisers. *Kongo* and *Haruna* destroyed 32 of the 37 US dive-bombers on Henderson Field with a bombardment of shocking intensity from their 14-inch guns. Cruisers returned the next night to continue the job. With the Cactus Air Force down – if not out – the Japanese were able to land so many reinforcements that Hyatutake had nearly 20,000 men, some artillery and even a company of light tanks to prosecute his attack.

The Japanese ground offensive ran from 23–25 October and resulted in another resounding defeat with very lopsided casualty rates: an estimated 1,500 Japanese soldiers (and all nine tanks) were lost in exchange for some 60 US fatalities. The 17th Army did not inform its own navy what had happened, despite knowing that the Imperial fleet had sortied in support. Yamamoto's all-out effort brought about the fourth action between US and Japanese aircraft carriers – the last they had any chance of winning.

Three Japanese aircraft carriers, two light carriers, four battleships, ten cruisers and thirty-one destroyers sailed, with a surface action group in the lead – unlike at Midway, where the battleships had remained far in the rear. The carriers were divided into two squadrons, operating 100 miles apart – three times average visual spotting distance from an aircraft. They could combine to attack a US task force, but an air strike sent against one of them would be unlikely to see the other. There were no troop transports to be guarded: this was a seek-and-destroy mission: its target was the US carrier force, in this case *Hornet* and the newly repaired *Enterprise*.

Shells in the South Seas

The fleets met on 26 October after a tense 24 hours of manoeuvre and air strikes that found no targets. Both launched reconnaissance flights at dawn. The Japanese soon discovered *Hornet* less than 200 miles away, and launched 67 aircraft from *Shokaku*, *Zuikaku* and *Zuiho* at 8.40 p.m. US dive-bombers on reconnaissance flights nevertheless carried a 500 lb bomb, and just as the Japanese got their last aircraft airborne, two Douglas SBDs spotted the fleet, reported what they had found – and swooped. They scored a direct hit on *Zuiho* that blew a hole in her flight deck aft and started a fire; the ship was saved but was unable to recover aircraft. On receipt of the SBD's signal, *Enterprise* and *Hornet* launched strikes of their own.

The rival air strikes passed close by, but not all pilots saw the enemy and only one flight – nine Zeros from *Zuiho* – left their formation to attack. They bounced *Enterprise's* nine Grumman TBF torpedo-bombers, shooting three into the sea and crippling a fourth before taking on the US escorts and downing three Grumman F4Fs and winging another.

Ninety minutes after they took off, the Japanese located *Hornet.* Eighteen Nakajima B5 torpedo-bombers from *Zuikaku* raced in at wave-top height while 22 Aichi D3 dive-bombers from *Shokaku* pounced from 17,000 feet. *Hornet's* anti-aircraft guns opened fire. Some gunners swore they hit the Japanese dive-bomber leader, others said he did it deliberately: all that is

> 'Guadalcanal was a very fierce battle. I do not know what to do next.'
>
> ADMIRAL YAMAMOTO, PRIVATE LETTER TO HIS FRIEND ADMIRAL SHIMIZU, COMMANDER OF JAPANESE SUBMARINE FORCES.

certain is that Lieutenant Commander Mamoru Seki's D3 plunged into *Hornet* without releasing its bombs. One exploded on impact, but the worst damage was done by the bomber's aviation fuel which acted like a giant flame-thrower on the crew of the signal bridge. Two of the torpedo-bombers scored hits, flooding the forward engine room and, as *Hornet* lost way, the last dive-bombers put three bombs through her deck. One torpedo-bomber, set on fire by *Hornet's* gunners, flew into the forward anti-aircraft battery, drenching more crewmen in blazing avgas. The way that another damaged B5 deliberately crashed into the destroyer *Smith* suggested that these Pearl Harbor veterans chose suicide attacks over crash-landing and possible surrender.

Hornet lay ablaze, at a cost of 25 Japanese aircraft and their crews. Her air group found the Japanese carriers half an hour later, the SBDs diving down to put three or more bombs through the deck of Nagumo's flagship, *Shokaku.* She survived, but would be unable to recover her aircraft. She was lucky that *Hornet's* torpedo bombers never found her, neither did the strike from *Enterprise*: both stooged about over empty ocean after failing to hear their comrades' radio messages.

Enterprise survived three severe bomb hits from *Zuikaku's* dive-bombers that arrived half an hour after the assault on *Hornet.* During her refit she had received new anti-aircraft guns and proximity-fused ammunition for her 5-inch guns. Now using radar fire control, they put up a deadly barrage that knocked down half the attackers.

Junyo's air group met a similar reception, some having a go at the escorting battleship *South Dakota* which suffered a direct hit on her forward 16-inch gun turret, jamming it in its tracks and nearly killing the captain. His throat was laid open by shrapnel, and only the quick reactions of his helmsman, clamping his finger over the artery, kept him alive long enough for the corps men to reach him.

The battlecruisers of the Japanese surface action group raced to close with the US task force while the *Shokaku* and *Zuiho* withdrew. Meanwhile, *Junyo* managed to launch a second strike and hit *Hornet* again. Listing and on fire, she had to be abandoned that afternoon. Japanese destroyers found her blazing hulk that night, and sent her to the bottom with torpedoes. The rest of the US task force had retired to avoid contact with the Japanese heavy units.

Losses, Sinkings and Closures

The action at Santa Cruz left the Americans with only one carrier in the South Pacific – *Enterprise* – and the US commander, Admiral Kinkaid, was relieved of his command. It was certainly a Japanese tactical victory, but while the Americans had lost 28 naval aviators, the Japanese had lost 148, including half their torpedo-bomber pilots. After this, the fourth aircraft-carrier fleet battle, the Japanese had lost more than half of the airmen who took part in Pearl Harbor. The Japanese had made no effort to create a reserve or expand their pilot-training system, so its main offensive weapon was now thoroughly blunted.

Admiral Yamamoto turned once more to his battleships. He ordered a renewed offensive: transports would ship an infantry division to the island, while shore bombardments took care of the Cactus Air Force. US signals intelligence enabled an American surface action group to be in place to intercept the Japanese on the night of 12–13 November. The squadrons shot it out at point-blank range until the Japanese withdrew; their damaged battlecruiser *Hiei* was too slow to escape and the Cactus Air Force finished her off. The next night two American battleships entered what had now been christened 'ironbottom sound' and met another Japanese bombardment group. USS *Washington* sank the Japanese battlecruiser *Kirishima*.

Japanese destroyers continued to resupply their troops on Guadalcanal, but they had lost the race to build up their forces on the island, and were forced on to the defensive. Rations were already very short; disease and malnutrition were rife. In December the Japanese high command accepted the game was up and ordered the evacuation of their remaining troops. The 17th Army fell back to the western end of Guadalcanal from where, in the first week of February, some 10,000 soldiers were taken off in a series of night voyages by destroyers from Rabaul.

In addition to the drastic losses suffered by their naval aviators, the Japanese lost many of their army aircraft during bomber raids mounted from Rabaul throughout September and October. The loss of the battlecruisers was symbolic – and a tonic for the US fleet – but of no strategic significance. Defeat at Guadalcanal ended the Japanese invasions, and left their once dominant carrier battle groups in poor condition to defend their conquests.

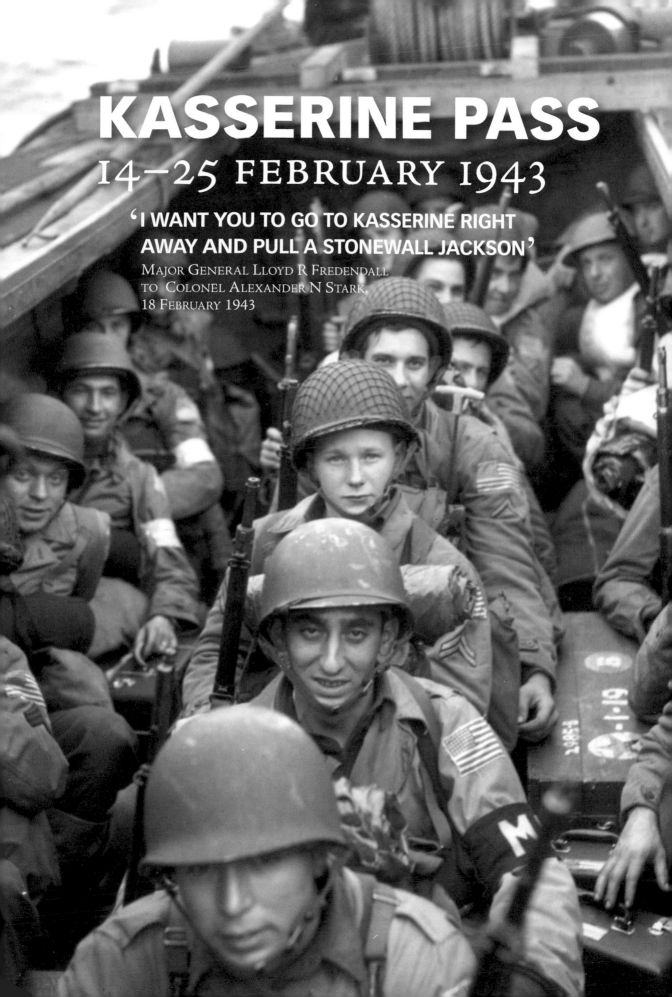

KASSERINE PASS
14–25 FEBRUARY 1943

'I WANT YOU TO GO TO KASSERINE RIGHT
AWAY AND PULL A STONEWALL JACKSON'

Major General Lloyd R Fredendall
to Colonel Alexander N Stark,
18 February 1943

The Battle of Kasserine Pass was the most dramatic defeat suffered by the US army at German hands during the Second World War. Driven back 85 miles in a week, and leaving more than 4,000 men behind as prisoners, it was a sorry way for Eisenhower's Mediterranean Command to start 1943; he speculated to his son that the debacle might result in his removal.

Several officers were subsequently transferred stateside, but their removal brought better commanders to the fore, most significantly General Patton. For the Germans, it was to be a last sweet moment of victory before the Allies closed in to crush their bridgehead in North Africa.

On 8 November 1942 an Allied Expeditionary force landed in Morocco and Algeria. For its commander, General Dwight D Eisenhower, this was the moment he had waited for his entire professional life, having been kept in America training new formations when US troops were deployed to Europe in 1918. The Allies put 65,000 men ashore in three widely separated groups: Major General Patton's Western Force occupied Casablanca; Major General Lloyd Fredendall's Central Force took Oran; and Major General Charles Ryder's Eastern Force seized Algiers.

Morocco, Algeria and Tunisia were controlled by France. Since the disaster of 1940, the French government had been led by the hero of Verdun, Marshal Pétain. Based at Vichy, rather than German-occupied Paris, his regime was collaborating more and more with the Nazis; nevertheless, the Allies hoped that the 130,000 Vichy French troops in North Africa would not fight, at least against Americans. Sadly, discreet diplomatic missions that included General Mark Clark slipping ashore from a submarine, failed to smooth the way. The French resisted the invasion with warships, including a semi-operational battleship that shot it out with the US fleet. Some 1,400 Americans and 700 French were killed.

> **'It looks like a dryland Dunkirk'**
> US TANK CREWMAN OBSERVING AMERICAN TROOPS FLEEING THE BATTLEFIELD.

German reaction to the Allied landings was typically vigorous. They won the race to establish a bridgehead around Tunis, frustrating the Allied attempt to seize the city at the end of November. Between then and January 1943, 81,000 German and 30,000 Italian troops were transported from Sicily to Tunisia, to form General von Arnim's 5th Panzerarmee. There would have been even more, but the massive Russian offensives at Rzhev and Stalingrad prevented the transfer of any troops from the Russian front.

OPPOSITE: *US soldiers landed in Algeria and Morocco in November 1942 but they failed to reach Tunis before German reinforcements arrived. Once joined by Rommel's retreating Afrika Korps, the Germans counter-attacked with tremendous effect around Kasserine Pass.*

'There'll Be Stukas Over . . .'

By January, the Allied forces in Algeria were deployed close to the Tunisian border, scattered over a wide front with units so intermingled as to defy the efforts of historians to untangle them. Battles in December had been notable for the local superiority of the Luftwaffe: Allied aircraft were few and far away, while the Germans had more than 800 aircraft in the Tunis sector, a few minutes' flying time away. Beaten back from Tébourba in December, disgruntled British troops made up new words to 'The White Cliffs of Dover', including:

> There'll be Stukas over the vale of Tébourba
> Tomorrow when I'm having tea
> There'll be Spitfires after, ten minutes after
> When they're no bloody use to me

Meanwhile in Libya, Rommel's Panzerarmee Afrika had completed its withdrawal along the desert coast, all the way from Egypt. The torpid British pursuit had enabled him to disengage and was now set to arrive in the Tunis sector, offering the possibility of a counter-attack to the west, before Montgomery's 8th Army arrived on his heels. Von Arnim had already planned a limited counter-attack, but Rommel argued for a more ambitious blow, aimed at Tébessa, where the Allies were stockpiling supplies for their own spring offensive. At one point, the Allies feared he might sweep north, up to the Mediterranean coast behind the British 1st Army to inflict defeat on a strategic scale, but the extent of his ambition died with him. In any case, many of his victories in the desert had come not by assiduous forward planning, but by seizing fleeting opportunities created by his first attack.

Promoted Beyond Competence

His opponent, Lloyd Fredendall, commanding the US II Corps, was the sort of impeccably dressed buffoon who often bullies their way to the top in a peacetime army. Eisenhower visited him the day before the battle, and came away impressed by Fredendall's knowledge of the battlefield area. 'He seems keen and fit,' he observed, although he was puzzled by his general's choice of command centre, more than 50 miles behind the front line. Using his only battalion of combat engineers, Fredendall had blasted out a warren of caves and tunnels in a remote ravine nine miles south of Tébessa, at the end of a winding gravel road. The ration strength of II Corps headquarters, including signallers, anti-aircraft gunners and all those engineers, exceeded 3,000 men.

Fredendall could paint his boss such a detailed picture of his forces' deployment because he had taken to micro-managing his command to an absurd degree. The US 1st

Armored Division suffered the most, divided into sub-commands which received orders direct from Corps, bypassing their own divisional headquarters. Working from his map, Fredendall issued orders to individual rifle companies that left his front line units poorly deployed to resist an attack.

On 14 February the 10th Panzer Division struck west through the Faïd Pass. To their front were two US infantry battalions deployed too far apart for mutual assistance. Tanks from the US 1st Armored Division advanced to support them, but were shot to pieces; the Germans supported their panzers with a handful of long-range 88mm anti-tank guns – and a platoon of Tiger tanks. The infantry were overrun and just seven out of 44 US tanks in action that day managed to escape. The 21st Panzer Division came through the Maizila Pass to the south, so the Germans assaulted the town of Sidi bou Zid from east and south.

Panzers and Shermans

The Germans readied themselves to meet an American counter-attack the next day, but Allied commanders from Major General Ward (1st US Armored Divison) to the commander of the British 1st Army to the north thought the whole thing was a diversion. Allied intelligence continued to report the presence of only one panzer division, the 21st. A single US tank battalion was ordered to attack on 15 February, in conjunction with a battalion of infantry in half-tracks and some self-propelled guns. They were outnumbered by the defenders, who were advised of the Americans' approach by German observation planes. Indeed, a dozen German aircraft strafed and bombed the Americans as they formed up to attack. The result was a massacre.

The 2nd Battalion, 1st Armored Regiment was wiped out: 40 Sherman tanks were destroyed and 4 escaped. They claimed 13 German tanks in return, but German records show no permanent losses; any damaged vehicles were operational again the next day. The loss of two infantry and two tank battalions in two days finally persuaded the Allied high command to order a withdrawal. They were lucky that Arnim's cautious chief of staff, Heinz Ziegler, was running the operation: he pushed out reconnaissance patrols, but kept his panzer divisions deployed defensively, expecting the sort of vigorous counter-stroke that would occur if roles had been reversed.

Cut Off at the Pass

Rommel was 60 miles to the south, where he began his part of the German operation. Fuming at Ziegler's lack of energy, he drove north with customary aggression, overrunning the Allied airbase at Thelepte and conducting a furious exchange of signals and telephone calls with von Arnim and their theatre commander, Field Marshal Kesselring. The 10th and 21st Panzer Divisions were transferred to Rommel, who had an Afrika Korps battle group supported by the new Italian tank division Centauro. The disunity of the German command was such that orders were not confirmed until 19 February when Kesselring flew to Tunisia. These delays reduced the damage the panzers would ultimately wreak on the fragmented Allied forces.

By the time the jovial Field Marshal touched down, Rommel's Afrika Korps veterans were probing into the Kasserine Pass. The American defence was co-ordinated by Colonel Alexander Stark, commanding officer of the 1/26th Infantry. In addition to his infantry battalion, he had a battalion of field artillery and one of US Combat Engineers, some self-propelled anti-tank guns and a French artillery battery. Stark was telephoned by General Fredendall on the night of 18 February, and ordered to 'pull a Stonewall Jackson' in the pass. He drove through a night of fog and rain to find the area shrouded in mist and the defences unprepared. Anti-tank mines had arrived, but were still on the trucks. When the troops tried to lay them, they found the rocky ground impervious to their entrenching tools, and ended up just laying the mines on the road and to either side in plain sight.

The Special Relationship

The British 26th Armoured Brigade was sent to defend Thala, and its CO, Colonel Dunphie, drove down to liaise with Stark. It was not a meeting of minds: Stark thought the British officer was 'a blockhead'; Dunphie's personal reconnaissance left him in no doubt that the Americans would lose and that Stark was 'out of his depth'.

Stark's scratch force held up the Afrika Korps battle group for a day, but by dusk German infiltration parties had scrambled up the hills to outflank them. A counter-attack

Kasserine Pass

1942

8 November Allied forces land in French North Africa.

1–3 December Allied advance into Tunisia stopped at the Battle of Tébourba.

1943

14 February Combat Command A/US 1st Armored Division attacked by German battle group at Sidi bou Zid.

15 February US counter-attack at Sidi bou Zid is defeated with the loss of a tank battalion.

18 February Rommel and von Arnim's forces meet at Kasserine. Rommel is appointed to command the Axis offensive.

19–20 February Rommel's Afrika Korps battle group defeats US forces defending Kasserine Pass.

21 February German attack towards Tébessa is halted by Combat Command B/US 1st Armored Division; German attack towards Thala is halted by British 26th Armoured Brigade.

22 February Both German spearheads go over to the defensive, ending Rommel's last battle in Africa.

25 February British and American troops re-occupy Kasserine Pass.

by some of Stark's infantry regained one hilltop during the night, only for more Germans to push past and isolate one of the American companies. On the morning of 20 February, the Germans renewed their attacks under the stern eye of Rommel himself. The American defence crumpled in what one observed kindly called an 'unco-ordinated withdrawal'. Even the US official history had to confess 'The enemy was amazed at the quantity and quality of the American equipment captured more or less intact.' Many of the 26th Infantry's half-track personnel carriers were captured at the foot of the hills and pressed into service by the Germans, giant iron crosses on the sides, giant swastika aerial recognition flags on the hood. By nightfall the pass was in Axis hands and an Italian tank battalion had pushed five miles westwards in pursuit.

The rains caused the Hatab River to flood and the US engineers blew the main bridge. Rommel did not stop to bridge the river, but allowed his forces to advance along divergent axes, either side of the river, the Afrika Korps battle group northwest towards Tébessa and the 10th Panzer Division north, heading for Le Kef where the Allies were concentrating their reserves. Kesselring meanwhile had an angry meeting with von Arnim, who he considered overly pessimistic, and recommended that Rommel be placed in charge of all Axis forces in the theatre.

The 10th Panzer Division's advance brought it up against Brigadier Dunphie's armoured brigade at Thala. His obsolete British tanks were outmatched by those of the Germans but they were ordered to hold their ground at all costs: 29 out of 50 were knocked out that afternoon. During the night, the Germans used a captured British tank to penetrate the lines of the Leicester Regiment and overrun the position by surprise. But when the Germans came to renew their attack on 22 February, Dunphie had been powerfully reinforced: the divisional artillery of the US 9th Division was deployed and in action after four days' gruelling driving over 700 miles of bad roads across the Atlas Mountains.

A suicidal attack by the British 2nd Lothian Tank Battalion that morning and a well-aimed artillery shoot led the CO of 10th Panzer to cancel his next assault, and go over to the defensive. Dunphie's cool handling of the defence won him promotion and before long a position as assistant chief of staff to Patton's US 2nd Corps: the usually Anglophobic Patton took a great liking to this British officer and gave him his own Silver Star when Dunphie was wounded.

Rommel Leaves the Scene

Rommel's push towards Tébessa with 21st Panzer was stopped at Sbiba and although he was placed in overall command of Axis forces in Tunisia on 23 February, he became ill and left for Germany a fortnight later, never to return. With fuel for only another 150 miles or so, Rommel's armoured forces fell back through Kasserine and by 25 February the surviving combat command of US 1st Armored Division and the British 26th Armoured Brigade were probing down the pass, past the wreckage of the previous battle.

The ground was soon retaken, but the US army had sustained 6,000 casualties and its lamentable battlefield performance left many British soldiers thinking their new allies were no better than the French. One American officer described Kasserine as 'a professional graveyard': Eisenhower sacked many middle-grade officers, including Colonel Stark (who redeemed his reputation in the Pacific theatre). In classic army tradition, Fredendall was given his third star and sent home, 'a hero' to command a training establishment in Tennessee. George Patton was put in command of 2nd Corps and immediately inflicted some heavy blows on the German defences. Kasserine was a tactical defeat, but it had major strategic consequences. It was, of course, the first time the German army had met the Americans on the battlefield in the Second World War. Being thorough professionals, they debriefed their men and issued pamphlets describing their experiences. They never updated them. So it was that the German units defending Normandy in 1944 expected the same shambolic performance exhibited at Kasserine: unfortunately for them, the US army learned its lessons well. Reorganized, re-equipped and with combat-proven leaders in command, it was a very different army that landed in France.

KURSK
4–20 JULY 1943

'WHENEVER I THINK ABOUT THIS ATTACK,
MY STOMACH TURNS OVER'
ADOLF HITLER, MAY 1943

The Battle of Kursk ended Hitler's dreams of conquering communist Russia. For the first time in two years of fighting, the Russians stopped a German summer offensive in its tracks. Before the battle was over, the Russians had launched an attack of their own, demonstrating that the Red Army now held the initiative. The scene was set for the remorseless Russian advance that would end in Berlin nearly two years later.

The famous Russian victory at Stalingrad destroyed the German 6th Army, and ended with a field marshal and 91,000 German and allied troops in captivity. But it did not blunt the German army's tactical and technical superiority. In the wake of Stalingrad, the Russians pressed on with a new offensive in March 1943. They recaptured Kharkov, and Hitler himself heard the sound of their guns from his temporary headquarters in the Ukraine. Then came the German counter-attack. Just as the Russians extended their forces across a wide front, the panzers struck, cutting off tens of thousands of Russians, capturing hundreds of tanks and guns and retaking Kharkov.

The ebb and flow of battle had left a deep bulge in the German front. For the Russians, this salient around Kursk was an ideal jumping off point for another thrust to the west; German generals could see that by attacking from north and south in a pincer movement, they could isolate and destroy the Russians around the city.

By early 1943 the Russians enjoyed a 2:1 advantage over the Germans in manpower: 6 million versus 2.7 million men under arms. They had an overwhelming superiority in tanks, with up to 15,000 vehicles against a little more than 2,000 German. In artillery, the Russians fielded more than 30,000 guns against some 6,000 German. Worse, from the German point of view, was the fact that the USA had now supplied tens of thousands of trucks, enabling the Russians to move their vast quantities of guns and ammunition at modern speeds. Most German guns were still pulled by horses.

Operation 'Zitadelle'

After recapturing Kharkov, Field Marshal von Manstein had launched the SS Panzer Corps onwards, retaking Belgorod on 18 March. The spring thaw then imposed its annual halt on military manoeuvres as the snow melted, the rivers flooded and the dirt roads turned into quagmires. On 12 April the German high command selected the code name 'Zitadelle' for its next operation, the crushing of the Kursk salient. It was scheduled for mid-May, as soon as the ground dried out.

In the summers of 1940, 1941 and 1942 the German tank formations had driven all before them, so the decision to attack Kursk did not appear unduly ambitious. However,

OPPOSITE: *Russian infantry follow T-34 tanks into battle. The Russians blunted the German offensive at Kursk at the expense of hideous losses, but were able to follow up with a massive offensive of their own.*

some German officers, including panzer expert General Heinz Guderian, argued against 'Zitadelle', wanting Germany to remain on the defensive, building up the strength of the panzer divisions for the day the British and Americans landed in western Europe.

Hitler's limitations as a strategist are clearly revealed by the Battle of Kursk. At the end of June 1943, British and US troops prepared to land in Sicily, Italian generals plotted to change sides, U-boat losses in the Atlantic reached an unsustainable level and Allied strategic bombers attacked the heart of the Reich. Hitler spent his days poring over maps and photographs of one sector of the Russian front. The Führer remained focused on the tactical minutiae of army operations in Russia. Germany's ever-bleaker strategic situation he ignored, spouting geopolitical nonsense or quoting tank production figures whenever senior commanders asked what the long-term plan actually was.

The first operational order for Operation 'Zitadelle' called for Army Group Centre, commanded by Field Marshal von Kluge, to attack the north flank of the salient with the German 9th Army: 12 infantry and 4 panzer divisions plus Kampfgruppe Esebeck (2 panzer divisions). The 5th and 8th Panzer Divisions were in Army Group reserve. The 2nd Army would hold the face of the salient with six infantry divisions. Von Manstein's Army Group South would assault the southern flank with the 4th Panzer Army: ten infantry, four panzer and five panzergrenadier divisions, plus the reconstituted 6th Army, including one panzergrenadier division, and the nine divisions of Armeeabteilung Kempf.

The attack was postponed several times to allow the new battalions of Tiger and Panther tanks to take part. The 147 Tigers performed well, but the 200 Panthers were reduced to 50 by the end of the second day. Mechanical problems dogged Panzer Regiment 39 for the duration of the battle. It fell to those workhorses of the Wehrmacht, the Panzerkampfwagen III and IV, to provide the bulk of the German army's tanks at Kursk. The 16 panzer and 5 panzergrenadier divisions taking part included a total of 115 Panzer IIs, 844 Panzer IIIs, 913 Panzer IVs and some 300 StuG III assault guns. The 2nd SS Panzer Division Das Reich even had 25 captured Russian T-34 tanks.

German delays gave the Russians ample opportunity to fortify the salient. Prodigious quantities of mines were laid – more than 1,800 per mile – and up to eight successive lines of defences bristling with anti-tank weapons awaited the German onslaught. This could not be disguised. By early May, many of those German generals initially in favour of a summer offensive were having second thoughts. Aerial photographs showed ominous lines of upturned earth, dug-in gun positions and evidence of increased troop levels. Manstein thought the moment for 'Zitadelle' had now passed and it should be cancelled. Even the combative Model got cold feet. On the other hand, General von Kluge was so confident he challenged Guderian to a duel after one particularly heated discussion! Significantly, Stalin had ordered his generals to prepare their own offensive – to liberate Orel – on the assumption that the German attack on Kursk would be defeated.

By July there were some 1.2 million Russian troops in the Kursk sector, with 3,500 tanks and 25,000 guns. The German assault force comprised no more than 600,000 men, with 2,750 tanks and 10,000 guns. Above the battlefield would be up to 2,000 German aircraft and nearly 3,000 Russian.

Konstantin Rokossovsky

On the northern side of the salient, Generaloberst Model's 9th Army faced the Russian Central Front under General Konstantin Rokossovsky, a half-Polish former tsarist officer who had been severely tortured by Stalin's secret police after his arrest in 1938. They broke his ribs, knocked out nine of his teeth, shattered his toes with a hammer and pulled out his fingernails, but Rokossovsky refused to confess he was a Polish spy. They sent him to Siberia. In 1940 he was released and rehabilitated. Placed in command of the new 9th Mechanized Corps, Rokossovsky survived the Kiev encirclement in 1941, and led the 16th Army during the defence of Moscow with great skill. In September 1942 he commanded the Don Front, retitled the Central Front in February 1943 – and had been preparing to defend the Kursk salient for nearly four months.

Rokossovsky had a very good idea of the German timetable and was able to order a bombardment of Model's start line two hours before the German offensive began. Nevertheless, the German artillery opened fire at 4.30 a.m. It was a short but intense bombardment, planned for maximum shock effect, with the Luftwaffe joining in after 40 minutes with 730 aircraft from Luftflotte 6. The ground forces commenced their assault under cover of both air and artillery bombardment. Model's assault was led by the most exotic combination of German heavy tanks: 89 Elefant assault guns of schwere Panzerjäger Abteilung 656, together with the 31 Tigers of schwere Panzer Abteilung 505 were used to spearhead the assault, supported by the 45 Brummbär assault guns of SturmPanzer Abteilung 216.

The Elefant Tank Destroyer

The Elefant, also known as the Ferdinand, was an assault gun based on the chassis of the unsuccessful contender for the Tiger heavy tank project. When Henschel's design was chosen for production, Porsche used the components of its prototypes to create a 65-ton tank destroyer with an 88mm PAK 43 anti-tank gun. Capable of knocking out any Allied tank at up to 3,000 yards, it was protected by 200mm of frontal armour, making it all but impervious to enemy fire. Designed in the wake of Stalingrad, the Brummbär (Grizzly Bear) or SturmPanzer IV was intended to support combat in built-up areas. It combined a Panzer IV chassis with an armoured fighting compartment fitted with a 150mm howitzer.

This battering ram of new heavy tanks made the initial penetration. Only one of Model's panzer divisions took part in the first day's fighting: the other five held back, ready

to pour through once a gap had been blown in the Russian defences. The Elefants suffered from a lack of defensive machine guns, a problem the Sturmgeschütz battalions had already addressed, and lost some of their number to Soviet infantry anti-tank teams. Many of the Tigers were disabled by mines, and their commanders complained that they were asked to do too much. However, Model's plan worked. The battalions of heavy tanks led the infantry through the first line of Soviet field works, and smashed a Soviet counter-attack. On 5 July, Model's 9th Army advanced about four miles against the Russian 13th Army. The Russian 2nd Tank Army, ordered to recapture the original front line, counter-attacked the next day, but it suffered such terrible losses that Rokossovsky sacked its commander. Rokossovsky ordered the surviving Russian armour to be dug in among the defensive positions and not to attempt to fight a mobile battle.

Tigers, Panthers and T-34s

Now the panzer divisions poured into the gap, ready to smash through the remains of the defences and break into open country. Between the small towns of Ol'hovatka and Ponyri, ten infantry and four panzer divisions battered their way forward, but although the Germans captured part of both towns, they could not wrest them completely from the defenders. Fighting from deep entrenchments, the Russian infantry kept firing, reducing German infantry companies to mere handfuls of men. Although the German tanks were knocking out impressive numbers of Soviet vehicles, they were suffering steady attrition themselves, especially track damage caused by land mines.

On 7 July, Model committed the 2nd and 18th Panzer Divisions, adding the 4th Panzer Division the next day. Rokossovsky responded by bringing up the 9th Tank Corps. Attack and counter-attack followed, hour after hour, in the baking heat of the steppe. The German 292nd Infantry Division, in action near Ponyri, identified 11 discrete Russian counter-attacks

LEFT: *Inside the cramped interior of a German Panzer III tank: the gunner has his eyes glued to the padded telescopic sights, while the loader pushes in another round. The picture is taken from the tank commander's seat. The battle of Kursk involved some of the largest tank actions in history.*

against it on 8 July alone. Each afternoon the atmosphere grew increasingly oppressive until the skies darkened and the day ended in a thunderstorm. Model halted his forces on the 9th, then resumed the offensive on the 10th, making the last minor gains, but his army never broke into the open. After a week of intensive fighting, day and night, his divisions had advanced only another couple of miles by 12 July when he suspended offensive operations. The Russian attack on the Orel salient forced Army Group Centre on the defensive. The ground won at such bitter cost was abandoned as Model turned his forces to help 2nd Panzer Army face the new threat.

The southern arm of the German pincer at Kursk was provided by Army Group South, which had more armour than Army Group North: 13 panzer and panzergrenadier divisions, including the SS Panzer Corps, as well as the 200 Panther tanks of Panzer Regiment 39. The Großdeutschland Division and the SS divisions Leibstandarte, Das Reich and Totenkopf each had a company of Tiger tanks while schwere Panzer Abteilung 503 had 45 Tigers. The Army Group was supported by 1,100 aircraft assigned to Fliegerkorps 8.

Field Marshal von Manstein conducted his assault very differently from Model, attacking with massed armour from the very first hour. The 4th Panzer Army under the veteran tank commander Generaloberst Hermann Hoth broke into the Soviet defences northwest of Belgorod under cover of an equally short but sharp artillery bombardment. The Soviet 6th Guards Army could not stop the onslaught and the Germans advanced up to six miles through the Soviet defences. General Vatutin, commander of the Voronezh Front, brought forward the 1st Tank Army (6th and 31st Tank Corps) with both his reserve Tank Corps (2nd and 5th Guards), a total of more than 1,000 tanks to block the approaches to Obajan.

The city of Belgorod lies on the west bank of the River Donets, and was just within German lines at the southern neck of the Kursk salient. The German Armeeabteilung Kempf (six infantry and three panzer divisions plus three assault gun battalions) had succeeded in bridging the river and establishing a bridgehead, but the forewarned Soviet artillery battalions delivered an intensive barrage just as the Germans tried to break out. Nevertheless, German engineers laid two more bridges south of the city and by noon on 5 July, the panzer divisions were crossing the Donets, poised to sweep along the east bank, guarding the flank of Hoth's 4th Panzer Army as it headed for Kursk.

Whether Vatutin or his tank commanders were aware of the fate of the 2nd Tank Army's counter-attack in the north, or were simply more cautious, the 1st Tank Army did not launch itself at Hoth's panzers. A counter-attack scheduled for 6 July was cancelled and the Soviet tanks took up defensive positions behind the infantry, the anti-tank guns, anti-tank ditches and minefields. The 1st Tank Army was on high ground overlooking the River Ps'ol, southwest of Obajan; the 2nd and 5th Tank Corps were behind the 69th

Army to the southeast. In reserve 90 miles further east lay the 5th Guards Tank Army of Konev's Steppe Front. If Hoth led 4th Panzer Army directly for Kursk, he would run into 1st Tank Army and leave his right flank exposed to the rest of Vatutin's armour, and the 5th Guards Tank Army. Instead, Hoth veered northeast, towards the small town of Prochorovka where the Belgorod–Voronezh road intersects the Kursk–Belgorod railway. Advancing in this direction also avoided further bridging operations. Hoth would pass between the Ps'ol and the headwaters of the Donets. Given the German dependence on heavy tanks that were too large for standard army bridging equipment, this was no small consideration.

Stalin, Zhukov and Vassilevski Watch

The 4th Panzer Army crashed through the Soviet defences with incredible skill and élan. Against the most formidable entrenchments, stubbornly defended, the 48th Panzer Corps and 2nd SS Panzer Corps advanced 19 miles in a week to reach a line running from Verhopen'e, along the high ground towards Prochorovka. At Verhopen'e, combat engineers repaired the bridge and the Großdeutschland Division rolled up the defences, taking numerous prisoners from the 71st Guards Rifle Division. The II SS Panzer Corps broke through to the west of Prochorovka. On its left, Totenkopf established a bridgehead over the Ps'ol on 10 July. For seven days, Stalin, Zhukov and Vassilevski monitored the progress of the battle, demanding hourly reports on 10 and 11 July. They were determined to preserve as large an operational reserve as possible, ready for their own offensive. The German attack in the north had been stopped without drawing on the reserves, but 4th Panzer Army was still smashing its way through one defensive line after another. The Soviet 69th Army, in danger of being cut off between Hoth's panzers and Armeeabteilung Kempf, was compelled to withdraw.

The 5th Guards Tank Army (18th and 29th Tank Corps plus 5th Mechanized Corps) was transferred to Vatutin's operational control on 9 July and ordered, as Hoth had predicted, to Prochorovka. The 5th Guards Army was despatched too, occupying the 28-mile front between Obajan and Prochorovka on 11 July. The 5th Guards Tank Army counter-attacked on 12 July, together with 2nd Tank Corps and 2nd Guards Tank Corps from Steppe Front's reserve. A monstrous tank battle ensued to the dramatic background of a summer storm as II SS Panzer Corps continued to attack as well. SS Leibstandarte inflicted severe losses on the 18th and 29th Tank Corps of the Soviet 5th Guards Tank Army. Totenkopf, delayed by getting its tanks across the Ps'ol, bludgeoned its way into the defensive positions of the 33rd Guards Rifle Corps.

The same day Field Marshals von Kluge and von Manstein were summoned to Hitler's headquarters in Prussia. A tense meeting ensued on 13 July. The British and Americans had landed on Sicily and Italian forces were just melting away. Army Group

South was ordered to despatch 2nd SS Panzer Corps to Italy, in the expectation of an attack on the mainland. That was the end of Operation 'Zitadelle'.

The Kursk Myth

The Battle of Kursk was hailed as a great victory in Russia, and Stalin ordered a triumphal salute to be fired in Moscow. The Red Army had received the most powerful blow the German army could deliver, parried it, and commenced two major offensives of its own. In the chaos of a great tank battle – as in an aerial dogfight – exorbitant numbers of 'kills' tend to be claimed. At Kursk they were inflated out of all proportion: the Russians claimed to have destroyed 2,952 tanks and 195 assault guns, killed 70,000 men and shot down 1,392 German aircraft.

These bogus figures created the often repeated fiction that Kursk was a mortal blow to the German army in general and the panzer divisions in particular. Army Group Centre reported the loss of nearly half its tanks; a total of 304, including 39 of the Elefants. Army Group South had 233 tanks destroyed, including 58 Panthers. By the end of July Army Group South had 500 operational tanks, roughly half as many as it began the battle with. In total, the Germans lost no more than 700 tanks and assault guns, of which about 300 were complete write-offs. German tank strength on the eastern front was approximately 1,500 at the beginning of 1943 and remained level at about 2,000 through the whole year as replacement vehicles arrived from the factories.

German manpower losses at Kursk were approximately 50,000 compared to 235,000 Russian killed, wounded and prisoners. The Russian armoured units in the forefront of the battle lost 1,600 tanks. In crude attritional terms, Kursk cost Russia proportionately far more than Germany: at this rate of exchange the 'Russian steamroller' would grind to a halt long before Hitler's war machine. But Germany now faced war on two fronts: the Allies were ashore in southern Italy and Mussolini's regime had been toppled. Kursk proved to be the last time Hitler's armies could concentrate a striking force of more than 500,000 men for a major offensive.

THE NORMANDY LANDINGS

6–30 JUNE 1944

'LITTLE FISH! WE'LL THROW THEM BACK
INTO THE SEA IN THE MORNING.'
SS-Brigadeführer Kurt 'Panzer' Meyer,
12th SS Panzer Division

On 6 June 1944, a massive Allied fleet closed on the coast of France: 958 British and Canadian warships and nearly 200 from the US navy. They subjected the German defences to a systematic bombardment, and prevented any meaningful intervention by German torpedo craft or submarines.

The warships escorted 6,000 other ships and amphibious assault vessels which landed five infantry divisions between the Cotentin peninsula and the River Orne. The US 4th Division came ashore on the eastern side of the peninsula, its invasion beach code-named 'Utah'; ten miles east, the US 1st Division landed at 'Omaha'. The three other beaches were another 10 miles further east: the British 50th Division at 'Gold', the 3rd Canadian at 'Juno' and the British 3rd Division at 'Sword'. By nightfall 75,000 British and Canadian and 57,000 US troops had landed from the sea. This, the biggest amphibious invasion in history, was co-ordinated brilliantly and appropriately by Admiral Ramsey, RN, who had managed the evacuation of the BEF from Dunkirk four years previously.

D-Day Dawns

Fighting had been going on inland since just after midnight. The US 82nd and 101st and the British 6th Airborne Divisions – 23,000 men – had flown in either side of the invasion beaches to seize vital ground and obstruct German forces heading for the beachheads. The liberation of France had begun.

Six months earlier, Hitler had told his chief of operations, General Jodl, that 'there is no doubt the attack in the west will come in the spring'. He thought the battle would decide the war, 'when that attack is beaten off, the story is over. Then we can take the forces away again without delay' – to Russia. The majority of the German army remained on the Russian front, and even as the Allied invasion loomed, German forces in the west were starved of men and equipment. When it came to it, they would fight with diabolical efficiency, but the story of the Normandy landings must be told in context: for every German division fighting the Allies in France there were five trying to hold the line in Russia.

'Overlord' was the code word for the Allied liberation of northwest Europe; 'Neptune' denoted the initial invasion and establishment of a sustainable bridgehead. Its timing was very tight and vulnerable to weather, since the airborne divisions required a full moon and the landings had to take place an hour or so after low water, just after dawn. These conditions left the Allies with a small window, 5–7 June, and in the event the attack had to be postponed 24 hours owing to heavy weather in the Channel.

German soldiers in Russia joked that '53 per cent of the army is fighting in the east for the existence of the German people; 47 per cent is standing around doing nothing'. In fact,

PREVIOUS PAGE: *US troops wade ashore on D-Day: the greatest amphibious operation ever attempted. Success was due in no small part to the excellent Allied deception plan that led the Germans to retain powerful forces around Calais, too far away to intervene when the landings began in Normandy.*

the incessant pressure in the east, as well as the defence of Italy and the Balkans left Field Marshal von Rundstedt thinly stretched to defend the coast of Europe from the Low Countries, the French Channel, Atlantic and Mediterranean coasts. Rehabilitated in March 1942 after falling out with Hitler over the conduct of the war in Russia, Rundstedt was a 67-year-old Prussian aristocrat and archetypal product of the Prussian War Academy. Privately very rude about the 'Bohemian Corporal' who was now head of state, Rundstedt did what he could with the forces Hitler allowed him.

A Variety of Weapons

More than half his divisions were static coastal defence formations of old, ill or wounded soldiers invalided from service with frontline units. Some of his active divisions were not much better. Battered formations were withdrawn from Russia to rest and refit in France; some were then transferred to Rundstedt's command, but he found many comprised nothing more than 'a divisional commander, a medic and five bakers'. They were re-equipped with whatever the Germans had to hand. Thus no two German divisions facing the Allied landings had the same type of field guns: supplying the mixture of captured French, Russian, Czech and Italian weapons with the right ammunition would have been a nightmare even without incessant Allied air attacks.

Rundstedt held southern France with a thin scattering of divisions comprising Army Group G. He was not to know that the Allies had abandoned plans for a simultaneous assault on both coasts, electing to use all available landing craft to get the largest possible force ashore in Normandy. The north coast was defended by Army Group B under the energetic Field Marshal Rommel. The 'Desert Fox' brought new energy to his command, installing underwater defences on likely invasion beaches, sowing minefields and improving the 'Atlantic Wall'. Since 1942 the Germans had expended 17 million cubic tons of concrete fortifying the coasts with artillery positions and blockhouses which made for great newsreel footage, complete with bombastic announcements about 'Fortress Europe'. The giant gun turrets looked formidable but were clearly visible to Allied photo reconnaissance aircraft, and individually marked on maps eventually issued to naval gunnery officers and bomber pilots. Rundstedt thought it a waste of time, likewise the creation of 'fortress ports' like Dunkirk, Calais, Boulogne and Le Havre: these were soon isolated by the Allied invasion along with 100,000 German troops garrisoning them. The wall, once breached, was useless. And a breach was inevitable.

Rundstedt accepted that he could not stop a landing, but planned to overwhelm the Allied beachhead with a concentrated force of tank divisions. However, micro-management by Hitler's headquarters which left even tactical decisions to the Führer – and a gigantic miscalculation – prevented the Germans delivering such a dramatic counterpunch.

The Normandy Landings

5 June Invasion ordered, then postponed owing to bad weather.

6 June Invasion begins with airborne landings in the early hours and seaborne assaults after dawn.

7 June British and Canadian forces link the beacheads 'Gold' and 'Juno'. Allied attack on Caen is foiled by the newly arrived 12th SS Panzer Division.

8 June British Marines close the gap to link 'Omaha' with 'Gold' beach.

9 June The first airstrips are established within the Allied perimeter; Allied aircraft outnumber the Luftwaffe in Normandy by 200:1.

10 June General Montgomery, Allied commander of 21st Army Group tasked with Operation 'Neptune' lands in France. US troops link 'Omaha' and 'Utah' beaches.

11 June Carentan is liberated by the US army.

13 June German 17th Panzer Divison makes determined counter-attack that comes close to re-occupying Carentan.

17 June US forces advance across the Cotentin peninsula, isolating Cherbourg.

19 June Bad weather in the Channel damages the 'Mulberry' artificial harbours.

25–27 June Battle for Cherbourg ends with the liberation of the first major French port.

30 June Remaining German forces in the northern Cotentin peninsula surrender.

Even once the Normandy landings were underway, the German high command clung to the belief that the real Allied assault would strike at the Pas de Calais. An attack there involved the shortest crossing of the English Channel; it was there that the German V-1 and V-2 rockets were being launched at London; it offered the most direct route to Germany's industrial heartland, the Ruhr. The Allies went to enormous lengths to confirm this error, radio trucks driving around Kent created enough signal traffic to suggest the presence of the fictitious '1st US Army Group' under the very real, and very frustrated, command of General Patton.

Mulberry Harbours and Amphibious Tanks

One reason the German high command doubted the feasibility of a landing in Normandy was the absence of major ports. However, the Allies had invented artificial harbours that could be towed across the Channel. Code-named 'Mulberries', these enabled heavy equipment to be unloaded from transport ships and driven onto the beach. Fuel was supplied to the troops ashore by a system of underwater pipelines. The gradient and composition of each invasion beach was sampled by British naval special forces. The British also developed a series of specialist tanks to help the infantry breach the German defences. Several battalions of M4 Sherman tanks were converted into amphibians of uncertain reliability – many sank like stones – others carried giant flails to batter a path through the German minefields.

The invasion caught the Germans by surprise. Rommel was in Stuttgart, visiting his family and many of his senior staff were in Rennes – ironically conducting an anti-invasion war game to test their plans. The airborne landings did not go according to plan, paratroops were scattered all over the countryside, but they created chaos for the Germans, and seized several strategically important features including the bridge over the Orne Canal. The seaborne landings did go as planned, with the exception of 'Omaha'. This sector was defended by the 352nd German infantry division, 7,500 men commanded by 55-year-old Lieutenant General Dietrich Kraiss, holder of the Knight's Cross with Oak Leaves.

Carnage on Omaha Beach

The US 1st and 29th Infantry Divisions expected to face one of the German static coastal units; US planners thought the 352nd was inland but would not be able to intervene until late in the day. However, Rommel ordered Kraiss's men to the coast as part of his plan to win the battle on the water's edge. Kraiss was reinforced with two German battalions and one of Russian volunteers, although by the time the assault began, one of his three regiments had been ordered away to deal with the airborne landings.

'When they attack in the west, that attack will decide the war'

ADOLF HITLER, DECEMBER 1943

Kraiss had built some new gun positions that were not targeted by the Allied preliminary bombardment. The initial landing was opposed by his 916th Grenadier Regiment commanded by Colonel Goth. The first two US Regimental Combat Teams ashore were shot to pieces, each suffering about a thousand casualties. Goth signalled that he could hold his ground, and US 1st Army commander General Bradley discussed evacuating the survivors and landing the rest of the force at 'Gold' beach. However, numbers eventually told and by nightfall there were more than 30,000 US troops on Omaha. Now facing odds of 5:1, Kraiss's men fell back in good order over the next 48 hours, still making sharp counter-attacks. The 352nd Division fought to destruction in the ensuing battle for Normandy; it was declared no longer fit for combat on 30 July. Kraiss died of wounds on 6 August.

The Germans never landed the sort of concentrated tank attack they planned and the Allies feared. Those units close to the coast were not released from reserve until too late on 6 June. Those stationed inland found it impossible to get forward. The Panzer Lehr Division took 72 frustrating and fearful hours to drive 90 miles from Le Mans to Caen. The Luftwaffe had been driven from the skies and the roads became a 'fighter-bomber race course' along which no German vehicle could move during daylight. By 10 June Rommel had recognized that the beachheads could not be destroyed by the forces he had available. Indeed, the Allies had landed 500,000 troops and 300,000 vehicles. All the Germans could do was to dig in among the small fields and high hedgerows of the Normandy countryside and try to hold them there.

The bulk of the German army consisted of infantry divisions with horse-drawn transport. They marched across France at a rate of 20 miles a night, lying-up by day as Allied aircraft passed overhead. Even panzer divisions struggled to move faster. In the two

Where is the Luftwaffe?

THE UNIVERSAL LAMENT of German troops in Normandy was 'Where is the Luftwaffe'. British and American aircraft flew some 49,000 sorties in the first week of Operation 'Neptune' and even German heavy tanks were unable to drive down a highway in daylight. Luftflotte 3 had no more than 300 operational aircraft on 6 June and was never able to mount a serious challenge to Allied control of the Normandy skies. The Allies were now benefiting from the savage air battles over north west Europe during 1943. Heavy casualties against the RAF and USAAF led more instructors to be returned to combat duties; severe fuel shortages further curtailed training programmes so that by D-Day, German trainee pilots were receiving half the hours' training provided to British and American fliers.

months before the landings, Allied aircraft had dropped 195,000 tons of bombs on the French road and rail network, knocking down bridges and paralysing rail transport.

'The Poor Bloody Infantry'

'Overlord' envisaged three stages: the break-in ('Neptune'), the build-up and the break-out. The second phase became a sanguinary attritional struggle in Normandy's bocage country. Daily casualty rates among British and German infantry battalions exceeded those of the Somme, Verdun or Passchendaele. Seven out of the nine German tank divisions despatched to Normandy were broken on the British front; while Montgomery's attacks were not conspicuous by their success, his defensive actions accounted for 350 German tanks and half the panzer divisons' personnel. The last German attempt at a major counter-attack – by the SS Panzer Corps – was defeated with heavy losses on 29 June. Unprecedented quantities of artillery fire support were the most important reason. The Allies were able to substitute capital for labour – firepower for bodies – thanks to their vastly greater material resources. A two-company British attack might be backed by 3,500 rounds of artillery fire. Divisional artillery regiments fired 4,000 rounds a day. This prompted an astonishingly naive lament by the CO of 2nd Panzer Division, General Lüttwitz, 'The Allies are waging war regardless of expense.'

Hell in the Falaise Pocket

'Neptune' officially finished on 30 June by which time 850,000 men had been brought ashore along with 570,000 tons of supplies. The battle for Normandy raged on for another six weeks before the German line was broken, but the end, if not the timing, was inevitable. The Germans would ultimately lose 20 divisions there, including 50,000 prisoners in the Falaise pocket. After the failure of the 29 June counter-attack and the fall of Cherbourg, Hitler's military chief Field Marshal Keitel called von Rundstedt in a state of some agitation.

'What shall we do?' he asked.

'Make peace, you idiots,' replied von Rundstedt, and put the phone down.

'A GREATER CATASTROPHE
THAN STALINGRAD'
GERMAN HIGH COMMAND WAR DIARY

OPERATION
BAGRATION

22 JUNE–
25 AUGUST 1944

To America, Britain, Canada and the other Western Allies involved in the Normandy landings, D-Day was the decisive blow against Hitler's Germany. Once the Allied armies were secure in their beachhead it was only a matter of time before their superior numbers and firepower overwhelmed the Wehrmacht.

However, before the Allies had managed to break out into open country, the Russians had staged three massive offensives, each one on a larger scale than the Normandy campaign. The most significant consequence was the destruction of Germany's Army Group Centre in western Russia.

War On Two Fronts

D-Day was not much of a secret. By spring 1944, it was obvious that the Western Allies were poised to liberate France by an amphibious invasion across the English Channel. With this in mind, the German and Russian high commands laid their plans for summer 1944. Stalin had of course been pressing for an Allied landing in France since 1942, increasingly suspicious that the British and Americans were determined to defend the world down to the last Russian soldier.

German strategy for 1944 was based on the assumption that the Allied invasion would be in the Pas de Calais, not Normandy. German intelligence also predicted that the Russians would follow up the spectacular success of their 1943 winter offensive that had brought them to the borders of Romania and Hungary. If they attacked in the south, the Russians could strike into southern Poland, cross the Carpathian Mountains into Hungary or advance into Romania to overrun the oilfields that sustained the German forces.

German intelligence was wrong on both counts.

The D-Day campaign is celebrated for the brilliant deception plan that played on German fears, fooling them into maintaining large forces around Calais even after the Allies were ashore in Normandy. The Soviet summer offensive of 1944 – called Operation Bagration after a heroic general killed fighting the French in the 1812 war – was preceded by an equally successful deception scheme. And even after the blow fell on 22 June, the anniversary of the German invasion three years earlier, German intelligence persisted in its belief that the major effort from the enemy was still to come. The result was the greatest German defeat of the war.

The Germans had 700 tanks and 1,000 assault guns with their armies in the East in May 1944. These were divided between 22 panzer and panzergrenadier divisions, deployed

PREVIOUS PAGE: *On 17 July 1944 the Russians paraded 57,000 captured German soldiers through Moscow to show the world who was beating Hitler. Operation Bagration, the great Russian offensive of that summer, drove the invaders out of Russia and deep across Poland.*

equally between north and south: nine in Army Group North Ukraine and nine in Army Group South Ukraine. Army Group Centre, in the middle, had very little armour, and what it did have was almost all provided by batteries of Sturmgeschutz assault guns, a tank chassis fitted with an armoured box instead of a turret, limiting the traverse of the gun but enabling the vehicle to carry a more powerful armament. These tank destroyers were also less vulnerable to tank shells.

Army Group Centre was commanded by 69-year-old Field Marshal Ernst Busch, who had won Germany's highest award for bravery, the Pour le Mérite, as a junior officer on the Western Front during the 1914–18 War. A committed Nazi, he commanded the 16th Army during the invasion of Russia in 1941. He was

The Discovery of the Concentration Camps

ON 23 JULY 1944, THE FULL HORROR of the Nazi regime was exposed by the rapid Russian advance. Just outside Lublin the Germans had built the extermination camp of Majdenek. Similar camps at Belzec, Sobibor and Treblinka had already been closed and burned down. There had not been time to do this at Majdenek. The machinery of death was all still in place – concrete gas chambers and a crematorium capable of burning 2,000 bodies a day. The Russians found a barn containing 850,000 pairs of shoes, and a fresh mass-grave where the remaining prisoners were shot before the SS fled. 'It was with a whiff of Majdenek in their nostrils that thousands of Russian soldiers were to fight their way into East Prussia', noted Alexander Werth the BBC journalist with the Russian army. (The BBC spiked his report, refusing to believe it.)

awarded the Knight's Cross with Oak Leaves for his stubborn defence at Demyansk, surrounded by the Russians in the winter of 1942–3. In June 1944 his Army Group included three armies, totalling 38 infantry and 2 understrength panzer divisions. His infantry divisions had six battalions each, rather than the nine which German divisions had fielded in 1941. Their average ration strength was down to 300 men, or about 40 per cent of their usual numbers.

The Russian offensive was conducted by four army groups, the 2nd Baltic Front (General Andrei Yeremenko), 1st Baltic Front (General Ivan Bagramyan), 3rd Belorussian Front (General Ivan Chernyakhovsky) and 1st Belorussian Front (General Konstantin Rokossovsky). Between them they had 2,715 tanks, including Guard battalions with IS-2 heavy tanks mounting 122mm guns that could knock out any German tank in service. Each of the eight tank corps had three regiments of assault guns, totalling 1,355 vehicles to provide close support and limited anti-tank capability to the infantry.

A Rumble in the East

From the night of 19 June, Russian partisans struck behind German lines, blowing up railway bridges, sabotaging the points and disrupting the rail network on which the German forces depended for resupply. Sharp clashes between German security elements

ABOVE: *Russian troops bring up a 45mm anti-tank gun during street-fighting in Latvia. The collapse of Germany's Army Group Centre left Army Group North isolated in the Baltic States until the end of the war.*

and the guerrillas continued until 22 June, the third anniversary of the German invasion of Russia. In the early hours of the morning, Russian bombers attacked German headquarters and known artillery positions while specialist reconnaissance troops probed the German defences. The Germans had become very skilled at dropping back from their front-line positions to escape the fearsome artillery bombardment with which the Russians traditionally began their attacks. The reconnaissance units effectively pinned the Germans in place, forcing them to hold their ground or find themselves progressively infiltrated. Once the Germans were located, there were some 24,000 artillery pieces on hand to pulverize them.

For the first time on the Russian front in summer, the German air force lost control of the skies above the battlefield. Huge swarms of Russian fighters rose to meet the few

German bombers that attempted to intervene. Even the latest Junkers Ju-188 bombers found themselves getting intercepted at 30,000 feet and high altitude reconnaissance aircraft came under attack too. The only German bombers that could get through were Heinkel He-177s, which relied on close formation flying and their heavy defensive firepower, but the Luftwaffe simply did not have enough of them.

The front collapsed within days. By 24 June, Vitebsk was all but surrounded. The Russians intercepted radio signals from Busch to Hitler, requesting permission to withdraw his troops from the city and the narrow corridor connecting it to German-held territory. Hitler's micro-management of the war hastened his defeat in 1944 as he continued to force his troops to hold positions that could be bypassed and encircled. In the event, the German garrison attempted to break out anyway, regardless of orders. Of the 30,000 German troops in the Vitebsk sector, about 5,000 escaped to the west; the remainder were taken prisoner.

The Russians advanced to Bobruisk and crossed the Dnepr River to bypass the Germans in Mogilev, who were also ordered to hold their ground to the last man – as if it mattered. Within a week, the ominous gaps between major German forces showed no signs of closing. The Soviet 5th Guards Tank Army drove a wedge between the German 3rd Panzer and 4th Armies; into the gulf between the 4th Army and 9th Army plunged the Soviet 4th Guards Cavalry Corps.

Russia Begins to Kick In the Door

Hitler's personal direction of the war in Russia was now so far-reaching that generals joked that they were afraid to move a sentry from the window to the door without the Führer's permission. Hitler's reaction to the unfolding disaster was entirely predictable. He sacked the commander of the 9th Army, General Hans Jordan, who was lucky enough to be summoned to Hitler's HQ to be dismissed – and thus survive the war. Field Marshal Busch was removed too, and Field Marshal Model placed in command of Army Group Centre. But not even he could salvage much from the wreckage. Although German reinforcements were ordered to Poland to stem the tide, the Soviet staff work was of a high order and their mechanized units exploited the open front with the same panache the panzers had demonstrated in 1941.

The Russians broke through to Minsk, the Belorussian capital, and overran the city on 3 July, the T-34s of 4th Guards Tank Brigade racing through the streets to occupy the major junctions and key buildings before many Germans realized what was happening. Its commander was made a Hero of the Soviet Union.

Most of the German 4th Army was cut off east of the city and compelled to surrender. Chernyakhovsky's 3rd Belorussian Front encircled Vilnius on 8 July, but the German garrison was not taken by surprise and tenaciously held its positions. German counter-attacks to relieve the city continued for several days, but the front line was already 20 miles to the west. The 5th Guards Tank Army joined in the assault, losing many of its tanks to concealed anti-tank guns and hand-held anti-tank rockets. On 13 July elements of the 6th Panzer Division briefly broke through to link up with the garrison; some lucky troops joined them and made their escape. The rest were overwhelmed.

The mass of German forces in Army Group North Ukraine were unable to help. On 13 July, Konev's 1st Ukrainian Front attacked into Galicia, liberating L'vov and pressing on to the River San and the old First World War fortress at Premysl. At the end of the month, the Soviet 1st, 3rd and 4th Tank Armies reached the Vistula around Sandomierz and established several bridgeheads. These were subjected to furious counter-attacks. However, as the Germans had learned, Soviet bridgeheads were all but impossible to dislodge, and despite intensive fighting, they failed to drive the Russians into the river.

Parade of Prisoners

It was not long before the Russians were approaching Warsaw. The Polish capital was at the heart of German road and rail communications and a key crossing of the Vistula. It was so strategically important to the Germans that they counter-attacked aggressively from 30 July. Newly arrived in the east, and with a full regiment of Panzer IVs and a battalion of JagdPanzer IVs, the Hermann Göring Division attacked alongside 4th Panzer Division and SS Wiking Divisions, both from Army Group North Ukraine. They drove the Soviet 3rd Tank Corps and 8th Guards Tank Corps ten miles back northeast of Warsaw.

So many German units were left isolated by the disintegration of the front that there was no prospect of a rescue mission. Since the local partisans had been subjected to the most savage counter-guerrilla operations earlier in the year, they seized the opportunity to take terrible revenge against those German soldiers unlucky enough to fall into their hands. Regular Russian forces discovered more than one train packed with Russian children, ready for deportation. Nevertheless, the Russians received the first mass surrenders by German units. Across Belorussia the Russians took 150,000 prisoners and they paraded 57,000 captured Germans through Moscow on 17 July. The German army had lost 450,000 men. Thirty divisions were removed from the German order of battle, of which 17 never re-formed. Russian losses were astronomical: approximately 250,000 killed and missing and 800,000 wounded. Stalin's decision to halt his forces at this point, enabling the Germans to crush the Warsaw uprising was purely political, but it came as a great relief to his soldiers.

Profligate Tank Tactics

Russian losses were so incredibly high because the tactical performance of most Soviet units remained dismal by German (or American) standards. The T-34 tank was one of the fastest main battle tanks of the war, but this advantage was seldom exploited because few tank drivers lived long enough to learn their trade. Instead, they drove slowly with poor tactical awareness, driving along the tops of ridges, where they were skylined and easy targets. The horrendously high turnover in personnel prevented the Russian army from improving at a tactical level. Anyone showing genuine competence tended to be promoted very quickly. Where the Russian army had improved enormously since the dark days of 1941–2 was at a higher level: the performance of its staff officers was much better. To deploy, move and resupply so many tanks, guns and mechanized units and sustain operations on such a vast scale required excellent staff work. There was still the odd Neanderthal, however; Rotmistrov, the commander of 5th Guards Tank Army, was sacked for losing most of his tanks in street fighting, but whereas Stalin tended to shoot generals for this sort of thing in 1941, this time he adopted a more American solution and promoted him to deputy chief of armoured forces, where he could do no more damage.

Two Huge Armies Slug it Out

The battles in Russia and eastern Europe in the summer of 1944 were on a far greater scale than D-Day and Normandy. August 1944 found 38 Allied divisions fighting on a 75-mile front in France; after 27 days' fighting, they destroyed 20 German divisions, taking 90,000 prisoners. At the same time the Soviet forces mounted three offensives. Operation Bagration involved 172 divisions and 12 tank/mechanized corps in an advance of 400 miles along a 600-mile front; it overwhelmed 67 German divisions, inflicting 450,000 casualties. Meanwhile on the Romanian frontier, 92 Soviet divisions and six tank/mechanized corps attacked 47 German and Romanian divisions on a frontage of 450 miles; they encircled 18 German divisions and took 100,000 prisoners in a week. The third great Russian offensive involved 86 Soviet divisions and 10 tank/mechanized corps attacking across southern Poland. This thrust was the one the Germans had expected, and prepared for; nevertheless they failed to stop it and lost another 40 divisions in the process.

By the end of 1944 there were 91 Allied divisions in France, Belgium and the Netherlands, facing 65 German divisions across a 250-mile front. In the east, 560 Soviet divisions were fighting 235 German divisions across a 2,000-mile front, and driving them rapidly westwards. Modern Russian claims that they effectively won the war on their own are more than mere post-Soviet chauvinism.

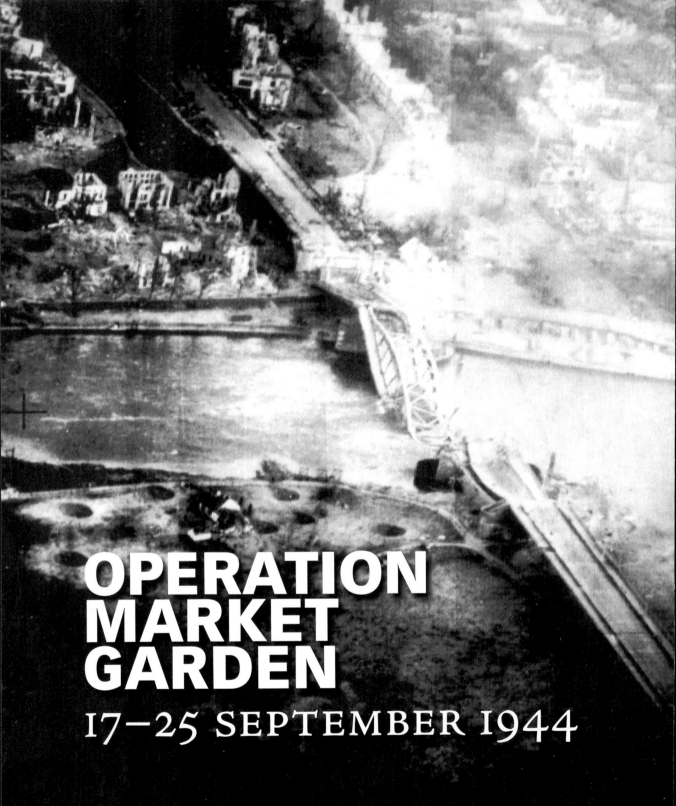

OPERATION MARKET GARDEN

17–25 SEPTEMBER 1944

'THE RED DEVILS STILL FOUGHT BACK AND
BATTLED FOR EVERY ROOM AND EVERY
HOUSE . . . LIKE CORNERED TIGERS'

SS BATTALION COMMANDER

Operation Market Garden is one of the most controversial battles of the Second World War. Immortalized by an international best-selling book and subsequent movie, *A Bridge Too Far*, it was a massive airborne assault intended to cross the Lower Rhine, thus outflanking the German 'West Wall' fortifications.

Had it succeeded, the Germans would have had no obstacle between the Allied armies and their industrial heartland, the Ruhr. Recriminations between the Allies began before the battle was over. However, arguments about who was to blame for the defeat rather miss the point. Allied errors only mattered because the German army mounted such a resourceful and aggressive defence: its last victory in the West.

Aiming at the Heart of Germany

After D-Day the US 82nd and 101st Airborne Divisions were withdrawn back to England in readiness for another parachute assault. Also in England by then was the US 17th Airborne Division, the British 1st and 6th Airborne Divisions and a Polish parachute brigade. Together they formed the 1st Airborne Army. Thus, while the British and American infantry divisions in Normandy were suffering terrible losses in the most savage fighting of the war, an all-volunteer force of elite Allied soldiers were enjoying the summer in England. US Army Chief of Staff George Marshall was not the only one pressing for these highly motivated troops to be employed as soon as possible. But as fast as parachute assaults were studied and planned, the advancing Allied ground forces reached the proposed drop zones. The British 1st Airborne were tasked with missions against Caen, St Malo, Quiberon and seven other targets, each time to be stood down at the last minute. Then Montgomery pressed for a very ambitious thrust across Holland in order to seize the newly built bridge across the Lower Rhine at Arnhem.

'They think it's all over . . .'

Montgomery's plan called for three and a half airborne divisions to be dropped in Holland to capture the towns of Grave, Nijmegen and Arnhem and the bridges over three canals and the Maas, Waal, and Lower Rhine rivers. The aerial drop would be Operation 'Market'; 'Garden' would be the code name for the advance by ground forces – the British 30th Corps – which were ordered to push north along Highway 69 from Eindhoven through Veghel, Grave and Nijmegen then on to Arnhem, 60 miles from the start line, by the fourth day of battle. This was far deeper behind enemy lines than any of the cancelled operations of the previous weeks. The assumption was widespread that the Germans

OPPOSITE: *Unable to capture Arnhem bridge, the Allies later bombed it. The British paratroops clung to the northern end (uppermost in the photo) with a tenacity that impressed the SS veterans of the Russian front.*

were finished, their helter-skelter retreat across France spelt the end of organized resistance; the war would be over by Christmas.

'Market' was the biggest airborne operation yet undertaken, but it was planned and launched in only seven days. There were no rehearsals; it was a 'come as you are' battle and voices of caution were ignored – or sent on leave as happened to one intelligence officer who claimed to have seen tanks in aerial reconnaissance photographs taken near Arnhem.

Lieutenant General Sir Brian Horrocks, the irrepressible commander of 30th Corps, recalled the bright sunny day of 17 September, 'at 2pm, precisely, there was a sudden deafening roar and a noise as though an express train was passing overhead'. The aerial armada took off from southern England, parts of it crossing London to the glee of schoolchildren who raced outside to watch a unique spectacle. There were 1,545 transport aircraft and 478 gliders, escorted by 1,313 fighters: a daunting formation 10 miles wide and 60 miles long. Before it reached Holland, 1,418 bombers attacked anti-aircraft gun positions and German airfields in the region.

In about 80 minutes, 20,000 Allied soldiers landed behind German lines. Dropping nearest to the front line to secure a 15-mile corridor from Eindhoven to Son, St Oedenrode and Veghel was the US 101st Airborne. The US 82nd Airborne dropped near Grave to seize the bridge there over the River Maas and the massive bridge over the River Waal at Nijmegen. The British 1st Airborne Division landed on the north bank of the River Rhine near Arnhem – but not near enough.

Delays and Near Misses

The main body of the British force landed up to eight miles from its objective, because its commander – and the RAF – believed that to site the drop zones closer to Arnhem would be an unacceptable risk, given the strength of German anti-aircraft defences. The British paras were superbly fit, and even with their customary heavy ammunition load, they could have reached the bridge quickly enough. Unfortunately, only half of them had been landed, and half of them had to stay to guard the drop zone where the rest would arrive the next day, weather permitting.

One battalion – 2 Para – force-marched to the bridge, picking up some stray British troops en route. Two others were blocked by a scratch force of German troops from the training and depot battalion of 16th SS Panzergrenadier Regiment. The small jeep-mounted reconnaissance force that was to have driven into Arnhem ran into opposition and fell back, awaiting orders. The brigade commander went forward to 3 Para to assess the situation only to agree with the CO's recommendation that they halt for the night. The delay was fatal and the caution in stark contrast to that of the Germans who knew that a company in the right place today is worth a battalion there tomorrow.

ABOVE: *The Allied Airborne Army descends on Holland, September 1944, in a daring operation, hastily improvised by its staff and relying for its success on the slowness of German reaction.*

Operation Market Garden

10 September Operation 'Market Garden' is approved.

11 September The first US troops enter German territory on the Luxembourg border.

12 September US 1st Army reaches German border at Aachen.

17 September 'Market Garden' begins.

18 September Ground forces link up with the 101st Airborne at Eindhoven.

19 September 2 Para holds the north end of Arnhem bridge but attempts by 1st Airborne Division to break through are repulsed.

20 September Nijmegen bridge is captured but 2 Para are finally overwhelmed at Arnhem.

21 September Polish Parachute Brigade is dropped to assist 1st Airborne.

22 September An attempt to get the Poles across the Rhine fails.

23 September The 82nd Airborne's 325th Glider Regiment is finally landed, too late to affect the operation.

24 September 4th Battalion, Dorsetshire Regiment attempts to cross the Rhine to join 1st Airborne but suffers severe losses.

25 September 1st Airborne ordered to withdraw during the night.

7 October RAF bombers destroy Arnhem bridge.

The 101st Airborne took four out of the five bridges they were tasked to seize intact. The fifth, at Son, was blown up by the Germans who had prepared all bridges in the area for demolition. The 82nd took the bridge at Grave and one over the Maas–Waal canal but failed to seize the one at Nijmegen. General Browning had diverted part of the 82nd to secure ground intended for his corps headquarters, pointlessly flown into the perimeter that day. The force assigned to take the bridge was reduced, and ran into staunch opposition, reinforced that evening by SS armoured cars.

The Germans had a Parachute Army in the region too, commanded by the pioneer of their Fallschirmjäger arm, General Student. But he could only lament to his chief of staff 'Oh how I wish I had such means at my disposal' when he saw the endless flights of aircraft pass overhead. His command was a heterogeneous collection of Luftwaffe ground crew, administrative staff, returning wounded – and a very few veterans of Germany's small but elite airborne force. He assembled what units he had, and what could be rushed to him, and spent the next week trying to hold up the advance of 30th Corps and cut Highway 69 – 'Hell's Highway' as the US paratroops soon christened it.

The Germans regarded Arnhem as a quiet sector and had sent two of the tank divisions from the 2nd SS Panzer Corps to refit there after their shattering defeat in Normandy. The 9th and 10th SS Panzer Divisions were at about a quarter of their authorized strength and were particularly short of tanks. Nevertheless the reaction of the SS Panzer Corps' headquarters to the crisis is a model of icy efficiency. The first situation report reached General Willi Bittrich at 1.30 p.m. Ten minutes later a warning order was despatched to all units. Bittrich identified the major road bridges at Arnhem and Nijmegen (both too big to be replaced by pontoon bridges) as the Allied objectives. He despatched the armoured reconnaissance battalion of 9th SS across Arnhem bridge to Nijmegen, and set about containing the British paratroops near Arnhem.

For all the professionalism of their response, the Germans did make one serious error, all too easy with overlapping commands and areas of responsibility. The SS vehicles roared over Arnhem bridge to Nijmegen, leaving it in the hands of a few guards. Each German HQ in the area assumed the defence of the bridge was someone else's responsibility. In the confusion, 2 Para seized the northern end of the bridge an hour or so after the SS had left.

A Panzer Too Many

The 9th SS Panzer's reconnaissance battalion was commanded by an archetypal 29-year-old Hauptsturmführer, Paul Gräbner, who had just been awarded the Knight's Cross for his bravery in the Battle for Normandy. Having seen the bridge at Nijmegen safe, he raced back overnight to Arnhem where a reported hundred or so British troops held houses around the north end of the bridge. He led his armoured cars and half-tracks in a high speed charge across the bridge, but there were more than 500 British troops there. Some of his armoured cars raced across and into the town but he and most of his command died in their vehicles in a hail of fire.

A renewed attempt by the British 1st Parachute Brigade to reach 2 Para was defeated with horrific losses. The decision to wait until daylight had enabled the Germans to thicken their defensive line and bring up heavy weapons. The plan for 'Market' envisaged the whole of 1st Airborne on the ground by day three, facing three or four enemy battalions. By the afternoon of 18 September, six British airborne battalions were fighting fourteen German battalions with tank and artillery support. The eventual arrival of 4th Parachute Brigade added 2,000 Paras to the battle, but by 19 September there was no longer any prospect of reaching 2 Para at the bridge. The rest of the British airborne force found itself clinging to a perimeter on the north bank of the Rhine at Oosterbeek.

> 'There is still little direct evidence that the area Arnhem–Nijmegen is manned by much more than the considerable flak defences already known to exist'
>
> INTELLIGENCE SUMMARY, BRITISH 1ST AIRBORNE DIVISION, 14 SEPTEMBER 1944

Operation 'Garden'

'Garden' fell behind schedule within hours. In many places the ground was too soft to support vehicles, restricting the tanks to a two-lane road raised above the surrounding fields and offering an easy shot to hidden anti-tank guns. For all their firepower, the ground troops found it impossible to progress as planned when the Germans contested every wood and farmhouse, and additional German units assembled on the flanks of the deepening salient.

The ground troops reached Eindhoven on the afternoon of 18 September, but had to stop at Son while the engineers brought forward a Bailey bridge. The following afternoon, they reached Nijmegen but were unable to dislodge the Germans around the vital bridge. Eventually US paratroops crossed the river in assault boats on the afternoon of 20 September and seized the northern end of the bridge. But it took until midday on 21 September for British tanks to resume their advance north, a delay much criticized by the 82nd Airborne – and the British paras at Arnhem. The logistical problems in advancing on such a narrow front had left tanks short of fuel and ammunition, but the ponderous pace was all too familiar. By the time the advance was renewed, 2 Para had been overrun and the Arnhem bridge was back in German hands. They rushed more troops over the bridge to thicken their defences between Arnhem and Nijmegen and the advance of 30th Corps was brought to a standstill again.

Without Supplies or Sleep

The Polish Parachute Brigade was finally landed on the afternoon of 21 September. It established a perimeter on the south bank of the Rhine opposite the beleaguered 1st Airborne, but brave efforts to cross the river were frustrated by heavy German fire. Advance elements of 30th Corps reached the Poles the following evening, but German armoured units kept stabbing at the base of 'Hell's Highway', interrupting the flow of fuel, ammunition and replacements. Another attempt to get troops across the river to join 1st Airborne led to the virtual massacre of the 4th Battalion, Dorsetshire Regiment, after which the surviving paratroops were ordered to retreat to the south bank. More than 2,000 men escaped on the night of 25–26 September but the rest of the 10,000-strong division was lost, dead or captured.

Montgomery claimed his operation had been '90 per cent successful' and Eisenhower put on an equally bold front, but the objective had been to cross the Rhine, opening the way into the German heartland, not just to liberate a narrow corridor across Holland. At the end of the operation they asked for an air attack on the Arnhem bridge, which was duly destroyed by RAF heavy bombers on 7 October.

A Luftwaffe intelligence summary circulated a few weeks later gave four reasons for the Allied defeat. Firstly, the landings were not concentrated on the first day but spread across three; the critical assault by British 1st Airborne was undertaken by a single brigade. The Allies had not realized 2nd SS Panzer Corps was in the area. To expect 30th Corps to advance 20 miles a day was wildly optimistic. Bad weather disrupted subsequent airborne drops, resupply and support by ground attack aircraft. But at the root of it all was the Allied belief that the German army was a spent force. Its powers of revival were to deliver another major shock before the end of the year.

LEYTE GULF

23–26 OCTOBER 1944

'THERE WOULD BE NO SENSE
SAVING THE FLEET AT THE EXPENSE
OF THE LOSS OF THE PHILIPPINES'
ADMIRAL TOYODA

The Battle of Leyte Gulf was the last – and biggest – naval battle of the 20th century. Fittingly, it involved almost every type of warship to fight in the Second World War, from battleships and aircraft carriers to cruisers, destroyers, submarines and torpedo boats.

More than 200 US warships and some 500 other vessels delivered the US 6th Army to the island of Leyte, in the central Philippines, on 20 October 1944. The 7th, 24th and 96th US Infantry Divisions and the 1st US Cavalry Division established large beachheads and were bringing vehicles and heavy equipment ashore by the afternoon. In what was arguably the most expensive photo opportunity in history, General Douglas MacArthur had himself filmed striding through the surf to announce, 'I have returned!'

The decision to liberate the Philippines by means of a ground invasion was controversial at the time – and since. The US naval command preferred to isolate the archipelago by air, submarine and surface-action group blockade. The capture of the northern Mariana Islands had already given America airbases from which heavy bombers could strike at Japan itself. US submarines had annihilated the Japanese merchant marine, above all the Japanese tanker fleet, choking off supplies of strategic materials, especially the precious resource for which Japan had gone to war in 1941 and without which it could no longer fight – oil.

Short on Training and Short of Fuel

By the summer of 1944 Japanese industrial output was in steep decline, its war effort hamstrung by fuel shortages. Lack of fuel restricted the training of new aeroplane pilots and contributed to the massacre of the Japanese naval aircraft in the Battle of the Philippine Sea in September. It was nicknamed 'The Great Marianas Turkey Shoot' as hundreds of barely competent Japanese airmen were shot down by US Navy fighter pilots. Lack of fuel also confined major Japanese warships to harbour; many heavy units swung at anchor off the Brunei oilfields and filled their bunkers with unrefined light crude for their final mission to Leyte Gulf.

If anywhere was to be the target of a ground assault, the US Navy argued, it should be Formosa, which would cut Japan's communications to its occupied territories throughout South Asia. But it was an election year, and MacArthur had his way. Ironically, his most famous operation went ahead without an overall naval commander, setting the stage for an almighty blunder.

Muddled command arrangements were a characteristic of the Japanese navy too. Its reaction to the Leyte landings was a typically complex plan, involving surface action

PREVIOUS PAGE: *A Japanese cruiser twists and turns under attack from US Navy dive-bombers. By the time US forces landed in the Philippines, American aircraft dominated the skies and the Imperial fleet's battle squadrons had to fight without proper air cover.*

groups scattered over an area the size of Texas, unable to communicate with each other, yet relying on a simultaneous attack to achieve victory. The elite aircrews that had struck at Pearl Harbor were almost all dead by October 1944, so the surviving aircraft carriers would be used as bait. They would lure the US carrier task force away to the north, while battleship and cruiser squadrons closed with the invasion beaches to destroy the support ships on which an amphibious invasion depends.

Admiral Kurita commanded the more powerful of the two surface action groups. He sailed from Brunei on 22 October, by which time the Americans had had time to establish airbases within their rapidly expanding beachheads. An air strike by 150 Japanese aircraft from the northern Philippines was met by 50 US fighters on 24 October, and cut to pieces. By the end of the naval actions off Leyte, so many land-based Japanese aircraft had been lost over Leyte that they ceased their attacks. The Japanese navy would be forced to fight its battle without air cover.

Huge Ships *Yamato* and *Musashi*

Kurita's command included the biggest battleships ever built, the 68,000-ton *Yamato* and her sister ship *Musashi*, plus *Nagato* and two modernized battlecruisers *Kongo* and *Haruna*. Ten heavy cruisers, including his flagship *Atago*, made this one of the most powerful surface squadrons assembled during the Second World War. However, lack of fuel forced the battleships to take the shortest route, via the narrow waters of the Palawan Passage to the Sibuyan Sea and the San Bernadino Strait. It also compelled the admiral to order his ships to cease zigzagging – the routine precaution against submarine attack.

A few minutes after midnight on 23 October, the massive warships appeared on the radar plots of two US submarines, *Darter* and *Dace*. By travelling at full speed on the surface for five hours, the submarines were able to position themselves directly ahead of the Japanese squadron and make textbook submerged attacks at dawn. *Darter* hit Kurita's flagship with four out of six torpedoes and the big cruiser sank immediately; a further salvo with the aft tubes crippled the cruiser *Takao*, which limped back to Brunei. *Dace* sank the cruiser *Maya*. Kurita survived, but to find himself swimming this early in the operation did not bode well. He was fished out of the water and hoisted his flag in the *Yamato*.

The other Japanese battle squadron, commanded by Vice Admiral Nishimura, comprised the modernized dreadnoughts *Fuso* and *Yamashiro*, the heavy cruiser *Mogami* and four destroyers. He was followed by Vice Admiral Shima with three cruisers and seven destroyers. Like Kurita, they were ordered to maintain radio silence. Nishimura's force was attacked without effect by American planes based on Leyte on 24 October, but pressed on towards the Surigao Strait.

Kurita's squadron was located by US Navy aircraft early on 24 October. It was now 48 hours since the Americans had landed on Leyte, and two of the US carrier groups

Leyte Gulf

23 October 1944

00.16 USS *Darter* detects Japanese surface ships by radar.

05.24 *Darter* and *Dace* commence attacks, sinking *Atago* and *Maya*, damaging *Takao*.

24 October

08.00 US air strikes against Kurita's squadron begin, ending when Kurita withdraws out of range.

09.38 Japanese aircraft attack from Luzon, one plane hits *Princeton*.

16.40 3rd Fleet aircraft detect Ozawa's carrier group.

17.15 Kurita resumes easterly course.

17.25 Battleship *Musashi* sinks.

17.50 *Princeton* is scuttled.

20.00 Japanese naval high command radios its admirals to press home their attack.

22.36 US PT boats observe Nishimura's battleships approaching up the Surigao Strait.

25 October

02.40 Admiral Halsey sends six battleships ahead to bring on a gun action with Ozawa's fleet.

03.00 US destroyers hit *Yamashiro* and *Fuso* with torpedoes; *Fuso* blows in half.

03.16 USS *West Virginia* detects Japanese warships by radar at 21 nautical miles.

03.53 *West Virginia* opens fire at 22,800 yards with a full salvo of her 16-inch main armament.

continued on opposite page

covering the invasion force had withdrawn to replenish supplies of fuel and ammunition. Admiral Halsey, commander of the US Third Fleet, recalled one group in the light of *Darter's* contact report, but delayed recalling the other for a crucial 24 hours. The US air attacks on Kurita would inflict significant damage, but had the carriers not been so dispersed, there could have been twice as many planes attacking.

USS *Intrepid's* air group struck first, two waves of aircraft scoring hits on three of the battleships and crippling the cruiser *Myoko*. *Essex* and *Lexington's* air groups launched too, *Essex's* Curtiss SB2C Helldivers hitting *Musashi* with ten bombs. The leviathan fell behind, her captain counter-flooding to maintain stability as more bombs and torpedoes slammed into her, while defending herself with San Shiki (bee hive) rounds – the biggest shotgun shells ever made – from her 18.1-inch main armament.

The intensity of the US air attacks persuaded Kurita to give up, and he reversed course with the rest of the squadron. By the time he reached the *Musashi* it was all but over: water was washing over the deck. After an estimated 20 torpedo hits and 17 heavy bomb hits, she capsized and sank at 7.25 p.m., taking 1,000 men with her. Another 1,376 were rescued by two destroyers Kurita detached for the purpose. Ten minutes earlier, he had reversed course again, intending to close with the Americans under cover of darkness.

Meanwhile the US carriers had come under sporadic attack by Japanese naval aircraft flying from shore bases on Luzon. They were shot down in droves by the US CAP but a lone Yokosuka D4Y put a bomb into the light carrier *Princeton* which triggered explosions and fires that ultimately sank her.

Admiral Halsey had a mighty force of battleships with his carriers, supporting them with their fearsome anti-aircraft gun batteries, but equally ready to do battle old style with Kurita's super-dreadnoughts. While his air strikes continued, he had issued a warning order to detach a battleship task force to intercept Kurita, but late on the afternoon of 24 October he received a contact report that a Japanese carrier group had been spotted to the north – and closing to strike range. He had no means of knowing their hangars were empty, but it did not seem to dawn on the admiral that Kurita might resume his charge under cover of darkness.

Admiral Halsey's Quest for Revenge

Confusing signal exchanges left US Naval Headquarters in Hawaii thinking Halsey had detached his battleships to cover against this eventuality. He had not; his whole fleet was steaming away from Leyte to smash the last carrier squadron of the Imperial Navy, avenging Pearl Harbor – as he had promised. Several of Halsey's senior officers feared their irascible boss had fallen for a decoy. Everyone knew Halsey had missed Midway through illness and nothing short of an Act of God would stop him going after the enemy carriers.

continued from previous page

04.20 *Yamashiro* sunk.

06.17 ASW flight from 7th Fleet observes Kurita's battle squadron off the east coast of Samar.

07.10 Halsey's carrier air groups locate Ozawa.

08.00 Halsey's air strikes begin, sweeping aside the Japanese CAP. The first reports of Japanese battleships off Samar arrive on board Halsey's flagship.

09.15 Kurita breaks off action against the CVEs and their destroyer escorts and retires towards the San Bernadino Strait.

11.15 Halsey orders his battleships to proceed at utmost speed towards Samar.

17.00 Halsey's cruisers finish off the Japanese light carrier *Chiyoda*.

23.10 Ozawa's surviving force is attacked by US submarine *Jallao*, which sinks the cruiser *Tama*.

Vice Admiral Nishimura's two battleships entered the Surigao Strait on the night of 24 October. The southern approaches to the invasion beaches were extremely well defended: Admiral Jesse Oldendorff had six battleships (five of them refloated or repaired after Pearl Harbor). Eight cruisers and nearly 30 destroyers tipped the odds to overwhelming, although the attacks by 39 torpedo boats fell far short of expectations. The US destroyer flotilla torpedoed *Fuso*, which broke in two. Nishimura gamely pressed on in *Yamashiro* until coming under radar-controlled gunnery from USS *West Virginia* at a range of ten miles – far beyond the distance at which the Japanese could return fire at night. After half an hour of furious pounding *Yamashiro* sank at 4.20 a.m. *Mogami* escaped, only to collide with Shima's flagship *Nachi* as the fourth Japanese squadron headed up the strait. Shima turned away, ending the Surigao Strait action, the last battleship versus battleship engagement in history.

'Combustible, Vulnerable, Expendable'

As Nishimura went down with his ship, Kurita found himself
rounding the north coast of Samar. And after dawn, the skies did not
darken with American aircraft as he had feared. All that lay between
his mighty fleet and the invasion beaches were the escort carriers of
the 7th Fleet. Built to operate as offshore airbases and give troops
ashore immediate air support, these were slow merchant ships,
converted into carriers. Their official designation CVE was rumoured
to stand for 'Combustible, Vulnerable, Expendable'. Seeing a scattering
of ships and not a battlewagon in sight, Kurita signalled 'General
Chase' and his ships broke formation to race after targets of their
choosing. However, the CVEs launched what aircraft they had, and
their attacks, even with inappropriate bombs, unnerved the Japanese.
The handful of escorting destroyers attacked with tremendous
panache, as if they had the whole US Navy behind them. The
aggression of the American squadron was one surprise. The dreadful
marksmanship of the Japanese gunners was another: photographs
show *White Plains* bracketed by towering fountains of water, but she
was not seriously damaged.

Admiral Kurita Thinks It Over

Yamato's skipper turned north to avoid a torpedo attack, taking
Admiral Kurita away from the action. Then, with the odds
overwhelmingly in his favour, Kurita ordered his squadron to
withdraw. He lived to a great age before commenting on his decision,
and his remarks in the 1970s were made in a very different era. Kurita
said then that he had thought the operation futile, since the
Americans were already well established ashore and he was risking
the lives of his men just to disperse empty transports. He certainly
assumed there was a major US battle squadron nearby, and his own
narrow escape from his flagship had probably focused his mind.
Relatively few Japanese admirals survived their defeats, yet three out
of four senior commanders at Leyte survived the war.

RIGHT: *General Douglas MacArthur returns to the Philippines, as he had promised.
The US Navy regarded the operation as a pointless sideshow as the Japanese
garrison there was already cut off from Japan, and US bombers were striking at the
Home Islands from the Marianas. Unfortunately, the admirals lacked MacArthur's
powers of persuasion with President Roosevelt.*

A third but now irrelevant action also began in the early hours of 25 October. Admiral Halsey detached a squadron of fast battleships ahead of the US carriers so they could finish off Ozawa's ships with gunfire if necessary. Ozawa launched his air group for a traditional dawn attack but his 75 aircraft were shot down for no effect. Halsey's air groups flew more than 500 sorties over the course of the day, sinking Pearl Harbor veteran *Zuikaku*, two light carriers and a destroyer. To the frustration of the US battleship squadron, it was withdrawn just as it closed on the Japanese and ordered to steam back to Samar at best speed. Further signals from the CVEs led Halsey to also detach his two fastest battleships, at that point still accompanying the carriers, to intercept Kurita. The Japanese had withdrawn before they arrived, so the *Iowa* and *New Jersey* never got their chance to fight *Yamato*.

The surviving Japanese warships dispersed to Japan or occupied ports near a fuel source, but there would be no more fleet battles. Most were sunk at anchor by Allied air strikes – or Royal Navy midget submarines in the case of *Takao*. The Japanese army reinforced Leyte until it had more than 40,000 men there, but they could not resist the 200,000-strong 6th Army which secured the island by the end of December.

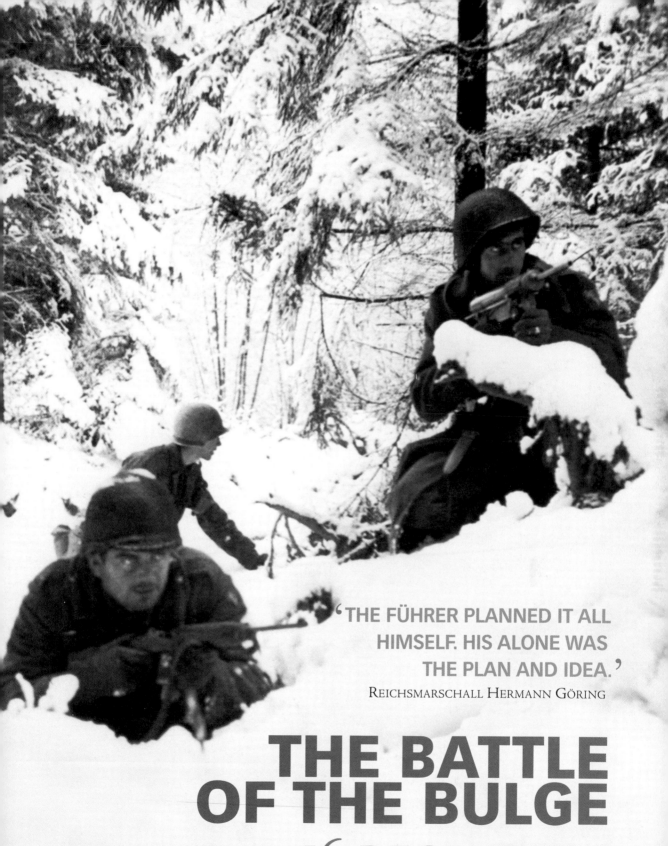

'THE FÜHRER PLANNED IT ALL
HIMSELF. HIS ALONE WAS
THE PLAN AND IDEA.'
REICHSMARSCHALL HERMANN GÖRING

THE BATTLE
OF THE BULGE
16 DECEMBER–
28 DECEMBER 1944

The Battle of the Bulge was the last major German offensive in western Europe during the Second World War. It caught the Allies by surprise and, within days, situation maps printed by newspapers showed a 20-mile bulge in the Allied frontline, expanding deeper westwards with every edition.

The US army did not lose as much ground as it had at Kasserine, but the forces involved were much larger and American casualties were officially recorded as 10,276 dead; 47,493 wounded; 23,218 missing. That a quarter of US casualties simply vanished – many taken prisoner – reveals how confused the fighting became. Although the battle involved the largest mass surrender by American soldiers in the European theatre of war, indeed, the biggest since Bataan, it was ultimately a disaster for the Germans. Milton Shulman called it 'the last violent convulsion of the Wehrmacht'. In fact there were further, savage death throes in eastern Europe, but the Battle of the Bulge marked the complete and irremediable defeat of the German armies in the West.

The Russians had already witnessed the astonishing capacity of the German army to recover from a terrible defeat and, like a wounded animal, round on its attacker with furious energy. It came as a most disagreeable surprise to the Allied command in 1944. The collapse of the German position in Normandy had triggered a wholesale disintegration, a stampede by disorganized survivors back to the Rhine and the first mass surrenders of German troops in western Europe. For a few heady weeks, it seemed the war would be over by Christmas. Even the notoriously cautious General Montgomery gave his blessing to an audacious airborne assault across the Netherlands – which ended in disaster at Arnhem. Suddenly the old German army was back with a vengeance. The British paratroops were surrounded and overwhelmed. Allied attacks met stubborn resistance all along the line.

Nazi propaganda made much of the German victory at Arnhem. It was certainly a fillip to the panzer divisions refitting in Germany. Many of the formations the Allies thought they had destroyed in Normandy – above all the 2nd SS Panzer Corps – were nearly back to full strength by December. Refitting and re-equipped, their morale was astonishingly high: Allied records document only five German soldiers deserting along the whole front during the first 12 days of the month. They had been told that they only had to hold a little longer before German secret weapons would change the course of the war. Already, their propaganda films boasted, large parts of London had been flattened by V-1 and V-2 ballistic missiles. And they were now fighting in defence of the German homeland, rather than conquered territory.

PREVIOUS PAGE: *Heavy snowfalls made for a picturesque battlefield, but the US Army's winter gear had yet to reach the frontline troops, and poor weather deprived the Allies of the air support they relied on.*

German Special Forces

THE GERMAN ATTACK FAMOUSLY involved a small number of English-speaking Germans, sent on sabotage missions behind Allied lines, wearing American uniforms. Most were caught and killed; others executed by firing squad later. Their military impact was small, but the paranoia they inspired led to many a nervous moment at sentry posts and the temporary imprisonment of Americans who could not remember the state capital of Illinois.

The battle also featured the last combat drop by German paratroops. While there were now whole armies of Fallschirmjäger in the German forces, very few had undergone parachute training by 1944. The transport pilots were woefully inexperienced too and only one plane in three found the drop zone on 16 December. Instead of blocking the Eupen–Malmédy road for 24 hours until relieved by German tanks, a few hundred disconsolate paratroops found themselves scattered in the woods with no blankets. Their radios did not work. Most were taken prisoner as they tried to escape back to German lines.

Panzer Tracks Through the Ardennes

As the striking force assembled, Hitler's headquarters discussed whether to retain it as a strategic reserve or deploy it to defend the east, where Russian forces were poised to invade Germany. To the astonishment of every senior officer, Hitler announced that it would be employed in the west – in the attack. He ordered his generals to repeat the victorious manoeuvre of 1940, by striking through the Ardennes. Calculating that the Allies would not position their best troops to defend the sector, he sketched out an insanely ambitious scheme in which two panzer armies would smash through to the River Meuse once more; this time pushing on to retake Antwerp and cut off the Allied 21st Army Group. From old school aristocrats like von Rundstedt and von Manteuffel, to hard-line Nazi loyalist Walter Model and bodyguard-turned-SS-general Sepp Dietrich, Hitler's generals were aghast. Field Marshal von Rundstedt, sacked (for the second time) after Normandy only to be recalled again, argued for what he called the 'small solution'. He sensed the opportunity to cut off US forces east of the Meuse. A dramatic blow there might inflict enough damage to disrupt the next phase of the Allied war plan. But nothing more.

Hitler overruled them all. Although the operational orders went out over the generals' signatures, the plan and the subsequent battle were conducted by Hitler and his personal headquarters, over the heads of the field commanders. The SS panzer divisions last seen in Normandy were regrouped as the 6th Panzerarmee under Dietrich. It also included a parachute division and several of Volksgrenadiers – new formations assembled from the

The Battle of the Bulge

17 September Operation 'Market Garden', the Allied airborne assault across Holland begins.

25 September The survivors of British 1st Airborne Division escape across the Rhine; Arnhem bridge remains in German hands.

23 November German 7th Army counter-attacks the US 9th Army, halting the Allied advance west of the Ardennes sector. Hitler orders a major offensive to begin there, but has to wait because it takes longer to assemble the forces than planned.

16 December German offensive begins, but makes slow progress.

17 December US 106th Infantry Division is cut off. SS troops shoot American prisoners at Malmédy.

18 December Kampfgruppe Peiper is halted by US troops.

19 December 101st Airborne Division stops the advance of Panzer Lehr division at Bastogne. Kampfgruppe Peiper is cut off by US advance.

20 December The US 1st Army is placed under operational control of British 21st Army Group, commanded by General Montgomery.

22 December General McAuliffe rejects German surrender ultimatum at Bastogne.

23 December Peiper's surviving men abandon their vehicles and retreat on foot.

25 December German assault on Bastogne beaten off.

continued on opposite page

cadres of disbanded regular divisions, air force and navy personnel, wounded veterans, teenage conscripts and rear echelon staff turfed out of their offices. Dietrich was to crash through the narrow valleys of the Ardennes, relying on severe winter weather to keep the Allied aircraft on the ground. He would cross the Meuse between Huy and Liège, then – to Antwerp.

Von Manteuffel's 5th Panzerarmee formed the southern arm of the pincer. With five tank divisions also reformed after their destruction in Normandy, it was also filled out with Volksgrenadier units. Following in its wake would be the 7th Army, intended to shield the deepening salient from US forces farther south. These were regarded as particularly dangerous as they were led by the only Allied officer they rated as a true panzer general: George Patton. Significantly, of all the Allied high command, only Patton had written down his suspicions that something was brewing in the Ardennes before the Germans struck.

Despite the events of 1940, the Allies regarded the Ardennes region as unsuitable ground for a major attack and stationed their weakest units there: green infantry divisions straight from training and exhausted, much reduced veteran formations that needed a quiet sector in which to absorb replacements. Only they did not call them 'replacements' now – 'reinforcements' was the politically correct expression. Simply, there had been too many. The US army had underestimated the casualty rate suffered by frontline infantry soldiers from 1943 onwards. The authorities had expected lower casualties than in the battles of the First World War, but rifle companies in Normandy suffered heavier casualties than on the Somme. Too many recruits had been posted as drivers, supply clerks or other supporting roles. Too few received rifle training, and many of those that did were men who had least impressed their recruiting officers in boot camp.

Low Light and Bleak Weather

Hitler had wanted to attack at the end of November, but it took longer than expected to assemble the forces – and the fuel and ammunition. On 16 December, they struck, achieving total surprise. Indeed, communications were so bad that it was not immediately obvious to Eisenhower's headquarters that the attack was on such a massive scale. The bitter winter weather forecast by German meteorologists had now arrived, so the troops went forward in thick snow, grateful for the heavy overcast weather that prevented Allied air attacks. On the other hand, it took until 8.30 a.m. for the sun to rise and it was dark again by 4.30 p.m. What followed was a story of short days, narrow roads and plentiful choke-points where a few determined men could hold up an army.

The green US 99th Infantry Division had just five battalions in line, but they held up the 6th Panzerarmee. The only too experienced US 28th Infantry Division had just lost 6,000 men in the ghastly battle for Huertgen Forest, but the survivors stubbornly resisted the attack of the 5th Panzerarmee. In 1940, German reconnaissance troops reached the Meuse in 24 hours. In 1944 they advanced just a few miles. By holding Clervaux so long, the 28th Division delayed the German advance on the key road junction at Bastogne just long enough for two US airborne divisions and a tank division to rush to the town's defence. By contrast, the confusion at US 1st Army headquarters was such that the 106th Infantry Division was left to be surrounded and destroyed.

GIs Trudge Through Snow

After three days' battle in the Schnee Eiffel, the US forces there were completely isolated and unable to fight on: 7,000–8,000 men surrendered to jubilant German infantry. The long columns of GIs shuffling through the snow to prison camps formed exactly the sort of image Nazi propaganda was looking for. However, by pushing on regardless, bypassing other positions still held by Americans, the spearhead German units were risking the same fate; most notoriously, a battle group from the 1st SS Panzer Division Leibstandarte under Joachim Peiper.

---

continued from previous page

26 December US 4th Armored Division relieves Bastogne.

6 January Von Rundstedt requests permission to withdraw from the 'Bulge' but Hitler refuses. Nevertheless, continuous Allied attacks retake position after position.

23 January St Vith liberated.

28 January The frontline is restored to that of 16 December.

Atrocity at Malmédy

A colonel (SS-Standartenführer) at 29, Peiper was the archetypal fanatical Nazi tank commander. He had expected to be forging westwards with his armoured column on 16 December, but it took all day to shuffle through a traffic jam of German vehicles. He reached the leading elements of the 3rd Fallschirmjäger Division at midnight, so the 100 tanks of his battle group now formed the spearhead of the German advance. His orders were to charge west, not worrying about his flanks, standard practice on the Russian front where he had learned his trade. Unfortunately, that was not the only aspect of the war in the east that Peiper brought to this battle: his men shot Belgian civilians at whim; at Malmédy one of his subordinates oversaw the murder of 85 American prisoners of war. Killing POWs was routine on the Russian front, but this atrocity led to reprisals by Allied troops once the tables were turned; it also stiffened the resolve of Allied forces under attack.

Peiper's advance brought him to Stavelot bridge, which he captured intact on 18 December, but the bridges at Trois Ponts were destroyed. A break in the weather enabled Allied aircraft to intervene briefly the next day and Peiper's battle group was bombed. On 19 December, US forces liberated Stavelot and cut him off. He hung on for another four days before blowing up his surviving tanks and escaping on foot.

The US army won the race to occupy Bastogne in force. Paratroop aggressiveness delayed the German assault too. Probing outside town to establish a perimeter, the US airborne troopers attacked what they thought was a roadblock: it was actually the spearhead of Panzer Lehr Division forming up to attack. Thinking they faced far larger forces than were actually present, the Germans paused to regroup. In the interval, the Americans were able to organize what would prove to be a very effective defence.

LEFT: *A German soldier guards a column of captured Americans. The 'Bulge' involved the largest mass surrender of US forces in the European Theatre of Operations, but while it made for a great Nazi propaganda reel, the battle ended in the loss of Hitler's last major operational reserve.*

Command of the sector fell to General Anthony McAuliffe, commander of the 101st Airborne Division's artillery (the divisional commander was away at a staff conference when the crisis broke).

By the early hours of 21 December McAuliffe's force was encircled. Panzer Lehr and 26th Volksgrenadier Division stabbed at the perimeter, but the lightly equipped paratroops were in luck. Inside Bastogne were four battalions of corps heavy artillery and a plentiful stockpile of 155mm shells. Probing attacks on 21 and 22 December were followed by an assault on Christmas Day by the Volksgrenadiers and 15th Panzergrenadier Division.

The Panzers Run Out of Gas

Help was already en route. Eisenhower convened a meeting of his senior commanders on 19 December. Patton irritated his chief by suggesting the Germans be allowed to advance as far as they liked: then a tank attack into the base of the salient would surround the lot. Eisenhower insisted they not be allowed to reach the Meuse. Patton's 3rd Army lay to the south of the battlefield. Asked how quickly he could intervene, he said 'on 2 December, with three divisions'. His boss dismissed this as characteristic bravado, but Patton's public persona masked a first-rate military mind. He had already issued warning orders, and was true to his word. His 4th Armored Division led the charge for 160 miles, breaking through the German encirclement on 26 December.

> **'I had nothing to do with it'**
>
> FIELD MARSHAL VON RUNDSTEDT

Thirty miles west, at Celles, a few miles short of the Meuse, the 2nd Panzer Division was defeated and dispersed by the US 2nd Armored Division and, thanks to clear skies at last, massive intervention by Allied air forces. Hitler's quixotic attempt to repeat 1940 in the Ardennes was over.

The Germans were pushed back from the salient they had won at such cost during January. By the end of the month the battle had cost the German army perhaps 100,000 casualties and left it unable to resist the invasion of its homeland.

IWO JIMA
19 FEBRUARY–
26 MARCH 1945

'ALL SHOUT BANZAI FOR THE
EMPEROR! I HAVE UTMOST
CONFIDENCE THAT YOU WILL
ALL DO YOUR BEST. I PRAY
FOR A HEROIC FIGHT.'
GENERAL TADAMICHI KURIBAYASHI

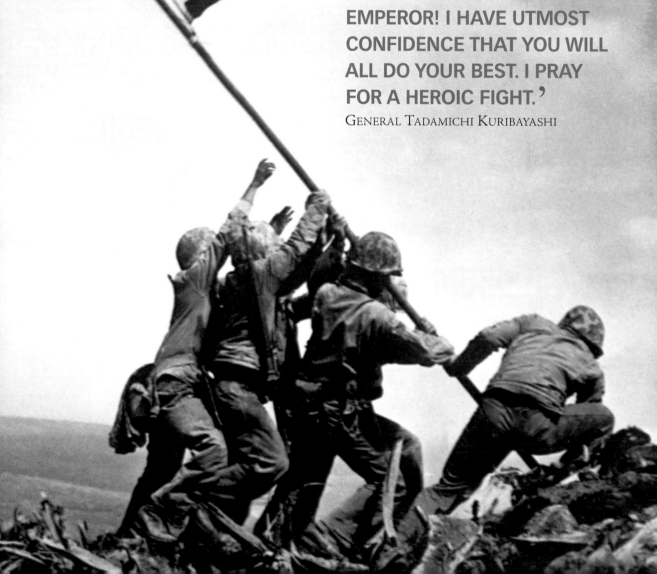

The Battle of Iwo Jima was the largest operation undertaken by the US Marine Corps during the Second World War. The 5th Amphibious Corps (3rd, 4th and 5th Marine Divisions) stormed what the Marines' official history calls 'an infinitesimal piece of land' that lies between the Mariana Islands and Japan. Joe Rosenthal's iconic photograph – and the intensity of the fighting – cemented its place in history.

It has been the subject of several major movies. John Wayne was nominated for an Oscar for his performance in the 1949 film *The Sands of Iwo Jima*, which featured some of the veterans from the battle. Clint Eastwood was nominated for an Oscar for directing *Letters from Iwo Jima* (2006) which showed the story from the other side of the hill. *His Flags of Our Fathers* (2006) focused on the men who raised that immortal flag.

The 'island-hopping' strategy of the US Navy involved a succession of amphibious assaults on Japanese-occupied islands across the Pacific. It was an extraordinary campaign, fought over unprecedented distances and only made possible by the enormous materiel resources of the United States. Many armies talk of resisting to the last man, but the Japanese forces really did, and US losses were correspondingly heavy. Nevertheless, every island attacked was taken. By mid-1944 the capture of the Marianas enabled US heavy bombers to make attacks on Japan itself. The occupation of Iwo Jima was mooted at this time, partly to provide an emergency landing strip for the giant B-29s, partly to enable long-range fighter escorts to accompany the 'Superfortresses' all the way to Tokyo.

Iwo Jima is one of the Volcano Islands, 660 miles south of Tokyo. They were colonized by Japan in the 19th century. Dominated by the extinct volcano Mount Suribachi, Iwo was named 'Sulphur Island' by a roving English sea captain who discovered it in 1673. Much of it is covered in volcanic ash. The thousand souls who eked out an existence on this remote rock in the 1930s had to import their rice from Japan. Roughly 4⅔ miles long by 2½ miles wide, the total surface area was no more than 7½ square miles. Even the tough soldiers of the Imperial Army baulked at the desolation that greeted them when they arrived, one major calling it 'an island of sulphur, no water, no sparrow, no swallow . . .'

Tadamichi Kuribayashi

After the invasion of the Marshalls in February 1944, the Japanese despatched army and naval personnel to the Volcano Islands. US amphibious landings took place too quickly for the Japanese to reinforce Saipan before it was attacked, and the troops went to Iwo where an airbase was constructed. The defence of the region was entrusted to the 109th

PREVIOUS PAGE: *Joe Rosenthal's famous photograph has been the subject of books and films in its own right. The scale of American losses suggested that an invasion of the Japanese Home Islands would result in hundreds of thousands of US casualties.*

Infantry Division, commanded by 53-year-old Lieutenant General Tadamichi Kuribayashi. A well-connected cavalry officer, he had served in Manchuria and China from 1938 to 1942 before commanding the Imperial Guards Division in Tokyo. He had spent 1928–30 in the USA and was one of the few Japanese generals to regard the attack on America as an act of insane folly. A good man, but one who knew how to take orders, his personal knowledge of US industrial might and technical know-how informed his battle plan on Iwo Jima. His command was a mixed bag, some veterans of the fighting in China but many conscripts. The naval forces, under their own officers, had no experience of ground combat.

Each island battle had ended with the annihilation of the garrison, so Japanese defensive tactics evolved slowly, if at all. However, Kuribayashi was a pragmatic and intelligent commander who concluded that the standard Japanese defensive method – fierce resistance from the water's edge – merely offered up his men as targets to American firepower. His naval counterparts disagreed, and built some concrete bunkers on the east and west beaches. But most of Kuribayashi's men would fight the Marines from a network of tunnels dug deep into the heart of the island. To the horror of many Japanese officers he forbade the sword-waving charges in which they preferred to die. Some were so deeply wedded to the death culture of the Imperial forces that they did so nevertheless, but most of his men fought as he trained them, resisting to the last from bunkers, caves and tunnels.

> '...the raising of that flag on Suribachi means a Marine Corps for the next 500 years'
>
> SECRETARY OF THE NAVY JAMES FORRESTAL, AFTER WITNESSING THE FLAG RAISING ON 23 FEBRUARY

To the Last Man . . .

General Kuribayashi anticipated precisely how the Americans would fight across the island. Halfway through the battle the Marines found a Japanese map showing the positions of the attacking and defending forces with great accuracy: but Japanese prisoners revealed that it dated from an exercise they had taken part in a month before the landings. While the Marines had been rehearsing their assault tactics on Maui, Kuribayashi had been drilling his men equally hard.

The tunnel complexes featured multiple fighting positions for infantry and heavy weapons. From small caves that could accommodate a few men, they ranged up to caverns that held several hundred. Most US casualties would be inflicted by machine guns and the 65 medium and heavy mortars dotted about the island but the defences incorporated 24 tanks, dug-in as static pillboxes, often in very inaccessible corners. Kuribayashi had 46 artillery pieces including a dozen giant 320mm mortars; the navy added 33 heavy guns and 94 heavy anti-aircraft guns. The coast defence batteries opened fire prematurely,

Iwo Jima

1944

15 June–9 July US Marines and army troops invade and capture Saipan in the Marianas.

15 June US Navy carrier task force strikes Volcano Islands.

11–12 November US Navy bombards Iwo Jima.

24 November B-29s make first Marianas-based air raid on Tokyo.

8 December US Navy surface units shell Iwo Jima.

1945

5 January US Navy surface units shell Iwo Jima.

24 January US Navy surface units shell Iwo Jima.

15–16 February 5th Amphibious Corps Landing Force departs Marianas after final rehearsals for assault on Iwo Jima.

16–18 February Amphibious Support Force (TF 52) bombards Iwo Jima.

19 February The 4th and 5th Marine Division assault Iwo Jima.

21 February Japanese kamikaze attacks against US ships off Iwo Jima.

23 February American Flag raised atop Mount Suribachi by the 28th Marines.

25 February The 3rd Marine Division committed to the battle.

4 March First B-29 lands on Iwo Jima.

continued on opposite page

revealing their positions which were destroyed by the US Navy's preliminary bombardment.

A Honeycomb of Tunnels

The Japanese airfield saw little use, few aircraft lasting long on an airstrip targeted on a daily basis by American B-24 heavy bombers flying from the Marianas. For 74 consecutive days the bombers pounded Iwo Jima while intelligence officers pored over aerial photos and a submarine photographed the beaches through its periscope. The planners recognized that the Japanese were tunnelling with great energy, and predicted a tough battle against an estimated 14,000 defenders. Unfortunately for the US Marines, there were more than 20,000 Japanese waiting for them in the hot sulphurous tunnels.

From 16–18 February 1945, US Navy warships pounded the island with heavy shells, aiming at every bunker and artillery position so far identified. The Marines had asked for seven days' bombardment but it is doubtful that any more shelling or bombing would have made a difference. The Japanese tunnels were so deep that anything short of a nuclear weapon – or the briefly considered option of poison gas – was incapable of inflicting lasting damage on the defenders.

On 19 February, 120 US Navy and Marine aircraft made low-level attacks with rockets, bombs and machine guns as the landings began. The awesome naval bombardment had convinced some Marines that there would be no one left to fight once they got ashore, but within two minutes of the first wave landing, beach 'Yellow 2' came under accurate Japanese mortar fire. The Marines suffered 2,420 casualties on the first day, including 501 killed:

8 per cent of the landing force. However, by nightfall six US Marine infantry regiments, six artillery battalions and two tank battalions were ashore, closed up in expectation of the Japanese banzai charge that had greeted most previous amphibious landings. It did not come.

On the second day, the Americans pressed south to take the dominant feature of Mount Suribachi and north towards the airstrip and the main defences. A kamikaze strike by 50 plus Japanese aircraft that afternoon sank the escort carrier *Bismarck Sea* and damaged the *Saratoga*. It was the first and last intervention from the homeland to support the garrison.

The Stars and Stripes on Suribachi

The Marines reached the summit of Suribachi and hoisted the Stars and Stripes. Joe Rosenthal took the world-famous photo on 23 February, but there were still Japanese in the hill. That night 122 Japanese were killed trying to infiltrate the Marines' lines, some with explosives strapped to them: suicide bombers bent on reaching American command posts or artillery positions.

continued from previous page

8 March Japanese night counter-attack (night of 8–9 March) repulsed by 4th Division.

11 March Iwo-based army fighter planes assume responsibility for providing air defence and ground-support missions when last navy escort carriers leave.

14 March Official flag-raising ceremony marks proclamation of US Navy Military Government in Volcano Islands.

16 March Iwo Jima declared secured after 26 days of combat.

20 March US Army's 147th Infantry Regiment arrives for garrison duty.

26 March Japanese survivors launch early morning attack in 5th Division zone against Marine and army bivouac areas near the west coast.

18 April Last Marines leave Iwo Jima.

The 3rd Marine Division was landed but took nine days of unremitting close combat to advance 3,000 yards. The northern part of the island was a warren of cliffs, ravines, gorges and crevices in and under which lay reinforced concrete bunkers. Many were unscathed by the bombardment. Capturing them required determined assault on foot, ferocious small-scale battles with rifle and bayonet, grenade and flame-thrower. Marine tanks were handicapped by the terrain. The few trails available were heavily mined and covered by anti-tank guns. Suicide anti-tank squads attacked them with bombs. One knocked-out American tank was taken over by a Japanese tank crew who engaged another Sherman until knocked out by a bazooka round.

Few Marines saw a live Japanese soldier. Even when they finally captured an enemy bunker, they often found nothing but heaps of empty cases and a few broken weapons. The surviving Japanese took their dead with them as they retreated deeper into the tunnels. Marine intelligence officers had realized the true size of the garrison by the end of February. What they did not know was that most were now dead: Kuribayashi's

command had been reduced to no more than 4,100 effectives by 4 March.

After two weeks' intensive fighting, the Marines paused for a day to reorganize, then made an all-out effort supported by the 11 artillery battalions they had brought ashore. Once again, for all its spectacular fury, the bombardment merely suppressed Japanese fire for its duration. As the Marines went forward, hidden machine guns and mortars raked them with pitiless efficiency. Casualties in the rifle companies were unprecedented, especially among NCOs, and combat efficiency declined as green replacements filled out the ranks. The men were willing but no advert for stateside training programmes; many were killed before they could learn proper use of cover and concealment.

'. . . Japanese and Marine fought hand-to-hand to the death'

Convinced the Americans would torture them if they surrendered, and subject to the draconian discipline of the Imperial Army, the Japanese soldiers fought on despite a chronic shortage of water. The longer they resisted, Kuribayashi had told them, the longer an attack on the homeland was postponed. But no one, from the senior commanders to the most recent conscript, had any doubt of the outcome now. Rear Admiral Ichimaru signalled Imperial headquarters with an update. 'The Americans only advance after making a desert out of everything before them. Their infantry advance at a speed of about ten meters an hour. They fight with a mentality as though exterminating insects.' But for all the napalm, heavy naval guns and artillery barrages, each Japanese position had to be taken by close quarter battle. 'Every cave, every pillbox, every bunker was an individual battle, where Japanese and Marine fought hand-to-hand to the death,' recalled the Marines' commander, Lieutenant General Holland Smith.

The runway that the Japanese had laboured to build was taken by the Americans and expanded. Before the last pockets of resistance had been crushed, B-29s were making emergency landings there after

LEFT: *US Marines unload supplies on the invasion beach. For all the bombs and bullets unloaded on Iwo Jima, the Japanese clung to their positions with incredible tenacity and Marines had to clear most enemy bunkers with grenades and bayonets.*

bombing Tokyo. Twenty of the giant bombers put down on Iwo on the 12th and 17th of March. By 14 March Kuribayashi had some 700 men remaining plus 200 naval personnel and with the airstrip operational the battle was now pointless. He sent his last signal to Tokyo three days later. Exhausted and emaciated after weeks underground, his final counter-attack was not the usual futile suicidal rush but a 'well-laid plan aimed at creating maximum confusion and destruction' according to the USMC Official History. Several hundred Japanese troops infiltrated along the west side of the island to attack US bivouacs near the western beaches at 5.15 a.m. In the confused fighting that followed Kuribayashi was shot in the leg but no eyewitness saw how he died. Although 40 of the Japanese dead carried swords, indicating that they were officers, Kuribayashi's body was never identified.

The Terrible Toll

Only 216 prisoners were taken by the end of the battle on 26 March, but there were many Japanese still hiding out in the tunnel complexes. Patrols and ambushes continued into April and May, resulting in the death of another 1,602 Japanese and – significantly – the capture of 867. The last stragglers holed up for several years before succumbing to lonely deaths or giving themselves up. Iwo Jima was the only battle of the Pacific War in which the number of US casualties – 27,909 – exceeded that of the Japanese. Kuribayashi was posthumously promoted to full general by the Imperial Army.

BERLIN
16 APRIL–26 MAY 1945

'SPEER, ONE OF THESE DAYS I'LL HAVE
ONLY TWO FRIENDS LEFT, FRAULEIN
BRAUN AND MY DOG'
ADOLF HITLER

By spring 1945 the German army had fewer than 2 million troops left on the eastern front. They faced 6 million Russians who had overwhelming numerical advantages in tanks, artillery and aircraft. The odds were worsened by Hitler's foolhardy insistence in clinging to strategically irrelevant lengths of the Baltic coastline: up to 750,000 German troops were trapped in various ports like Königsberg, and in Army Group North, now renamed Army Group Kurland, after the remote peninsula on which it was now doomed to sit out the rest of the war.

In March 1945 British and American armies reached the Elbe, 75 miles from Berlin. The Russians were much closer, about 40 miles east of the city, and Stalin was determined that his forces would take the 'lair of the Fascist Beast'. In the Kremlin it had not gone unnoticed that while German units were capitulating readily in the west, they fought with incredible tenacity to keep the Russians at bay.

Zhukov's 1st Belorussian Front consisted of nine armies, including two tank armies, formed up directly east of Berlin along the River Oder. Konev's 1st Ukrainian Front was to the south and comprised eight armies, two of which were tank armies. Close up to the River Neisse, Konev's forces had the River Spree to cross before they could sweep up to their objective.

As preparations for the final Soviet offensive began, the fighting continued unremittingly along the Baltic coast. Unlike many cities declared a 'fortress' by Hitler, Königsberg did actually have some modern concrete forts, rapidly augmented by every defensive measure German engineers could devise. With the sea at their backs and evacuation impossible under constant air attack, the German garrison defended itself with skill and bravery. When the casemates were destroyed by heavy artillery and the defensive guns silenced, Russian troops swarmed forward, but there were always handfuls of survivors fighting on with sub-machine guns and grenades. Despite the fearful odds, they continued to counter-attack, disputing every yard until 9 April when the Soviets finally broke into the middle of the city. When General Lasch and 92,000 German soldiers eventually surrendered, 42,000 troops lay dead in the ruins, along with an estimated 25,000 civilians – a quarter of the city's population. During and after the battle Russian troops committed the most appalling atrocities on German soldiers and civilians alike. The gross details were widely reported, so Berliners knew what lay in store if the capital fell.

PREVIOUS PAGE: *Red Victory: an appropriately named Stalin tank covers the Reichstag with its 122mm main armament as Russian soldiers scramble over the rubble and Russian bombers fly overhead.*

7.1 Million Rounds Loosed

The Soviet attack on Berlin involved more than 2 million Russian troops, led by 6,000 tanks and self-propelled guns and supported by 40,000 guns, mortars and rocket-launchers. To defend Berlin, the Germans were reduced to between 750,000 and 1 million troops, with about 500 tanks and 1,000 assault guns. Zhukov opened his part of the offensive with an artillery barrage of ferocious power: with up to 295 guns per 1,000 yards of front, his gunners fired 7.1 million rounds of ammunition.

The German forces were under the command of Army Group Vistula, briefly commanded by the head of the SS, Heinrich Himmler, who had no experience of senior military command and was busily trying to negotiate his way out of the war. Army Chief of Staff General Heinz Guderian shrewdly persuaded Himmler to step aside; the defence would be masterminded by Generaloberst Gotthard Heinrici, for two years the commander of the 4th Army on the Moscow front. Heinrici's first task was an impossible counter-attack at Küstrin, demanded by the Führer, undertaken with great courage but which, nevertheless, ended in failure – and with heavy casualties. Hitler called the generals traitors and their soldiers cowards, but Guderian (who had been drinking brandy with Göring) snapped back and ended up in a shouting match with the Führer. He was sacked, for the second and final time in his career.

Heinrici and other senior commanders like Busse, commander of the 9th Army, and Wenck, 12th Army, came to accept that the war was lost and Hitler was doomed. All that mattered now was to save as many people as they could from the revenge of the Russians. Heinrici's forces conspicuously failed to put themselves between Berlin and the advancing Russians; instead, they fought instead to preserve escape routes either side of the city. The Führer's devoted generals Keitel and Jodl scented treachery. Keitel visited Heinrici to demand adherence to the Führer's orders, but he was met with drawn weapons by Heinrici's and Manteuffel's staff officers.

Konev's troops stormed across the River Neisse on 16 April. His engineers laid 60-ton bridges that afternoon and his tanks were ready to go all the way to the River Spree. Meanwhile, Zhukov's attack faltered, notwithstanding the intensity of his artillery barrage. On the Seelow Heights, enough German defenders emerged from their bunkers to cut down the Soviet infantry. Typically, Zhukov allowed his impatience to overcome his judgement, and with a great deal of swearing at subordinates down the telephone, he ordered both his tank armies – six corps including 1,337 tanks/assault guns – to attack, without waiting for the infantry to break into the defences.

Panzerfausts and Tank-Killers

Zhukov could override both the battle plan and bully his commanders, but he could not force the Germans to give in by willpower alone. German anti-tank guns and a few surviving tank destroyers inflicted terrible slaughter on the Russian tanks as they struggled across the swampy plain below. Then, when the tanks fought their way into the German positions, they found themselves trapped in minefields where they were attacked by tank-killer teams with Panzerfausts (hand-held anti-tank weapons). Now it was Zhukov's turn for a roasting: Stalin phoned him from Moscow and ordered him in coarse, peasant Russian to break through immediately or face the consequences.

Stalin chose this moment to stoke the notorious rivalry between Marshals Zhukov and Konev. Still suspicious that the Western Allies might drive on to Berlin – Eisenhower's willingness to give the Soviets a free run at the city appeared too naive to be true – Stalin removed the agreed front boundaries just in front of Berlin. Whichever Russian commander advanced the fastest would have the honour of storming the Nazi capital.

Zhukov's men stormed the Seelow Heights the next day, after 800 aircraft carpet-bombed the ridge and his gunners delivered another massive bombardment. However, Konev's tanks had not only reached the River Spree, but a T-34 had taken the plunge and driven straight into the river where the map marked a ford. It roared across, under fire, water surging around its hull until it clattered up the opposite bank, firing its machine guns. Konev's armour headed north where Rybalko's 3rd Guards Tank Army met Katukov's 1st Guards Tank Army, part of Zhukov's Front, and encircled the remains of the German 9th Army.

At the daily briefings in the Berlin bunker where Hitler had withdrawn in mid-January, Generaloberst Hans Krebs, Guderian's replacement, brought a welcome professional calm to a headquarters so often the scene of histrionics. He never complained when Hitler demanded the impossible. Albert Speer realized it was a cunning game. Hitler continued to issue a stream of orders, sending this or that division to fall back on Berlin, others to hold on to 'fortresses' from Pomerania to Czechoslovakia and Krebs played along. It was all fantasy. While Speer raced around Germany, countermanding Hitler's vindictive orders to demolish all factories still standing, all bridges, power-plants and indeed anything of value, so Krebs kept Hitler busy manoeuvring phantom armies across the briefing maps. It diverted Hitler from issuing more lunatic orders that the SS were still all-too-ready to insist were obeyed. Field Marshal Kesselring played along too: during his last visit to the bunker he committed his forces in the west to a massive counter-attack, with not the least intention of carrying it out.

Dreams and Delusions

The 20th of April was Hitler's birthday: in 1945 he was 56 years old. He attended a brief party in the Chancellery then a military briefing in the bunker. Before he vanished underground for the last time, cameras recorded Hitler's final public appearance. He

ABOVE: *A T-34/85 wades a river: the turret sports a schnorkel device for deep wading and carries external extra fuel tanks of the sort that enabled the Russian tanks to sustain their advance, albeit at great cost if attacked from the air.*

shambled along, distributing medals to 20 teenage boys from the Hitlerjugend. Once back in the bunker with his generals, Hitler committed himself to dying in Berlin, disagreeable news to those in his entourage all set to fly to safety in Bavaria.

The US Army Air Force marked Hitler's birthday with the last of its daylight bombing raids. For nearly two hours, American heavy bombers plastered the city centre with high explosives. Night-bombing attacks by the RAF throughout 1944 and daylight raids by the Americans had already knocked out water, gas and electricity supplies to large parts of the city.

On 21 April the Soviet 3rd Guards Tank Army stormed Zossen, just 15 miles south of Berlin. Hidden beneath this leafy hamlet was the very brain of the Wehrmacht. Forty feet underground, its entrances hidden among the trees, was a gigantic labyrinth of tunnels, conference rooms, and the largest telephone exchange in Europe, code-named 'Zeppelin'. In continuous operation since 1939 and connected to every major German headquarters, it was to here that Hitler had been urged to retreat, rather than the cramped and incomplete shelter beneath the Berlin Chancellery. While the Nazi leaders had been gathering for Hitler's birthday party, German officers had been racing to sort out their paperwork. They piled what they had time to grab on lorries bound for Berlin, but the evacuation was carried out in such a rush that when Rybalko's men broke into the complex they found telephones still ringing and teleprinters churning out signals. And a couple of very drunk sentries.

On 22 April the bunker echoed with the incongruous sound of children's laughter as Magda Goebbels shepherded her family inside. She carried a small case with just one spare dress for herself; the six children were allowed one toy each. By 24 April the last roads out of Berlin were cut, and on 25 April the Russians overran Templehof airport. In its last aerial resupply missions of the war, the Luftwaffe delivered crates of anti-tank shells from Junkers Ju-52s, landing on the Unter den Linden. Hans Baur, Hitler's personal pilot, still had several long-range aircraft at Gatow, the last city airfield in German hands, including a Junkers Ju-390 with enough fuel to reach Manchuria. But the perimeter was steadily shrinking and the Russians were on the edge of the Tiergarten, no more than two miles from the bunker.

The atmosphere among Hitler's remaining entourage was doom-laden, claustrophobic and poisonous. Treachery was in the air. Hitler ordered the arrest of both Göring and Himmler, for secretly trying to negotiate their own peace deals with the Allies. Himmler's liaison officer, SS Gruppenführer Hermann Fegelein, was shot outside the bunker on the orders of Gestapo chief Müller. He was married to Eva Braun's sister, but being caught in civilian clothes, bags packed, did not help.

The troops defending Berlin were an uneven mixture of teenage conscripts, old men recruited into the Volkssturm, and hard-bitten army veterans like the men of the 9th Parachute and 18th Panzergrenadier Divisions. There were a remarkable number of non-German units, men for whom surrender was never going to be easy. The 11th SS Panzergrenadier Division Nordland was originally a regiment in the SS Wiking Division. In 1943 it had been expanded to divisional size, with a regiment of Danes and one of Norwegians. The 23rd SS Panzergrenadier Division Nederland consisted of Dutch volunteers. The 15th SS Waffengrenadier division Lettische Nr.1 was recruited in Latvia and its soldiers now had no home to return to. These units were joined in Berlin by one foreign company that actually fought its way into the city from the west. It was the surviving men of the French SS Division Charlemagne, a truly fanatical group that included a tank-killer team, each of whom had won the Iron Cross 1st class.

A Race for the End

Zhukov and Konev's armies remained neck-and-neck as they fought their way into the Berlin suburbs. Although the battle for the Seelow Heights cost his men vastly excessive losses, Zhukov pushed on to assault Berlin from the north and east, while Konev's men attacked from the south. Zhukov's post-war attempts to claim sole credit is petty in the extreme: Konev's front line was within 200 yards of the Reichstag when the fighting ceased.

The German defenders included some of the most lethal killers the world has ever seen. What some of the others lacked in professional skills, they made up for with the courage of despair. As the perimeter steadily shrank, each city block, each storey, each room, cost the Soviets dearly. Even once a street was captured, the Russians often found themselves being picked off by snipers, or assailed by small commando teams that had crept back through alleyways or even the sewers.

The Russians had arrived in Berlin ready to exact revenge for the sufferings of their country in general, and their own agonies in particular. Their own propaganda machine egged them on. The deaths and injuries sustained by so many of their comrades were avenged by systematic atrocity, mass murder of prisoners and gang rape of so many German women that the Roman Catholic bishop of Berlin gave Catholic doctors permission to perform abortions.

The Reich Draws to a Close

At 6.00 a.m. on Monday 30 April, SS Brigadeführer Mohnke, the commander of the Chancellery area defences, was woken by a telephone call from the Bunker. Hitler had asked Mohnke to report when, in his professional judgement, the enemy was within 24 hours of attacking the bunker itself. Since the Russians had captured the Tiergarten and now entered the subway under the Friedrichstrasse, Mohnke had no choice but to tell Hitler it was finished.

Mohnke returned to his headquarters to conduct a last-ditch defence. Hitler and his new bride committed suicide that afternoon. Mohnke returned to the Bunker the following evening, shortly after Magda Goebbels systematically murdered her sleeping children with cyanide capsules. Then he watched Joseph and Magda Goebbels walk upstairs to the courtyard where they committed suicide. General Krebs, who spoke fluent Russian, had already opened negotiations, coming face-to-face with none other than General Chuikov, defender of Stalingrad. In teams, in groups, in ones and twos, the surviving Nazi leaders, SS bodyguards, soldiers, Hitler's secretaries and cook crept away into the darkness, many to vanish for ever. German resistance in Berlin ceased on the 2nd of May. The hammer and sickle floated above the Reichstag.

'ALL REVOLUTIONARY
VICTORIES HAVE TO BE PAID
FOR WITH SACRIFICES'
General vo Nguyen Giap, Vietnamese
People's Army

DIEN BIEN PHU
20 NOVEMBER 1953–
7 MAY 1954

Dien Bien Phu was the most significant battle of the post-war era, an Asian Yorktown which ended with the total defeat of a European colonial army. The victors were not only Asian – they were communists. The triumph of communist guerrillas over French regular soldiers overturned two centuries of Western military and political supremacy.

It exerted a profound influence on policymakers from leaders in Moscow, Beijing and Washington, to African and Arab anti-colonialists. Fear of a repeat Dien Bien Phu stalked the Johnson administration during 1968 when US forces were besieged in a superficially similar situation at Khe Sanh. Yet, as often happens in Asia, this decisive military victory did not deliver an equally decisive political result. It triggered intervention by other powers, messy political compromise, and a peace treaty that led to another long war.

A Colonial Legacy

France colonized Vietnam in the mid-19th century but the Japanese conquest in 1941 fatally undermined their rule. In March 1945 the Japanese massacred the French garrison and established a notionally independent Vietnamese Empire under the same puppet emperor who had served as a figurehead for the French. The burgeoning communist resistance movement seized its chance when Japan surrendered, deposed the Vietnamese emperor and proclaimed independence on 2 September 1945. French troops arrived in the country again a month later, ordered to resume control. Negotiations took place through 1946 but ended when the French navy bombarded Haiphong in November. A national uprising began, and from 1947 the Viet Minh fought a guerrilla war against the thinly stretched colonial forces. The communist victory in the Chinese civil war in 1949 gave them a sanctuary, training area and source of significant military aid.

From 1950 the Viet Minh fielded an increasingly well-equipped army including five infantry divisions and artillery and engineer assets. Early attempts to take on the French in conventional battles were hit and miss. The French 1st Foreign Legion Parachute Battalion was martyred at Lang Son as the far north was overrun by the communists, but a premature thrust on Hanoi was smashed by French airpower, artillery and the legionnaires. In France governments came and went, few administrations lasting more than a couple of months. Militant left-wing opposition to the 'dirty war' in Indochina led to a ban on the deployment of conscripts to the region. The war would be fought by regular soldiers, most conspicuously the Foreign Legion, but also locally raised units from Vietnamese parachutists to pro-French partisans among the mountain tribes.

OPPOSITE: *French paratroops drop into Dien Bien Phu as part of a French plan to smash the communist guerrilla forces in advance of the Paris peace talks that were intended to resolve the six-year war in Indochina.*

In May 1953 General Henri Navarre was transferred from a NATO post to take command in Indochina. By then the French war effort was 75 per cent funded by the United States, which was itself fighting in Asia to defend South Korea against communist attack. An international peace conference was due to begin in April 1954 at Geneva. Navarre's instructions were to improve the military situation in order that the French could negotiate their exit from a position of strength. But they left dangerous room for interpretation and the military chain of command was not clear either. The tragedy that followed was the subject of public rows and court cases between generals and politicians for many years afterwards.

Navarre ordered two major offensives. His main effort would be Operation 'Atlante', which would 'pacify' the four Annam provinces south of the 16th parallel, hitherto a Viet Minh stronghold that effectively cut the country in half. The first step, Operation 'Aréthuse', opened in January 1954 with some 25,000 troops sweeping into Phu Yen province. Step two began in mid-March with Operation 'Axelle', involving 40,000 men and an amphibious assault on Qui Nhon. But 'Axelle' was terminated early; the grand finale, Operation 'Attila', was cancelled. Navarre's other operation, on the Laotian frontier at a remote border town called Dien Bien Phu, had gone horribly wrong.

The Unforeseen Problem of Artillery

In order to draw off the main Viet Minh forces while 'Atlante' was underway, the French airborne forces conducted a parachute assault on Dien Bien Phu in November 1953. An airstrip was established and some fighter-bombers from the French navy landed. Artillery positions were established and ten light tanks were dismantled, flown in on huge transport aircraft and reassembled in the valley. Striking out from this secure base, the theory went, the French would hit the Viet Minh on their home ground and draw them into a battle in the open. As at Na San (December 1952) the Viet Minh would be broken by the hammer of aerial and artillery firepower on an anvil provided by dug-in paratroops and legionnaires. The first part of the plan worked only too well: the Viet Minh sent all their best troops to the region. Within weeks of landing, a veteran airborne battalion had the battle of its life to get back to the airbase and movement of any distance from the perimeter drew heavy fire. Intelligence reports on 3 December identified four Viet Minh divisions closing on Dien Bien Phu.

The French had fatally misjudged their enemy. Ten thousand of the best soldiers in the French army were now dug-in around a remote jungle airstrip deep in hostile territory. It was overlooked by the surrounding hills on to which the Viet Minh dragged 24 American 105mm howitzers captured in Korea. Thousands of labourers dragged the guns into position, and stockpiled ammunition. The Viet Minh commanders studied the French positions and conducted exhaustive rehearsals with their battalions. By March

there were 50,000 Viet Minh in the sector and on
the afternoon of 13 March the Viet Minh
artillery opened fire.

Position 'Béatrice' Falls

The French had entrenched themselves in a
series of battalion strongpoints, each named (so
the rumour went) after a mistress of their
flamboyant, thrice wounded, general Christian
Marie Ferdinand de la Croix de Castries.
'Béatrice', in the northeast corner of the valley,
was held by a full battalion of the French Foreign
Legion. To the horror and amazement of the
garrison, the position was overrun and the
legionnaires wiped out. The next night, 'Gabrielle'
was overrun with the loss of a battalion of
Algerian colonial troops and heavy losses among
a Vietnamese parachute battalion that tried to
counter-attack. Artillery fire on the airstrip made
it dangerous for aircraft to land. The fighter-
bombers departed. When French bombers swooped on the Viet Minh gun positions they
were greeted by a hail of fire from anti-aircraft guns also supplied by the communist bloc.
French airpower was unable to silence the guns.

The Viet Minh sapped forward, digging trenches ever closer to the French positions.
The southernmost strongpoint, 'Isabelle', was isolated. The evacuation of wounded
became a hideously dangerous business on the airstrip, and more and more supplies had
be dropped by parachute. The French had wanted a set-piece battle dominated by artillery,
but this was not how they had envisaged it. The French gun batteries were clearly visible
while their opponents remained hidden in the jungle. The French were handicapped by
ammunition shortages while the hail of fire from the hills never seemed to diminish.

Navarre's masterplan had been derailed. The siege of Dien Bien Phu made world
headlines. With mountainous jungle instead of snow-swept steppe, this was a latter-day
Stalingrad, the drama played out in full view of the cameras. French aircraft photographed
the valley, dropping the pictures to de Castries so he – and the high command in Hanoi –
could see how the sinuous Viet Minh trench lines entangled the surviving strongpoints.
As the perimeter contracted, so aerial resupply drops fell into no-man's-land or straight
into the hands of the enemy.

Led by one or two 'bisons' as they dubbed their tanks, the French regained the cratered

The Survivors of Dien Bien Phu

ONLY A HANDFUL OF MEN succeeded
in escaping from Dien Bien Phu. The
only officer to do so was sous-lieutenant
Mackowiak of the 3rd Thai battalion – a
veteran jungle fighter who spoke fluent
Thai. Sergeant Ney, one of the tank crew,
escaped from his guards when they
brought him to strongpoint 'Gabrielle' to
repair the sabotaged tanks. He joined up
with a handful of other survivors, only to
be recaptured. However, he overpowered
a guard one afternoon and they took to
the hills. The party split up, two engineers
managing to reach a French special
forces patrol and the others, guided by
anti-communist Méo tribespeople, were
rescued by helicopter on 5 June after
walking for 125 miles.

ruins of their fallen strongpoints. It grew so hot inside the tanks that thirst became a critical problem. The crews were reduced to urinating in a helmet liner, adding powdered coffee and drinking the only fluid remaining to them. But the infantry had to refortify the position under artillery fire, knowing they would face another ferocious 'human wave' assault the next night. This was the attritional rhythm of Dien Bien Phu. It became impossible to evacuate the wounded once the airstrip was unusable; hundreds of injured soldiers were crammed head to foot in the medical dugouts. Yet such was the spirit of the French colonial army that men volunteered to parachute into the cauldron right until the bitter end. For some this was their first parachute jump.

'Human Wave' Assaults

At the end of March the Viet Minh had restocked their ammunition enough to make another massed assault. French efforts to interdict their supply routes by air involved a few dozen second-hand Second World War aircraft using bombs that were often not properly fused. Furious battles took place over the Eliane strongpoints some of which changed hands several times a day. Time and again, handfuls of paras, legionnaires, Algerian or Vietnamese riflemen would hurl themselves against the enemy, tactical skill and élan making up for their lack of numbers. Two weeks of high tempo operations came tantalizingly close to breaking the Viet Minh. The well-trained shock troops of 13 March were either dead or wounded – and their medical facilities were extremely primitive. They had suffered something like 20,000 casualties and still the French endured, the ghosts of Verdun beside them in the stinking mud of the trenches.

> ' It's all over – they're at the command post. Adieu . '
>
> MAJOR ANDRÉ BOTELLA, (FRENCH) 5TH BATTALION VIETNAMESE PARACHUTISTS

Negotiations between France and the Viet Minh were already underway. Both sides would meet formally at an international peace conference about to begin in Geneva. The communist leadership redoubled its efforts to overrun Dien Bien Phu in advance of the talks. There were other moves behind the scenes. Pro-French partisans and special forces struggled through Laos to form a rallying point in case of a breakout. The French made overtures to the USA for the loan of B-29 Superfortress strategic bombers: 60 were assembled in the Philippines, some possibly got as far as receiving French air force roundels. Requests for the use of a tactical nuclear bomb met with a flat refusal from President Eisenhower.

Ammunition and Water Running Out

Deliberations in Swiss hotel rooms were of little concern to the dwindling band of survivors in the waterlogged trenches and bunkers. The Viet Minh overran the French defences to the west of the airstrip and so compressed the perimeter that it became all but

ABOVE: *Viet Minh soldiers smile for the camera during a filmed reconstruction of the battle, made a few weeks after the surrender of the surviving French troops. Viet Minh casualties were horrendous: as were their calculated acts of revenge on the captured garrison.*

Dien Bien Phu

1953

20 November Operation 'Castor': in the biggest airborne landing of the war, the French occupy the valley of Dien Bien Phu.

3 December French intelligence identifies four Viet Minh infantry divisions en route for Dien Bien Phu plus the 351st Division (artillery). Navarre accepts battle.

7 December General de Castries appointed to command Dien Bien Phu.

28 December Lieutenant Colonel Guth, de Castries's chief of staff, is killed on the road between the airstrip and strongpoint 'Gabrielle': the French are under siege.

1954

12 January The 1st Foreign Legion Parachute Battalion conducts a sweep outside the perimeter and meets heavy resistance, losing 5 dead and 33 wounded.

20 January Operation 'Atlante', Navarre's main effort begins.

13-14 March Viet Minh launch all-out assault, taking 'Béatrice' and wiping out a battalion of the Foreign Legion.

14-15 March: A second human wave assault submerges 'Gabrielle'.

30 March–5 April 'The battle for the five hills' – attack and counter-attack over the low hills surrounding the airstrip. French supplies and replacements now arrive by parachute.

1 May All-out Viet Minh assault further reduces the perimeter. The French 1st Colonial Parachute battalion parachutes into the position to bolster the defence.

7 May Final battle: last positions are overrun.

impossible to parachute in further supplies. 'Isabelle' was so tightly invested that it could not be resupplied either. Bandages and painkillers were long exhausted; ammunition and water all but gone. The Viet Minh marked May Day with another all-out assault that engulfed most of the remaining strongpoints.

Even that iron-willed paratrooper Major Marcel Bigeard had to bow to the inevitable. One of his junior officers was quite prepared to 'faire Camérone' and die with his command, but Bigeard declined to give the order. Resistance ended on 7 May and the Viet Minh found themselves with some 12,000 prisoners of which more than 4,000 were wounded. Some 3,000 were Vietnamese: they were executed or vanished into concentration camps. Forced marches, systematic torture and starvation diets killed more than half the other prisoners within a couple of months.

Vietnam Fatefully Split

The surviving prisoners were released in the wake of the Geneva Accords, signed on 21 July 1954. Although they had won a signal victory, the Viet Minh left the peace talks with an acute sense of betrayal. Russia and China used the occasion to leverage deals of their own; without superpower backing, the Viet Minh were compelled to accept the partition of the country into a communist North Vietnam and, from the 17th parallel southwards, the Republic of South Vietnam. The French army of the east broke up. Many landed in Algeria, determined never to cede another centimetre of French territory. Within the year, France found itself embroiled in another dirty war.

THE SIX-DAY WAR
6–10 JUNE 1967

'NOTHING WILL BE SETTLED BY A MILITARY
VICTORY. THE ARABS WILL STILL BE HERE.'
Israeli Prime Minister Levi Eshkol

General Rikhye commanded UNEF – the United Nations Emergency Force – an international peacekeeping mission deployed to Egypt in the wake of the 1956 Suez Crisis. In May 1967 Egypt expelled the peacekeepers, and began to concentrate its army near the Israeli frontier. The war of words that had intensified through the mid-1960s threatened to escalate to armed conflict. Egypt, Syria, Jordan – and Israel – mobilized their armies.

The Israelis seized the initiative on 6 June attacking Egypt, then Jordan and Syria, shattering the armies of all three in quick succession, and redrawing the map of the region. Israel trebled in size, capturing 42,000 square miles of territory that provided vital strategic depth to the country. But they brought a million Arabs within their new borders, including the Gaza Strip, described at the time by Israel's prime minister as 'a bone stuck in our throat'. As we approach the second decade of the 21st century, Rikhye's prediction, quoted on the opposite page, is beginning to look like an underestimate.

The Six-Day War led to the capture of Gaza and the West Bank by Israel. The political future of these territories dominates the politics of the region today. But when the war took place, the military and political map of the Middle East was very different. Iran was still ruled by the Shah, and quietly supplied much of Israel's oil. The Soviet Union armed and equipped most of the Arab forces, regarding Egypt in particular as a regional ally with which it could pursue the Cold War by proxy. It was the high tide of Arab secularism; a time when the ruling junta in Syria published anti-Islamic propaganda in its party newspaper – one article so gratuitously offensive it triggered a riot in their own capital.

Colonel Nasser's Ascendancy

Above all, it was the time of Nasser. The first native-born ruler of Egypt for 150 years, the handsome army officer was just 34 when he came to power. A brilliant orator in classical and colloquial Arabic, he ejected the British and strode the international stage as a champion of the 'non-aligned movement'. He created the biggest army in the region, more than 150,000 strong and equipped with Russian weapons. Both he and his army commander were made 'Heroes of the Soviet Union', the first foreign citizens to receive the honour. Faithfully married and personally incorruptible, he enjoyed genuine popularity, not just in Egypt but across the Arab world which hailed him as a latter-day Saladin.

PREVIOUS PAGE: *In 1967 Israel was threatened by vast Arab armies, supplied, equipped and advised by the Soviets. The controversial decision to launch a pre-emptive strike won great military victories but these Israeli Shermans are entering the Gaza Strip, beginning decades of trouble.*

Nasser's friend, political ally – and self-appointed field marshal – 'Abdel Hakim Amer, was not so scrupulous in his public or private affairs. The army became his personal fiefdom, in which officers were appointed and promoted according to family or political connections rather than merit. Intervention against the Saudi-backed royalists in Yemen embroiled 50,000 Egyptian troops in an intractable guerrilla war that no amount of bombing – even with poison gas – could resolve.

Soviet and Western Powers Stir

The early promise of Nasser's revolution petered out in the 1960s and by 1967 the once dashing colonel had ballooned into a corpulent, vindictive military dictator –increasingly out of touch. The Arab countries had accepted the ceasefire in 1956 but still refused to recognize Israel as a state or abandon plans to drive the Jews into the sea. Russian advisers prepared an operational plan for Syria, Operation 'Victory,' which called for a blitzkrieg assault by three divisions: a 40-mile advance would bring them to Haifa and Nazareth. The kingdom of Jordan had no such plans, but King Hussein's army held the West Bank, a mere nine miles from the Mediterranean coast. The Egyptians also had a Russian blueprint for victory, although in their case it was initially defensive. Operation 'Conqueror' involved three lines of fortified

'I think you're going to have a major Middle East war and I think we will be sorting it out 50 years from now'

GENERAL INDAR JIT RIKHYE, UNITED NATIONS PEACEKEEPER, 1967

positions: the first, outpost line would absorb the Israelis' initial blow, assuming they tried to repeat their dramatic offensive of 1956; the second was the main line of resistance on which they would become stuck, deep into the Sinai desert away from their supply lines. A counter-attack from the third line would overwhelm them.

Between conspiracies to overthrow the moderate King Hussein, Nasser and the Syrian junta poured out increasingly bellicose rhetoric, egged on by their Russian sponsors. The Russians repeatedly told the Syrians that the Israelis were massing for an assault on the Golan Heights. There were daily exchanges of fire between the Israelis and Syrians there, both sides equally bent on provocation, but Tel Aviv was certainly not preparing an invasion.

Nasser Adds the Last Ingredient

Nasser piled on the pressure in May, expelling UNEF peacekeepers and ordering his army forward from the still incomplete 'Conqueror' defensive positions. On 22 May he announced the closure of the Straits of Tiran to Israeli-flagged shipping: a violation of international law that he knew Israel, and quite possibly the United States, would contest. War seemed inevitable. US Secretary of State Dean Rusk observed the paradox of that spring: 'Each side appears to look with relative equanimity upon the prospect of major

The Six-Day War

1966

4 November Egypt and Syria sign mutual defence pact.

13 November Israeli retaliatory raid into West Bank backfires.

1967

January–April Frequent mutual provocations and exchanges of fire along Syrian–Israeli border.

13 May Russia tells Syria that Israel is poised to invade.

14 May Egypt mobilizes and deploys its troops in forward positions near the Israeli border.

16 May Egypt expels UN peacekeepers.

22 May Egypt closes Straits of Tiran to Israeli-flagged ships.

24–31 May Egypt, Syria and Jordan and Israel deploy their armies for attack.

30 May Egypt signs defence pact with Jordan after visit by King Hussein.

5 June Israel airstrike attacks, destroying the Arab air forces and attacking Egyptian forces in Sinai.

6 June Israeli armoured divisions destroy the retreating Egyptians, killing thousands.

7 June Israeli troops capture Jerusalem.

8 June Israeli troops overrun the West Bank.

9 June Israeli troops attack the Golan Heights.

10 June Israel captures the Golan region, routing the Syrian army.

hostilities and each side apparently is confident of success. Someone was clearly making a major miscalculation.' The US ambassador in Jordan thought the frenzied atmosphere reminiscent of Europe in 1914.

For ten years the Arab armies had been modernized and trained by the Russians. The fiery rhetoric of their leaders suggested they were finally ready to reverse the result of 1956. Frontline Arab forces included some 130,000 Egyptians with 900 tanks and 1,100 guns; Syria's 50,000 with 260 tanks; Jordan's 56,000 plus 270 tanks, and four brigades of Iraqis. Israel had mobilized its reserves, but while that put up to 275,000 men and women into the field, with 1,100 tanks and some 200 combat aircraft, it cost the economy $20 million a day to keep so much of the workforce in uniform.

The Israeli and Arab armies fielded a mixture of Second World War surplus – from helmets to Russian T-34 tanks and the Israelis' up-gunned Shermans – and new weapons from around the world. Jordan and Israel both had US-supplied M48 tanks; Egypt had Russian T-55s as well as the Dvina surface-to-air missile systems (NATO reporting name, SA-2 'Guideline') – by that time horribly familiar to US pilots over Vietnam. With more than 300 MiGs, the Egyptian air force outnumbered that of Israel, which was almost wholly supplied by France.

The IDF (Israeli Defence Force) knew who was miscalculating. Its field commanders were brimming with confidence, even if the chief of staff was briefly hospitalized with acute anxiety. Its forces were well trained, well led and convinced they could repeat or improve on their performance in 1956. The IAF (Israeli Air Force) could refuel and re-arm a fighter-bomber in eight minutes; Egyptian aircraft seldom flew more than once a day. Intelligence reports revealed at least a quarter of the Egyptian tanks, guns and aircraft were non-operational because of shoddy maintenance. To retain his throne, King Hussein was obliged to enter the war alongside Nasser but he recognized at the time that the Egyptian closure of the straits 'would only lead to disaster because the Arabs were not ready for war. There was no co-ordination, no co-operation, no common plan amongst them.'

Train Hard, Fight Easy

THE SIX-DAY WAR was not the first time governments had brought about a war only to have their armed forces exposed as a shambles. From Imperial France in 1870 to the Argentinian junta in 1982 and Saddam Hussein in 1991, history affords plenty of examples. Yet the contrast between Nasser's bellicose rhetoric and the tragic-comic performance of his useless army surely provides the yardstick. The IDF trained hard and fought easy against enemies who failed to conduct basic maintenance; never conducted serious rehearsals; and, above all, packed their officer corps with family, friends and political cronies. One former Egyptian brigadier noted how 'Israel spent years preparing for this war, whereas we prepared for parades. The drills for the annual Revolution Day parade went on for weeks . . . but there were no preparations for war.'

Israel's Air Force Strikes

Nasser warned his generals on 2 June to expect war within 48–72 hours but when the Israelis struck none of his senior commanders were at their posts. Abdel Hakim Amer partied late into the night on 5 June then flew out to visit the troops in Sinai in the morning – just as the IAF launched an all-out attack on Egyptian airfields. The Egyptian aircraft were not in hardened aircraft shelters, but lined up on concrete stands where 205 of them were destroyed in the first strike. Their runways were torn up by Durandel bombs specially designed to crater concrete. The strike was timed for early Monday morning, just after the MiG fighters had returned from routine dawn patrols. Eight of the 200 Israeli aircraft were lost, some to accidents and one to an Israeli SAM fired at a returning plane that flew too close to the Dimona atomic reactor. A second strike increased the tally to 286, including all 30 of Egypt's Tupolev Tu-16 heavy bombers and 185 MiG fighters.

Some Egyptian command centres were paralysed with panic, some thought a military coup was in progress, but a strange calm reigned at supreme headquarters. A communiqué announced that an Israeli attack had been defeated and 86 Israeli aircraft destroyed. Jubilant crowds poured on to the streets in Cairo, then in other Arab cities. Lies were so much easier for governments to peddle in those pre-Internet days: all Cairo needed to do was disconnect international telephone lines.

An Israeli ground assault began, bypassing Rafah and fighting its way through the Egyptian 7th Armoured Division to reach al'Arish that night. Major General Suliman was killed and his forces dispersed with some 2,000 casualties and 40 T-34s destroyed. Israeli losses were disproportionately smaller: 66 dead, 93 wounded and 28 tanks knocked out.

ABOVE: *The Russian-supplied MiGs of the Egyptian air force were mostly destroyed on the ground. Israeli air superiority played a key role in their battlefield successes on both fronts.*

Fortified by victorious broadcasts from Cairo, Jordanian, Syrian and Iraqi aircraft attacked targets across Israel, but hit little and lost many aircraft in one-sided engagements with IAF interceptors. The heaviest loss of life occurred when an Iraqi Tu-16 bomber crashed, killing 12 people on the ground. Retaliatory strikes by the IAF caught Jordan's 24 Hawker Hunters as they refuelled and destroyed them all.

Nasser discovered the true picture during the course of the afternoon, but the sudden annihilation of his air force – after all his overblown rhetoric – was a tricky story to spin.

He fed 'the Arab street' a propaganda story that was accepted even by people who should have known better, claiming the attacks were carried out by the US Sixth Fleet from the Mediterranean and by RAF bombers flying from Cyprus.

A Massacre in the Desert

The rapidity of the breakthrough at al'Arish led the Israelis to cancel a planned airborne and amphibious assault and send the 55th Parachute battalion to Jerusalem instead. The confused reports from the front led Nasser to order his army to retreat from Sinai the next day. He had managed to present the rout of 1956 as a successful withdrawal that kept the army intact for another day. However, with the Israelis in full command of the air, and aggressive tank commanders determined to land a definitive knock-out blow, the result was a massacre. The IDF reissued a directive threatening severe punishment for personnel who killed men who had surrendered. The Israelis reached some of the desert passes before the retreating Egyptians could pass through these strategic bottlenecks. Other Egyptian columns were bombed from the air in a manner that would be seen again on the road from Kuwait to Iraq in 1991. Between 10,000 and 15,000 Egyptian soldiers were killed and some 85 per cent of their Russian equipment was lost: 320 tanks, 480 heavy guns and 10,000 vehicles. Some Egyptian generals blamed the Russians, disparaging the weapons they had been given; Russian ambassador Pojidaev retorted that they had given the same to the North Vietnamese and they seemed to be doing just fine.

A Hostage to Fortune

Jerusalem, which had remained divided for 19 years, was united under Israeli control and the West Bank overrun by IDF units before their own government could react, let alone the outside world. Having dealt with two out of three opponents, the IDF then turned on Syria, shattering the units stationed on the Golan and driving them – and thousands of refugees – off the heights that were to remain Israeli occupied for 30 years. Syrian losses were the lowest of all belligerents; the junta and the ordinary soldiers agreeing that preservation of Arab manpower was their true priority. Some 118 Russian tanks were captured on Golan, along with 470 guns.

King Hussein lost 700 of his soldiers dead, perhaps 6,000 were wounded. He had lost half his kingdom, not to mention the Old City of Jerusalem. He would survive several more Egyptian and Palestinian-backed assassination attempts before ejecting the PLO from his territory in 1970. Field Marshal Abdel Hakim Amer committed suicide later that year after an unsuccessful attempt at a coup d'état. The IDF's victory engendered a dangerous overconfidence that would be punished in 1973. The future of the Arab territories it occupied have remained a thorny political issue ever since.

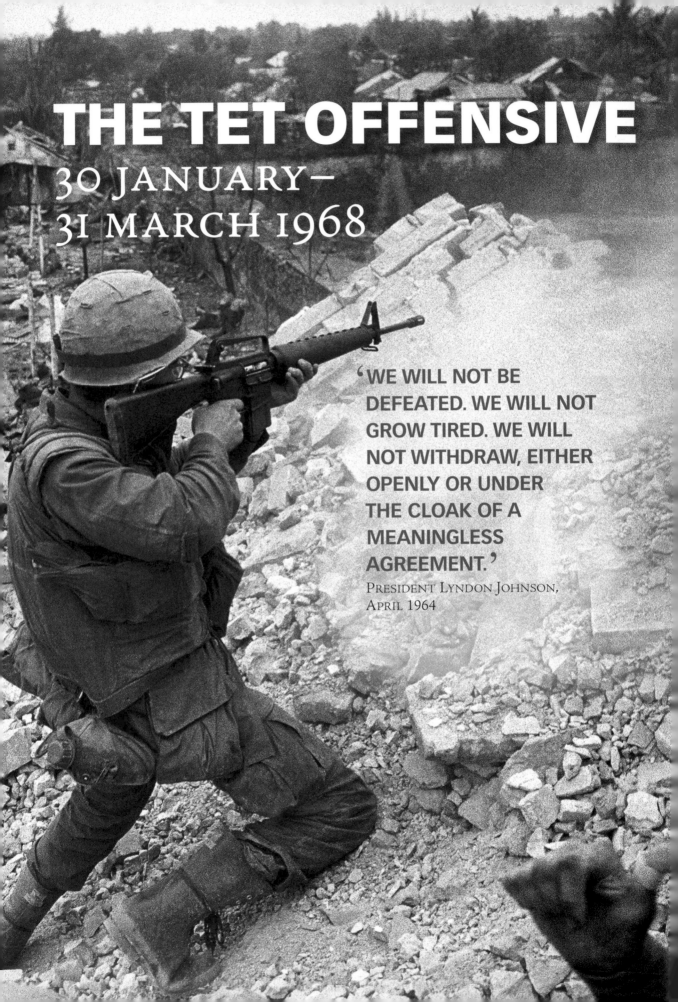

THE TET OFFENSIVE
30 JANUARY – 31 MARCH 1968

'WE WILL NOT BE DEFEATED. WE WILL NOT GROW TIRED. WE WILL NOT WITHDRAW, EITHER OPENLY OR UNDER THE CLOAK OF A MEANINGLESS AGREEMENT.'

PRESIDENT LYNDON JOHNSON, APRIL 1964

Like the Battle of the Bulge in 1944, the Tet Offensive was a last-ditch effort to end a war, launched by the army that was losing. However, while it ended in a crushing defeat just like the Nazi offensive, the North Vietnamese leadership were able to convert their blunder into a political triumph. The disconnection between what happened on the battlefield and what followed in the media and the political sphere have made this the most famous battle of the Vietnam War.

The Republic of Vietnam was invented in 1954. Under the terms of the Geneva Conference, the former French colony of Vietnam was ordered to be divided at the 17th parallel, pending nationwide elections in 1956. The north remained in the hands of the communists, flush with their great battlefield victory at Dien Bien Phu. Nearly a million people, mainly Catholics, fled communist rule to live in the south – internationally recognized as the Republic of South Vietnam. A referendum there saw Ngo Dinh Diem installed as president, in place of the former emperor Bao Dai. The countrywide elections were never held.

> '‌It became necessary to destroy the town in order to save it'
>
> UNIDENTIFIED US ARMY MAJOR, INTERVIEWED IN BEN TRE, SOUTH VIETNAM, FEBRUARY 1968

VC, NVA and ARVN

Determined to reunify the nation under their rule, the communists re-established a military command within the South in 1959. Local guerrillas, the Viet Cong, increasingly supported by NVA (North Vietnamese Army) units gradually gained the upper hand over the ARVN (Army of the Republic of Vietnam). American military advisers, special forces units and massive arms shipments slowed, but did not halt the communists. Diem's deeply corrupt government seemed to have no answer, and was ousted in a coup d'état, to which President Kennedy gave the green light. Diem and his brother were murdered on 2 November 1963 but it proved easier to change the leaders than reform the regime.

On 2 March 1965 President Johnson ordered aerial attacks on North Vietnam and landed US Marines in the South a week later. From 1965–7 the US deployed ever larger forces, peaking at more than 500,000 men inside South Vietnam. US troops led operations against the Viet Cong and NVA while – in theory – ARVN forces 'pacified' the countryside. Supported by heavy artillery and the world's most powerful air force, US forces inflicted terrible casualties on the NVA in a series of pitched battles. In 1966 the North Vietnamese suffered 93,000 dead; in 1967, 145,000. North Vietnamese conscripts marched south knowing that few, if any, would return home.

OPPOSITE: *A US Marine fires into the citadel at Hue, still held by the North Vietnamese after 18 days' fighting. The Tet Offensive was a catastrophic defeat for the North Vietnamese, turned into a victory by the US media.*

'Plausible deniability'

President Johnson refused to formally declare war, initiate full conscription and treat the conflict for what it was. American unit cohesion was undermined by a bizarre policy whereby individual soldiers were posted to Vietnam for a year, then replaced. By the end of 1967, as the election campaign began, Johnson claimed America was winning. The 'light at the end of the tunnel' was observed – more than once, corners were turned – several times. But neither the media nor the public could see what had been achieved by the deaths of 16,000 Americans in a remote Asian jungle. Public approval of Johnson's handling of the war fell from 75 per cent to 53 per cent over the year.

A CIA report that suggested the number of NVA troops inside South Vietnam was rising – not falling – was suppressed. Johnson, who had coined the expression 'plausible deniability', seemed surprised that statements from the White House were no longer believed, and that military communiqués issued from the US headquarters in Vietnam were regarded as the '5 o'clock follies'. The deep distrust between the media and the Johnson administration would play an important role in what followed.

Factions and Fanatics

For many years afterwards the Tet Offensive was regarded as a triumph of far-sighted Marxist strategy over American optimism and ethnocentricity. However, we now know the NVA plan for 1968 to have been the product of factional disputes within the communist hierarchy, fought with the usual ploys of secret denunciations, show trials and murder. Many senior figures argued for negotiations to begin, as the casualty rate was unsustainable and foreign support by Russia and China unreliable. They were shouted down by militants, whose glassy-eyed fanaticism contributed enormously to the 1.1 million casualties the North Vietnamese would ultimately suffer – although not admit until the late 1990s.

The militants' plan was to stage attacks all over South Vietnam over the national holiday period, Tet, a religious festival and celebration of the Lunar New Year. The intention was to trigger a nationwide revolt against the American 'occupiers' and their Vietnamese 'puppets'. By striking at the South Vietnamese Presidential Palace, the old imperial citadel at Hue, and government buildings throughout the country, the intention was to decapitate the South Vietnamese government; subsidiary attacks were made at American targets like air bases, logistical centres – and the US Embassy.

From the frontier with North Vietnam to Da Nang, the Central Highlands and the Mekong Delta, local Viet Cong and NVA units attacked with everything they had on the night of 30–31 January 1968. An estimated 84,000 communist troops were involved: their targets included five out of six autonomous cities, including the capital, Saigon; 36 out of 44 provincial capitals; and 64 of the 242 district capitals.

Rolling Thunder – The Bombing of North Vietnam, March 1965–October 1968

ON 2 MARCH 1965 PRESIDENT JOHNSON announced the beginning of Operation 'Rolling Thunder', aerial attacks on selected targets in North Vietnam intended to dissuade the Hanoi government from its onslaught against the South. Railway bridges, oil storage depots and various military facilities were attacked in order to prevent exactly the sort of mass assault represented by Tet. The targets were selected by a small team in the White House, not by the military. Missions were organized by a remote, cumbersome command structure. Unsuccessful attacks were often ordered to be repeated, maximizing the danger for American fliers who faced heavier anti-aircraft defences than the Nazis had built around Berlin. President Johnson halted the bombing so often that even the USAF official history cannot decide how many 'bombing halts' there were. They were intended to encourage the North Vietnamese to stop the war, but the 'ignorant' communists just interpreted them as lack of resolve. Nearly a thousand US aircraft were lost and hundreds of airmen killed in a pointless exercise that Johnson finally cancelled in October.

Thirteen of the sixteen provincial cities in the Delta were assaulted; many of the attacks failed, but they did capture part of the river city of Ben Tre. Artillery and air strikes helped US and ARVN infantry retake it, but many buildings were levelled, leading to the unfortunate comment by an American major to a reporter that 'It became necessary to destroy the city in order to save it.'

In the Central Highlands, Ban Me Thuot's city centre changed hands four times before the ARVN 23rd Infantry Division regained control. The Lang Vei Special Forces camp near Khe Sanh was overrun on 7 February; the attack led by Soviet-supplied light tanks. This seemed to confirm US theatre commander General Westmoreland's mistaken judgement that the whole offensive was a diversion to draw away his reserves – then repeat the Dien Bien Phu victory by overwhelming Khe Sanh. But by 21 February the NVA accepted it had lost the battle for the highlands.

US Embassy, Saigon

Thirty-five Viet Cong and NVA battalions attacked targets in and around Saigon. One team seized the radio station, intending to play a taped message from President Ho Chi Minh. They took the building, but were frustrated in their mission by a South Vietnamese officer who had issued orders to cut the power to the station if it was captured. Another team assaulted the Presidential Palace, but were driven off and besieged in a nearby building for 48 hours: 32 out of 34 were killed. A 19-man unit attacked the US Embassy, blowing a hole in the compound wall with a satchel charge

The Tet Offensive

July 1967 North Vietnamese government begins planning for all-out offensive against South Vietnam.

August 1967 President Johnson claims that America is winning the war in Vietnam.

November 1967 General Westmoreland states that US troops can begin to withdraw from Vietnam within two years, mission accomplished.

10 January 1968 Westmoreland authorizes redeployment of US forces from Cambodian frontier to the vicinity of Saigon.

20 January North Vietnamese forces lay siege to Khe Sanh.

29 January Tet holiday season begins. Allies begin 36-hour ceasefire.

30 January Communist attacks begin.

8 February Of all the positions attacked, only Hue and some Saigon suburbs remain in NVA/VC hands. Communist losses run into tens of thousands in one week.

21 February Viet Cong high command orders a return to guerrilla warfare.

31 March President Johnson announces he will not run for a second term. He orders yet another partial bombing halt.

and rushing through, led by their officers. Two US Marines were killed in a furious exchange of fire, but they did manage to shoot down the first men through the gap; without their officers, the surviving Viet Cong milled about the grounds, firing on the building, but were never able to gain entry.

There were many Western journalists living nearby. Within 15 minutes, Associated Press issued a bulletin falsely claiming the Viet Cong had seized part of the US Embassy. It arrived in America just in time to make the headlines in the east coast newspapers. The Viet Cong had failed to get inside their key targets, but they were inside the news cycle. General Westmoreland gave an impromptu press conference outside the compound at 9.20 a.m. Filmed with dead Viet Cong, broken glass and rubble in the background, and coming from a man who had claimed to be winning the war, it failed to quell the impression that the communists had caught everyone napping.

It emerged later that the critical decision had been made three weeks earlier. On 10 January, Lieutenant General Weyand, commander of the III Corps district that included Saigon, had told General Westmoreland that he suspected a VC attack on the capital was imminent. He was authorized to withdraw 15 battalions from their positions near the Cambodian border, and station them nearer Saigon. Weyand's own HQ came under rocket and mortar fire as he struggled to make sense of the reports of multiple attacks, but before dawn 5,000 US troops were already on the move to threatened locations. There were fierce battles too at Long Binh, where a VC regiment attacked the logistics hub and the 2/47th US Infantry counter-attacked in armoured personnel carriers, and the 11th Armored Cavalry made a 12-hour high-speed drive to intervene with characteristic panache.

The Bien Hoa air base was attacked by another VC regiment and might well have been overrun but for a vigorous defence by the 1/5th Armored Cavalry which fought through an ambush to support the 2/506th Infantry. The one tank supporting the 506th was hit 19 times and the crew replaced twice by the end of the day. By the end of 1 February, there were 500 American combat vehicles fighting in and around Saigon and the VC assault teams were everywhere on the defensive. The Viet Cong leadership recognized the game was up. No significant locations remained in their hands, no ARVN units had come over to them or deserted en masse; there had been no sign of civilian support for the communist cause.

The City On the Perfume River is Ruined

The longest-running battle during Tet took place in the old imperial city at Hue. The headquarters of the ARVN 1st Division was inside the ancient citadel, and on the south side of the Perfume River was an Allied command centre housing US and Australian military advisers and staff. Half the men of the ARVN division were on leave; most of those on duty were posted outside the city where their commander thought the enemy might attack. As a result, two NVA regiments and two battalions of local VC met little opposition when they assaulted the heart of the city in the early hours of 31 January.

So confused had the situation become that morning that the US counter-attack to relieve the embattled command post comprised A Company 1/1 Marines and four M-48 tanks. A Company's advance soon ran into ferocious opposition. By midday, G Company 2/5 Marines was ordered in to support A Company and eventually both units made it to the compound. The ARVN HQ and the Allied command post remained isolated within the communist perimeter, but most of the city was now in enemy hands.

The communists opened the jail to release 2,500 prisoners, some of which joined the battle. Their troops fortified their positions to await the Allied counter-attack while their commissars gave the world a foretaste of what communist rule would mean. Working from extensive lists prepared beforehand, they arrested hundreds of government officials, teachers, students (the dreaded 'intellectuals') and anyone who could identify the local VC who had been living in the city before the battle. The first mass graves were found at the end of February and excavations could continue until 1970: 2,810 people were murdered by the communists at Hue.

Propaganda Twists and Turns

It took three weeks of house-to-house fighting to overcome the NVA and VC battalions holed-up in the city. On 16 February the NVA command post signalled Hanoi, requesting permission to withdraw and admitting that the senior officer commanding had been killed. Permission was denied and the battle went on another ten days, by now concentrated in and around the stone-walled citadel. The ensuing casualties were reminiscent of the Pacific War: 5,000 NVA were killed and just 89 taken prisoner. The ARVN lost 384 dead and 1,800 wounded, belying the NVA briefing which expected no serious resistance from the 'puppet forces'. US losses were 216 dead and 1,364 wounded.

Tet had not triggered a popular uprising: the communist forces had suffered a terrible defeat. Their casualties were approximately 50,000 dead; total US losses were about 4,000 killed and wounded; ARVN deaths about 6,000. Damage to infrastructure was significant and several hundred thousand South Vietnamese were left homeless by the destruction. Unfortunately for South Vietnam and the United States, the mere fact that the North Vietnamese had been able to mount such a massive operation when – according to President Johnson and his generals – they were on their knees, had profound consequences. The media began to preach that the conflict was lost; policymakers from both parties in America began to lose faith in the war. Popular reaction in America was mixed, many of those professing themselves 'anti-war' simply meant opposing the way the war was being fought.

The collapse of Johnson's own morale was more significant. He hid from public view for weeks, contributing to a decline in his approval rating to 47 per cent in February. On 31 March President Johnson gave up and announced he would not seek re-election. Other than the White House staff, the one important group of people to feel they had lost were the communist soldiers. Some 47,000 subsequently deserted to embrace the 'open arms' amnesty programme in 1969.

By the time President Nixon withdrew US ground troops they had done their job: the North Vietnamese Army had lost more than 1 million men and its last hurrah, the 1972 offensive, was repulsed with horrendous losses. However, Nixon's fall and disgrace led to a congressional ban on US military aid to the South; the 1973 Arab–Israeli war sent the price of oil spiralling, while Russian and Chinese support for the North was stepped up. Events very far from Saigon reversed the verdict of Tet and enabled North Vietnamese tanks to crush the Republic once and for ever in 1975.

THE FALKLANDS WAR

2 APRIL–20 JUNE 1982

'BE PLEASED TO INFORM HER MAJESTY
THAT THE WHITE ENSIGN FLIES ALONGSIDE
THE UNION JACK IN SOUTH GEORGIA. GOD
SAVE THE QUEEN!'

MAJOR GUY SHERIDAN, ROYAL MARINES, 25 APRIL 1982

In 1982 Argentina's ruling military junta invaded the Falklands, desolate windswept islands in the remote South Atlantic, farmed by some 1,800 souls: one of the last residual outposts of the British Empire. Had General Galtieri waited but a few months, his country's dubious claim to the islands might well have achieved international recognition.

Instead, to his bewilderment, and the whole world's astonishment, the moribund British state suddenly came to life, and mounted a liberation mission from the other side of the world. A Royal Navy Task Force steamed 8,000 miles, defeated the Argentinian naval and air forces and landed an infantry brigade on East Falkland. As one Royal Marine remarked from his landing craft in San Carlos Water, 'The Empire strikes back!'

Signals Are Crossed

The British had given the junta every reason to believe that an invasion would not be contested. In 1968 they had signed a memorandum of understanding with a previous junta in which they agreed to recognize Argentinian sovereignty at a future date, when it was in 'the best interests' of the inhabitants. The 1981 British Nationality Act denied the islanders' children British passports, unless the birth took place in the UK. The retreat from empire, assiduously managed by the British Foreign Office, had such momentum by the 1970s that only the personal intervention of a prime minister could stop it. That prime minister was James Callaghan, who cut the bureaucrats off at the knees with his trenchant refusal to 'hand over one thousand eight hundred Brits to a gang of f****** Fascists.' Nevertheless, the subsequent Conservative government of Margaret Thatcher resumed talks with the Argentinians, who can be forgiven for believing that a deal would eventually emerge.

British defence spending had been slashed throughout the 1970s, and with their 1981 defence review, the Conservatives were poised to bang the final nail in the coffin. Of the Royal Navy's three operational aircraft carriers, one was to be scrapped and one sold. The fleet's amphibious assault ships were to go too, threatening the very survival of the Royal Marines. Near the bottom of the list of the cuts was the *Endurance*, a patrol ship stationed in the South Atlantic. To Buenos Aires its proposed deletion seemed a clear signal that the UK was abandoning the Falklands. London appeared to have no interest in the region, and was jettisoning its out-of-area capability.

The military junta had seized power in 1976 and amid economic meltdown, social unrest and terrorism it conducted a hideous war on its own people. Up to 30,000 people were murdered by the secret police and armed forces. In late 1981 General Galtieri sought

PREVIOUS PAGE: *HMS* Antelope *explodes and sinks in San Carlos Bay after Argentinian air strikes against the British fleet off the Falklands, 25 May 1982.*

Muerta Negra

SINCE THE 1960S ROYAL NAVY FLEET AIR ARM AIRCRAFT had worn a standard scheme of blue-grey upper surfaces with white lower surfaces and brightly coloured national markings. But on the way south in 1982, the Sea Harriers were repainted in a very dark sea grey all over, with low-profile markings. The Argentinian air force lost 41 fixed wing aircraft in the battle, of which 21 were shot down by the Royal Navy's Sea Harriers, understandably dubbed *Muerta Negra* ('black death') by the Argentinians. The adoption of these unique aircraft had been highly controversial, their carriers having to be designated 'through-deck cruisers' in the Alice-in-Wonderland world of UK defence procurement. By 1980 when the Sea Harriers entered service, the Royal Navy was essentially the anti-submarine and mine countermeasures arm of the US Atlantic Fleet. Nobody had anticipated relying on Sea Harriers to defend a task force against sustained attack by land-based aircraft. Ironically, the Sea Harriers were withdrawn from service in 2002 with nothing to replace them. The very future of the Fleet Air Arm is open to doubt.

to restore the popularity of the regime with a final solution to the Falklands problem.

The plan was to seize the islands in May 1982 at the onset of the southern Atlantic winter – heavy seas and frequent storms would make any reaction impossible. The defence of the islands rested in the hands of a single platoon of Royal Marines, so resistance could only be token. The invasion was brought forward because it had become open knowledge in Argentina and – the junta assumed – in London. When it came, the assault on the Falklands on 2 April was a model of efficiency. There were no British fatalities, military or civilian – no mean feat given the robust stand made by the tiny garrison – so the British could accept it as a fait accompli.

Galtieri's Mistake

However, newspaper photographs of Royal Marines lying in the mud surrounded by heavily armed Argentinians did not play well in Britain, nor did the sight of a general on a balcony haranguing a baying mob. Galtieri relished the adulation of the crowds that poured into the streets of Buenos Aires, but the spectacle looked disturbingly familiar. Even a Chilean officer thought it was all too Mussolini-like and agreed to help the representative of British intelligence who visited him the next day.

The British foreign and defence ministries had cautioned the government against a military response. A policy of craven appeasement was championed with equal loquaciousness by Margaret Thatcher's enemies on both sides of the House, above all by the 'wets' within her own cabinet. Even once operations were underway, the new foreign secretary appeared to champion UN intervention; it is hard to disagree with Alexander Haig's description of Francis Pym as 'a duplicitous bastard'. Significantly, the life-long pacifist Labour leader Michael Foot sided with Margaret Thatcher. Britain had been

The Falklands War

1981

20 December: Unauthorized Argentinian landing on South Georgia.

1982

9 February Thatcher confirms retirement of HMS *Endurance*.

25 February Sovereignty talks resume between Britain and Argentina.

31 March Chief of Naval Staff Admiral Sir Henry Leach presses Thatcher to send a task force if the islands are invaded.

2 April Falkland Islands and South Georgia occupied. Brigadier General Mario Menéndez is appointed governor of 'Islas Malvinas'.

3 April UN Security Council passes Resolution 502 demanding immediate Argentinian withdrawal.

5 April Aircraft carriers *Hermes* and *Invincible* sail from Portsmouth.

25 April South Georgia recaptured by Royal Marines.

1 May First Vulcan bomber raid on Stanley airport.

2 May HMS *Conqueror* sinks the cruiser *General Belgrano*.

4 May HMS *Sheffield* sunk by an Exocet missile.

21 May San Carlos landings.

25 May British container ship *Atlantic Conveyor* is sunk.

continued on opposite page

attacked by the same enemy she had faced in 1939–45: the response had to be the same.

American aid was generous and vital. Caspar Weinberger was awarded a KCB after the war, while Thatcher's own defence secretary received nothing. If there was a delay, it was understandable since successive British governments had given every indication they would cave in. Once there proved to be some fight in the old dog still, weapons, fuel and intelligence data flowed without pause – or paperwork. (Had the Royal Navy still possessed the manpower to crew the aircraft carrier it was offered, the subsequent story would have been very different.) As it was, the supply of state-of-the-art AIM-9L Sidewinders gave the Royal Navy's Sea Harriers far better air-to-air missiles than the older ones fitted to Argentinian jets.

Sea Harriers v Mirages

With the decommissioning of HMS *Ark Royal* in 1978, the Royal Navy lost its last fleet carrier and with her the ability to operate supersonic fighters and – crucially – airborne early warning aircraft. The air defence of the fleet would rest with a very small air group of just 24 Sea Harriers: subsonic V/STOL aircraft of revolutionary design, but never before tried in combat. The Task Force faced a formidable challenge: to make an opposed amphibious landing thousands of miles from a friendly harbour, and within range of enemy land-based aircraft. The Argentinian air force had 15 Mirage interceptors and 33 Mirage 5 (Dagger) fighter-bombers, both capable of Mach 2. Its primary strike aircraft was the tough little Douglas A-4 Skyhawk, of which they had 52; along with 10 Canberra bombers. The navy had eight A-4Qs, bought from the US Navy in 1972, and five French-built Super Étendard bombers. The latter were built to launch the Exocet anti-ship missile, but only five had been delivered when the war – and an arms embargo – began.

When it became clear that the British would fight, the Argentinian army commanders reacted with the same combination of bombast and incompetence displayed so often in the Middle East. Instead of shipping in the engineers and materiel to extend Stanley's runway and enable the air force to base its jets there, Galtieri packed the island with soldiers and broadcast rabidly patriotic speeches. He remains one of the few heads of state in recent times to have refused to take a phone call from the president of the United States. The garrison on the Falklands dug in, mostly around Port Stanley, but carried out no training or rehearsals. The soldiers shivered in their waterlogged trenches while many of their officers and senior NCOs stayed inside in the warm.

The Argentinian air force and naval air arm proved altogether more professional. Some of the navy's newest warships were British-built, so the air force was able to practise attacking a destroyer of the same class they would soon face in anger. The results were depressing: attacking with 1,000-lb bombs – unguided freefall weapons straight out of the Second World War, and ironically also supplied by Britain – they estimated they would suffer 50 per cent casualties against the warships' guns and missiles. They could not even try to overwhelm an isolated ship with a mass attack: the islands were at extreme range for their single-seater aircraft. The Skyhawks and Étendards could refuel in mid-air but they had only two KC-130 tankers in service. The Daggers and Mirages required two drop-tanks to reach the Falklands, and if they cut in their afterburners for supersonic flight, they probably would not have enough fuel to get home.

As the British fleet approached the Falklands, the Argentinian navy countered with two task forces: a surface action group comprising the cruiser *General Belgrano* and two Exocet-armed destroyer-escorts; and another including their sole aircraft carrier *25 de Mayo*. The carrier had eight A-4Qs aboard, an elderly SP-2 Neptune scouted far ahead to track the British; and the stage was set for the first carrier versus carrier battle since the Second World War. Luckily, the wind dropped and without the extra lift it was not possible to launch an A-4 and its 2,000-lb bomb load. The ancient steam catapults aboard *25 de Mayo* were too weak for the Étendards in any condition, and they flew from the mainland.

continued from previous page

28 May 2 Para launch attack on Goose Green.

8 June *Sir Galahad* and *Sir Tristram* are bombed at Fitzroy.

12 June 3 Para take Mount Longdon; 42 Commando take Mount Harriet; 45 Commando take Two Sisters.

13 June Battles for Tumbledown, Wireless Ridge and Mount William.

14 June Argentinian forces on the Falklands surrender.

17 June Galtieri resigns.

11 July *Canberra* brings 40, 42 and 45 Commando into Southampton amid rapturous reception.

12 October Victory Parade in London.

ABOVE: *British soldiers had spent a generation training to meet a Russian invasion of Western Europe, only to find themselves on the far side of the world fighting much the same enemy their fathers fought in 1940. The ensuing battles showed the advantages of hard training over theatrical posturing.*

The Exocet's Moment

In the vastness of the ocean even the biggest fleet can be hard to find, as the Pacific War battles had demonstrated. On 1 May the Argentinian air force made a maximum effort but its first two strike forces failed to locate the Task Force before their fuel levels compelled them to return. Subsequent flights were intercepted by Sea Harriers which shot a Mirage and a Dagger; another Mirage was shot down by an Argentinian missile battery when it attempted an emergency landing at Port Stanley. One of two attacking Canberra bombers was also destroyed by a Sidewinder from a Harrier; the other was damaged by a SAM from the fleet and limped back to Argentina. The next day, the British submarine *Conqueror* torpedoed and sank the *General Belgrano*. Stooging about in waters full of hungry British submariners had little to recommend it, so the Argentinian squadrons returned to port.

On 4 May the weather cleared and the Argentinian Étendards tried their luck again. Two aircraft headed for the reported position of the British carrier *Hermes*, launched their Exocets at maximum range – about 20 miles – and lit out for home. They hit the destroyer *Sheffield* which was consumed by fires started by the unexpended rocket fuel as much as the warhead. The Exocet – hitherto an undistinguished weapons system – became a household name.

Boots On the Ground

The decisive battle of the campaign took place on 21 May as the British carried out their landings not, as the Argentinians had expected, directly into Port Stanley, but the other side of East Falkland at San Carlos. The assault ships and the horribly vulnerable liner *Canberra* anchored in the narrow waters, where the surrounding hills would prevent an Exocet from locking-on. The Argentinians launched 60 aircraft that day, of which 44 reached the islands, where they pressed home their attacks with great courage at very low level. They sank the frigate *Ardent* and damaged several other warships, but failed to hit the transports unloading the invasion force. Four Daggers and four Skyhawks were shot down by Sea Harriers en route, one Dagger fell to a SAM from HMS *Broadsword*. Five infantry battalions were ashore by the end of the day and under cover of bad weather on the 22nd, more stores and equipment piled up on the beachhead.

Air strikes on 23 and 24 May failed to stop the progress of the landings, despite finally achieving some hits on the logistic ships. Their exercises had suggested that by coming in at wave-top height, the pilots would make it very difficult for British missiles to track them. That worked better than they had hoped, but it gave insufficient time for the bombs to arm. Many failed to detonate and their targets survived to fight another day. On 25 May the Étendards tried again for a British carrier but their missiles launched at *Invincible* were deflected by counter-measures and sank the cargo ship *Atlantic Conveyor*. The loss of the helicopters she carried would bedevil the British operations ashore; nevertheless the Argentinian defensive positions fell one-by-one to infantry who had not spent all those years training in the wettest parts of Wales for nothing. The Argentinian garrison surrendered on 14 June.

Democracy Makes a Comeback

Galtieri's gamble backfired spectacularly and he was forced to resign, the junta toppled and democratic government was reinstated. Thatcher was re-elected in 1983, but her victory owed more to the collapse of the Labour vote, rather than increased support for her. However, after the dismal decline of the 1960s and 70s, such a vigorous reassertion of the national interest was as welcome as it was unexpected.

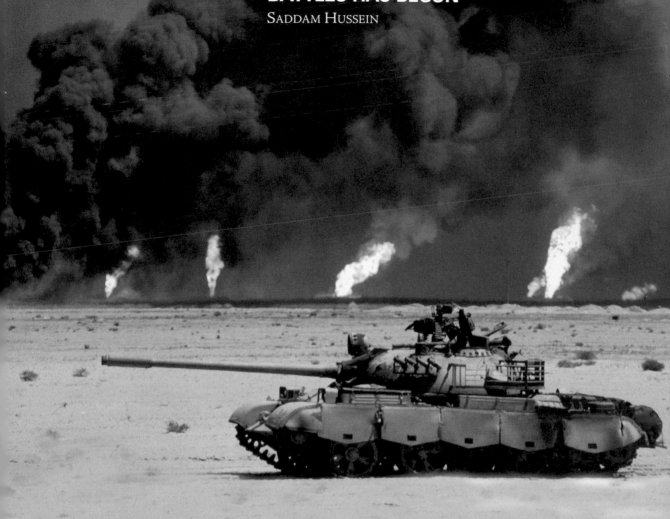

THE GULF WAR
2 AUGUST 1990–
28 FEBRUARY 1991

'THE MOTHER OF ALL
BATTLES HAS BEGUN'
SADDAM HUSSEIN

The Gulf War was the last great coalition war of the 20th century, the breadth of the international alliance assembled by the United States a testimony to the diplomatic abilities of President George H.W. Bush and Secretary of State James Baker. Military contingents from 34 countries assembled in the Middle East to liberate Kuwait from Iraqi occupation.

Other nations contributed financially. Iraq entered the war an international pariah, supported only by the Palestine Liberation Organization (which never missed an opportunity to miss an opportunity). Yet, as so often before in the region, even this most decisive military victory failed to deliver lasting peace. Kuwait was liberated, but Saddam Hussein's murderous regime survived.

Saddam's Rise

Saddam Hussein was 19 years old in 1956 when President Gamal Abdel Nasser emerged triumphant from the Suez Crisis. Nasser's secular pan-Arab vision of the Middle East won him legions of admirers, and the young Iraqi had similarly messianic ambitions. By 1959 he was part of a CIA-funded assassination squad in Iraq and by great political cunning and a fearsome capacity for personal violence he rose through the Ba'athist ('renaissance') Party, survived periods of exile and imprisonment, and became the republic's strongman during the 1970s. In 1979 he ousted his president in a bloodless coup, purged the senior ranks of the party and installed his own henchmen in their place.

Saddam was a modernizer in the Nasser mould. He established a public health system that put all others in the region to shame. A trenchant secularist, he abolished Islamic law and introduced free education for girls as well as boys, recognizing that the country's widespread illiteracy was a weighty block on progress. His emancipation of women extended beyond education: they were promoted to responsible jobs in business, government and the health service. It infuriated religious conservatives, and Islamic fundamentalists hated him more than Israel or the United States. The very real threat of assassination left him on the move every day, seldom sleeping in his grandiose palaces and developing a network of safe houses that would prove their value later. His secret police shrank at nothing in their efforts to crush dissent.

A Move Too Far

Saddam followed Nasser's model too closely, and overreached himself in a foreign war. Iraq's invasion of Iran in 1980 failed to produce the snap victory he had sought, instead bogging down into an eight-year war of attrition that involved the first mutual use of

PREVIOUS PAGE: *An Iraqi tank, abandoned in the lee of a burning oil well. As in the wars of 1956, 1967 and 1973, imposing Arab tank fleets do not last long against competent armies and air forces.*

chemical weapons since the First World War. Saddam also employed poison gas to crush a Kurdish revolt in northern Iraq in 1988. Yet his aim of overthrowing the Islamic regime in Tehran was not unpopular in other capitals: Saddam's war received financial aid from the USA, Saudi Arabia and the Gulf States. It was not enough. By the end of the war Saddam's once wealthy state was virtually bankrupt. He had nothing to show for hundreds of thousands of casualties, and found himself looking at a war debt of perhaps $75 billion.

About a third of the debt was held by Kuwait, a country whose borders had been drawn up by the British deliberately to restrict Iraqi access to the sea – and which had enormous oil reserves of its own. On 2 August 1990 the Iraqi army occupied Kuwait and declared it to be the nineteenth province of Iraq. Saddam had persuaded himself that – as a counterweight to Iran – Iraq was more valuable to the USA than Kuwait. His regime seemed quite unprepared for what followed: international condemnation; diplomatic isolation; stark warnings of military action.

Saddam wrapped himself in the flag, but his pose as Arab champion fell flat. The borders of the Arab world might have been imposed rather haphazardly in the 1920s, but the idea they could be redrawn with tanks was not something any regional power wished to encourage. He took Western hostages, some of which he paraded on television in what remains one of the most self-defeating propaganda campaigns of modern times. Within days of the occupation of Kuwait, US troops arrived in Saudi Arabia in case Saddam's ambitions stretched further. USAF aircraft patrolled the border.

Momentum Gathers

By the end of November Saddam had run out of diplomatic road and faced a UN resolution demanding the withdrawal of Iraqi forces from Kuwait by 15 January 1991 – and authorizing their removal by military action. The months of negotiations enabled the US to deploy more than 500,000 troops to the theatre of operations, above all massed armoured formations. Allied intelligence estimated that 100,000 Iraqi troops had taken part in the invasion, but Saddam continued to reinforce the occupation force and to deploy more of his army. By the end of the year an estimated 430,000 Iraqi troops were positioned along the Saudi border.

President Bush's administration assembled a formidable coalition including some unlikely partners: Syria, Argentina, Belgium, Italy, Egypt – even France. The biggest Allied contingent came from Britain which deployed 45,000 men including a full armoured division under command of the US 7th Corps. On 12 January the US Senate voted – by a narrow margin – to authorize the use of force.

While the coalition forces had trained together, and rehearsed their tactics, the Iraqi army remained in its positions, dug-in across the desert in the standard Soviet defensive

The Gulf War

1990

2 August Iraqi invasion of Kuwait. UN demands Iraq withdraw.

6 August UN imposed economic sanctions on Iraq.

7 August US troops arrive in Saudi Arabia.

1991

17 January Coalition air and missile attacks begin.

18 January Iraq fires seven Scud missiles at Israel.

29 January Iraqi army raids Saudi border town of Khafji.

22 February Iraq accepts Russian peace plan.

24 February Allied ground forces invade Iraq.

26 February Iraqi garrison in Kuwait starts to flee back to Iraq under concentrated air attack.

27 February Kuwait City is liberated.

28 February President Bush halts the fighting.

positions they had favoured against Iran. Like the Arab armies that had attacked Israel so often, it was an impressive force on paper. Iraq had nearly 1 million men under arms. There were several thousand tanks in service, mostly obsolete Chinese and Russian types but including 500 Russian T-72s of more recent vintage. Supporting the tanks and infantry were hundreds of heavy artillery pieces, and an integrated air defence system of surface to air missiles (SAMs) and guns. The Iraqi army had killed hundreds of thousands of tactically unskilled, but fanatical Iranians. How it would fare against a modern army was unknown, but it was equally unclear if the political resolve of the coalition would survive serious casualties.

Iraq's air force had several hundred Russian aircraft, but everyone from Western analysts to their own pilots knew what was likely to happen if they went up against the United States Air Force.

'Smart' Bombs and B-52s

The USAF opened proceedings in the early hours of 17 January with air strikes across occupied Kuwait and deep into Iraq. Lockheed F-117 Stealth bombers struck Baghdad while Iraq's aircraft were systematically picked off in their hardened shelters. Those Iraqi MiGs that rose to challenge the Allies over the next few days were shot down with ease, and the surviving aircraft fled – bizarrely – to Iran, which imprisoned most of the aircrew and confiscated the planes. Boeing B-52 bombers returned to their Vietnam role, deluging the Iraqi defences with their enormous bomb loads. Cruise missiles were fired from the navy's last serving battleships.

Saddam's response to the bombardment was subtle and unexpected: the next day he launched one Scud missile at Saudi Arabia – and seven at Israel. These crude ballistic missiles, supplied by Russia and locally modified, were similar to the German V-2s fired on London in 1944–5. Fired from large trucks that nevertheless proved very elusive in the Iraqi desert, they were so inaccurate that even a target the size of a city proved hard to hit with consistency. Saddam calculated that the Israelis would respond in kind with retaliatory air strikes, likely to cause civilian casualties which could be on television by the time the all-clear sounded. The involvement of the Israelis would jeopardize the coalition, but they bowed to US pressure. Coalition aircraft and special forces units scoured western Iraq for the elusive missile transporters, but 81 Scuds were successfully launched over the next five weeks. Many fell in the desert but on 25 February one struck a US base in Saudi, killing 28 Americans.

Schwarzkopf's 'Shock and Awe'

The coalition air campaign struck Iraq's infrastructure hard, destroying the country's power stations, dams, telecommunications facilities, oil refineries, railways, bridges and the highways to neutral Jordan, likely bolt-hole for the regime's senior figures. After two weeks, Iraqi towns and cities struggled to get power, sewage plants had ceased operation and drinking water was running short. Several thousand Iraqi civilians were killed or wounded, most notoriously in Baghdad on 13 February when as many as 200 people died in a blockhouse struck by two laser-guided bombs.

Most Iraqi aircraft were destroyed on the ground, although 29 were shot down by USAF fighters. In late January about a hundred Iraqi aircraft flew to Iran. Their escape route to Jordan was intensively patrolled by coalition aircraft, but most of the pilots were held prisoner for some years. The aircraft were confiscated.

Allied artillery in Saudi Arabia joined in the barrage, subjecting the Iraqi positions to a fearsome weight of high explosive. On the 7th Corps front, it added up to the equivalent of 75,000 Scud missiles. The British 1st Armoured Division had more artillery firepower at its disposal than Montgomery's entire army at El Alamein.

The day the bombardment began, the US 18th Airborne Corps and the 14,000-strong French contingent started to drive westwards. The coalition commander, General H Norman Schwarzkopf, planned an extremely wide flanking manoeuvre, beginning some 200 miles to the west and hooking around Kuwait to cut the Iraqi forces' supply lines. Meanwhile the heavy armour of 7th Corps would make a frontal attack, while the US Marines threatened an amphibious assault that compelled the Iraqis to hold the coastline in strength.

> 'We don't want to pay a terrible price to get it over with quickly'
> GENERAL H NORMAN SCHWARZKOPF

On 22 February, Iraq announced it would accept a Russian-brokered peace plan in which it would withdraw from Kuwait. However, the plan also demanded a ceasefire which was not a precondition of the UN resolution. President Bush gave Saddam until noon the next day to retreat. At 4 a.m. on 24 February the 1st and 2nd US Marine divisions went into action to liberate Kuwait, the tank crews wearing NBC suits against the chemical weapons it was feared Iraq would employ. Three hundred miles to the west, the US 82nd Airborne and French 6th Light Division invaded Iraq and seized As-Salman airfield. The US 101st Airborne conducted a heliborne assault 70 miles into Iraq to establish a forward logistics base. In the centre of the Allied line, the 1,200 tanks of 7th Corps headed north, then east intending to strike the Iraqi Republican Guard divisions outside Basra.

'The pilots said it was a turkey shoot because the Iraqis were like sitting ducks'

GLR RADIO, LONDON, JANUARY 1991

General Schwarzkopf and his staff planned the battle to liberate Kuwait with the assumption that the Iraqis would fight hard. Combat supplies for 60 days had been laboriously stockpiled across the desert. Yet within hours of the ground fighting beginning it was obvious they would not be required. By noon on the first day of battle, more than 5,000 Iraqis had surrendered. The coalition forces kept up a furious pace of operations, not ceasing at nightfall but pressing on, relying on night vision gear and stimulants to maintain the advance. By the third day of unrelenting battle, the British tank division commander instructed his units to write down all messages and check them before transmitting. Exhausted men make mistakes, and with the enormous firepower at their disposal, the potential for the world's worst 'blue-on-blue' was all too real. Nine British soldiers died on 26 February when their vehicles were attacked by US bombers. Nevertheless, the 1st Armoured had knocked out 300 Iraqi AFVs and captured 8,000 men.

Push-Button War

THE WIDESPREAD USE OF GUIDED WEAPONS, satellite intelligence and electronic warfare made this the most technologically advanced battle of the century. Patriot air defence missiles were used to shoot down incoming Scuds, cruise missiles and laser guided bombs targeted specific buildings in downtown Baghdad. F-117 Stealth bombers operated with virtual impunity over heavily defended air space; the strength of the defences was demonstrated by the RAF which, lacking modern electronic counter-measures, attacked at low level and had several jets shot down by ground fire. The disparity in both technology – and commitment – between the two armies was enormous. The coalition expected to suffer many thousand casualties, but losses were not much greater than on an exercise of this scale: slightly more than 200. Some 20,000 Iraqi troops were killed, possibly 60,000 wounded.

Unfinished Business

Kuwait City was liberated on 27 February. Fifty thousand Iraqi soldiers had been taken prisoner and 29 out of 42 Iraqi divisions had ceased to exist as combat formations. By the early hours of 28 January (local time) the 24th Division was poised to assault the Republican Guard units around Basra, but the operation was cancelled. After 100 hours' combat, President Bush had declared a ceasefire. Kuwait had been liberated, Saddam's army was shattered

ABOVE: *General H Norman Schwarzkopf in characteristically ebullient pose. Although upbeat throughout, he had stockpiled combat supplies for 60 days' fighting before unleashing his ground offensive.*

and Bush had no desire to embroil his forces in a battle for Basra – or Baghdad. To do so would go beyond the remit of the UN resolution. It is fair to assume that intelligence predicted Saddam's speedy fall and execution by his own generals: the traditional fate of defeated Iraqi leaders. Unfortunately, the wily dictator survived, crushed internal revolts and endured until President George W. Bush's controversial decision to invade Iraq in 2003.

INDEX

Page numbers in *Italics* refer to illustrations

PICTURE CREDITS

8 Getty Images; 15 Hulton-Deutsch Collection/Corbis; 19 Popperfoto/Getty Images; 22, 27 TopFoto; 30 Getty Images; 37 PA/Tophams/Topham Picturepoint/Press Association Images; 43 AP/Press Association Images; 47 Bettmann/Corbis; 51 R Tomasi; 57 Bettmann/Corbis; 64, 69 Ullstein Bild/TopFoto; 71, 76 Bettmann/Corbis; 79 DPA/Press Association Images; 84 Bettmann/Corbis; 86, 91 Getty Images; 94 Bettmann/Corbis; 101 US Army; 108 RIA Novosti/TopFoto; 112 R Tomasi; 117 CPhoM. Robert F. Sargent/Corbis; 123 Interfoto/Alamy; 126 The Print Collector/Alamy; 130 AP/Press Association Images; 133 Lightroom Photos/TopFoto; 137 Bettmann/Corbis; 143 US National Archives; 145, 150 Bettmann/Corbis; 153 Joe Rosenthal/Corbis; 158 Bettmann/Corbis; 161 Yevgeny Khaldei/Corbis; 165 TopFoto; 168 AP/Press Association Images; 173 AFP/Getty Images; 175 Ullstein Bild/Photo12.com; 180 Getty Images; 183 Bettmann/Corbis; 189 Martin Cleaver/AP/Press Association Images; 194 Getty Images; 196 Lightroom Photos/TopFoto; 203 David Turnley/Corbis.

Quercus Publishing Plc
21 Bloomsbury Square
London
WC1A 2NS

First published in 2010

A catalogue record of this book is available from the British Library

ISBN: 978 1 84916 068 1

Designed by Patrick Nugent
Picture research by Claudia Tate

Printed and bound in China

10 9 8 7 6 5 4 3 2 1